Miller, Tim (Timothy
Jon), 1970- author.
Barbecue

D0955385

BARBECUE

The Meals Series
as part of the Rowman & Littlefield Studies in Food and Gastronomy

General Editor: Ken Albala, Professor of History, University of the Pacific
(kalbala@pacific.edu)
Rowman & Littlefield Executive Editor: Suzanne Staszak-Silva
(sstaszak-silva@rowman.com)

The Meals series examines our daily meals—breakfast, lunch, dinner, tea—as well as special meals such as the picnic and barbecue, both as historical construct and global phenomena. We take these meals for granted, but the series volumes provide surprising information that will change the way you think about eating. A single meal in each volume is anatomized, its social and cultural meaning brought into sharp focus, and the customs and manners of various peoples are explained in context. Each volume also looks closely at the foods we commonly include and why.

Breakfast: A History, by Heather Arndt Anderson (2013)

The Picnic: A History, by Walter Levy (2013)

Lunch: A History, by Megan Elias (2014)

Barbecue: A History, by Tim Miller (2014)

BARBECUE

A HISTORY

Tim Miller

ROWMAN & LITTLEFIELD
Lanham • Boulder • New York • Toronto • Plymouth, UK

Published by Rowman & Littlefield
4501 Forbes Boulevard, Suite 200, Lanham, Maryland 20706
www.rowman.com

10 Thornbury Road, Plymouth PL6 7PP, United Kingdom

British Library Cataloguing in Publication Information Available

Library of Congress Cataloging-in-Publication Data
Miller, Tim (Timothy John), 1970-
  Barbecue : a history / Tim Miller.
    pages cm. — (The meals series)
  Includes bibliographical references and index.
  ISBN 978-1-4422-2753-8 (cloth : alk. paper) — ISBN 978-1-4422-2754-5
(electronic : alk. paper) 1. Barbecuing—History. 2. Cookbooks. lcgft I. Title.
  TX840.B3M53 2014
  641.7'6—dc23   2014007968

Printed in the United States of America

CONTENTS

SERIES FOREWORD

Custom becomes second nature, and this is especially true of meals. We expect to eat them at a certain time and place, and we have a set of scripted foods considered appropriate for each. Bacon, eggs, and toast are breakfast; sandwiches are lunch; meat, potatoes, and vegetables are dinner, followed by dessert. Breakfast for dinner is so much fun precisely because it is out of the ordinary and transgressive. But meal patterns were not always this way. In the Middle Ages people ate two meals, the larger in the morning. Today the idea of a heavy meal with meat and wine at 11:00 a.m. strikes us as strange and decidedly unpleasant. Likewise when abroad, the food that people eat, at what seems to us the wrong time of day, can be shocking. Again, our customs have become so ingrained that we assume they are natural, correct, and biologically sound.

The Meals series will demonstrate exactly the opposite. Not only have meal times changed but the menu as well, both through history and around the globe. Only a simple bowl of soup with a crust of bread for supper? That's where the name comes from. Our dinner, coming from *disner* in Old French, *disjejeunare* in Latin, actually means to break fast and was eaten in the morning. Each meal also has its own unique characteristics that evolve over time. We will see the invention of the picnic and barbecue, the gradual adoption of lunch as a new midday meal, and even certain meals practiced as hallowed institutions in some places but scarcely at all elsewhere, such as tea—the meal, not the drink. Often food items suddenly appear in a meal as quintessential, such as cold breakfast cereal, the invention of men like Kellogg and Post. Or they disappear, like oysters for breakfast. Sometimes an entire meal springs from nowhere under unique social conditions, like brunch.

Of course, the decay of the family meal is a topic that deeply concerns us, as people catch a quick bite at their desk or on the go, or eat with their eyes glued to the television set. If eating is one of the greatest pleasures in life, one has to wonder what it says about us when we wolf down a meal in a few minutes flat or when no one talks at the dinner table. Still, meal-time traditions persist for special occasions. They are the time we remind ourselves of who we are and where we come from, when grandma's special lasagna comes to the table for a Sunday dinner, or a Passover Seder is set exactly the same way it has been for thousands of years. We treasure these food rituals precisely because they keep us rooted in a rapidly changing world.

The Meals series examines the meal as both a historical construct and a global phenomenon. Each volume anatomizes a single meal, bringing its social and cultural meaning into sharp focus and explaining the customs and manners of various people in context. Each volume also looks closely at the foods we commonly include and why. In the end I hope you will never take your meal-time customs for granted again.

Ken Albala
University of the Pacific

ACKNOWLEDGMENTS

I would like to thank Ken Albala, the content editor for this series, for the opportunity to write this book. I first heard about the series on a mailing list, where Ken posted that he was looking for someone to write a book on the history of barbecue. I replied with an e-mail explaining just how I would approach writing the book, Ken said that the approach was good but he wanted more details, and over the course of a few weeks that e-mail turned into a prospectus that, a year and a half later, expanded into this book. I am very grateful for Ken's original support for this book, and for his many helpful suggestions during the writing process.

I would also like to thank Suzanne Staszak-Silva, the editor at Rowman & Littlefield, for her guidance and patience with a first-time author.

Dr. Lola Norris, on the faculty at Texas A&M International University in Laredo, Texas, was immensely helpful in translating parts of *A General and Natural History of the Indies*, by Gonzalo Fernandez de Oviedo y Valdés, the first book to mention *barbacoa*, the Spanish root of "barbecue." Her work helped me to get a better understanding of the many meanings the early Spanish explorers ascribed to the word.

Finally, I would like to thank my wife Janet for her love and support during the time it took to write the book. Without her, the book probably would have still gotten finished, but it may have been a few years late.

INTRODUCTION

Barbecue as a Meal

This book is part of the Rowman & Littlefield meals series, and it exists along with books on breakfast, lunch, brunch, and dinner, so the main point of the book is to look at barbecue in the context of a meal. As an entry in a series it is more informative than argument driven; to some extent it sums up the history, culture, and content about barbecue rather than advancing a brand new argument.

However, a thread of an idea can be followed through this book, and it is this: Just like a good barbecue meal, eaten with one's hands with a supply of paper towels nearby, the history of barbecue in America is a messy affair. For much of its history the story has been simple, with a single storyline, but in the first half of the 20th century barbecue fractured into several competing pieces that make for a confusing story (or, at least, make extra work for anyone writing a single history of barbecue in America).

Much of the confusion exists at the linguistic level. For example, there is a quote from an acquaintance of mine who lived near Atlanta, Georgia, where barbecue has been a part of the culture for several hundred years. The acquaintance had a friend from the North who wanted to buy a house with a big backyard so, as the friend said, he "could put in a barbecue." The Georgian couldn't quite understand what the northern friend meant: to the southerner, "barbecue" only refers to a food that can be eaten, not a place where one could cook barbecue. There is also the comment from a restaurateur from Memphis, Tennessee, quoted in Lolis Eric Elie's excellent exploration of American barbecue,

Smokestack Lightning, who said "listen. . . . If you're gonna write a book, do me one damn favor. Explain to people that barbecue is a way of cooking. So don't walk into a place and say, 'Give me a barbecue.' Give me a barbecue what? It's like walking into a place and saying, 'Give me a fried.' A fried what? That's very important to help barbecue along."[1]

Barbecue probably would be helped along if there was not so much confusion over the word, but the fact is that "barbecue" has numerous meanings that change in different situations. The creation of these different meanings is intimately tied to barbecue's history, so a quick explanation of that history, and the various meanings attached to the word, will be useful here.

First, a look at the meanings. The online version of the Merriam-Webster dictionary gives five meanings for "barbecue," two of which treat the word as a verb and three of which treat it as a noun. For the verbs, barbecue is either "to roast or broil on a rack or revolving spit over or before a source of heat (as hot coals)" or "to cook in a highly seasoned vinegar sauce."[2] As a noun, barbecue can be "a large animal (as a steer) roasted whole or split over an open fire or a fire in a pit," "a social gathering especially in the open air at which barbecued food is eaten," or "an often portable fireplace over which meat and fish are roasted." To summarize those definitions, a barbecue is either roasting a large animal over a fire or cooking food in a vinegar sauce, or it is the animal being cooked, the things the animal is being cooked on, or the social gathering where the cooking is taking place.

Those definitions are precise but problematic. Dictionaries attempt precision, but words are slippery and malleable. Consider the Texas BBQ Whopper, a burger being sold at Burger King restaurants across the country as this book is being written. The sandwich's connection to barbecue is that it includes barbecue sauce. Purists may be outraged but Burger King continues to advertise and serve it—is it barbecue? If the grill where food is cooked is known as a "barbecue," and chicken is grilled on the barbecue, is the chicken "barbecued"? As stated above, barbecue's definition fractures during the first half of the 20th century, so maybe it would be helpful to take a quick look at the history of barbecue to see the effect of historical change on the definition.

"Barbecue," it is fairly clear, descended from the Spanish word *barbacoa*, which in turn seems to have come from a term used by Native Americans. The early history of barbacoa is complicated and shrouded in the mists of time (at this point it was simply too long ago to see how the word jumped from the Native Americans to the Spanish), but the process of slow roasting large animals was well established in the American colonies by at least the mid-1700s. The practice gradually disappeared from the North but became well established in the South, particularly in Virginia, and as Virginians migrated south and west they usually took the tradition with them.

By the mid-1800s "barbecue" had a couple of meanings, all of which were fairly clear cut. To barbecue meant to roast a fairly large animal (pig, goat, sheep, or beef) over a low fire (usually, hot coals) for a long period of time—as barbecuers say today, cooking it "low and slow." There was a social element to a barbecue. A barbecue was either a political meeting (a rally or a debate), a celebration (July Fourth was particularly popular), or a more general social gathering (a dance or corn husking, where bushels and bushels of corn kernels were separated from corncobs).

In the late 19th century the first barbecue restaurants appeared, and the definition for barbecue became somewhat unstable. These early restaurants were usually just a stand along the road, or even simply an open pit where, a few days a week, someone sold barbecued meat. The restaurants divorced barbecue from the social element and made barbecue grossly capitalistic. They also created the idea that, in different regions of the country, barbecue was not simply an animal that was barbecued, but was instead a particular type of animal: whole hogs, or parts of hogs, or parts of beef, or sheep—anything else was not real barbecue. Sauces, also, became identified with certain regions or, rather, people in different regions began to see certain sauces as being the correct kind of sauce: tomato based, mustard based, vinegar based, hot sauce, or no sauce at all.

If the creation of restaurants made the definition of barbecue unstable, the mass popularity of barbecue in the years after World War I, and particularly after World War II, blew it apart. Barbecuing as a mass movement was originally identified with the West, not the South, and it swept across the country until it seemed that everyone wanted a barbecue grill in the backyard to entertain both the kids and the boss. During this time barbecue, to most Americans, became anything prepared on a grill, either inside or outside of a building, and then, by the 1960s, anything with barbecue sauce on it. The "low and slow" technique of barbecuing still existed, and has had a considerable amount of aid from barbecue competitions since their birth in the 1970s, but since the 1950s that older definition of barbecue was eclipsed by the newer definition. Today, the two main definitions of barbecue—as a synonym for outdoor grilling, and "low and slow" cooking—exist together uneasily, and the confusion in our language is a reflection of barbecue's tangled history.

Likewise, there are a number of cooking techniques that have been used over the years to produce what we today would call barbecued food. The earliest technique, written about by the Spanish who first encountered Native Americans, seems to have been a kind of smoke cooking. Fish, iguanas, and other types of meat were arranged on wooden racks (which were called barbacoas), under which was a long-burning, low fire that both dried and smoked the meat. Later, through the late 1800s, Americans used pit roasting. Long trenches were dug and filled with logs, which were set ablaze and burned down to coals. Meat was then set at ground level, either on metal grills or spits, and roasted for hours.

Today, two kinds of cooking dominate when it comes to barbecue. Traditional-style barbecue, used by most restaurants and by barbecue competitors, is indirect grilling. The fire is contained in a box with the meat but is not directly below the meat, heating the meat at a constant temperature of about 250 degrees. The intention here is to not just cook the meat but also to smoke it, by using charcoal or wood from a few types of trees (oak, mesquite, apple, etc.) as the main fuel, or by burning a small amount of that wood while the meat cooks. Because of the long cooking time tough cuts of meat work best for this type of cooking, which is why cuts like brisket are so popular for traditional barbecues.

The second type of cooking today that falls into the category of barbecue is simple outdoor grilling, either using direct heat (the meat sits just over the fire) or indirect heat in an enclosed grill. This gives no smoky flavor to the food, but it also requires much less time—cooking time is usually somewhere between ten minutes and an hour, depending on the size of the food being cooked.

Of course, this book is a history of barbecue, and the history briefly sketched here is told in more detail in chapter 1. That chapter moves from the earliest usages of "barbecue" in European languages to the most recent developments in competition barbecue. Along the way many factors in the growing popularity of barbecue are outlined, showing that barbecue, as a cultural movement, has been influenced by the wider American culture.

Chapter 2 goes deeper into the history of the particular dishes associated with barbecues. Certainly, the meat is important, but then there are the side items as well, such as potato salad, coleslaw, and baked beans (this is also the chapter with the recipes in it). Again, historical changes are observed, including the popularity of serving grilling canned meat (such as Spam) and boiled coffee at barbecues in the 1950s.

Chapter 3 deals with barbecue restaurants, and is roughly divided into two parts. The first part examines the history of barbecue restaurants, from their beginnings as roadside shacks in the late 19th century to their transformation into respectable restaurants in the 1980s, proper enough to take out-of-town visitors. The second part of the chapter is a closer analysis of barbecue restaurants: the similar origins for many of them, a look at the menus of various restaurants, and, finally, brief biographies of some of the more famous restaurants, and restaurant chains, in America.

Chapter 4 examines barbecue worldwide. While many other countries have barbecue traditions, for the most part this is outdoor grilling, often on a skewer. International barbecue has not penetrated very far into American culture by this point, although it is possible to find barbecued dishes from around the world at some restaurants.

Chapter 5 looks at barbecue's appearances in popular culture. Barbecues are social events, and some movies and television shows have set scenes at barbecues to show characters coming together and mingling at barbecues. Reality shows have focused on barbecue, and there is even one reality program that is centered on barbecue competitions. In barbecue's appearances in popular culture, one can see barbecue's place in American culture.

1

THE HISTORY OF BARBECUE

B arbecue is a prime example of how cooking can be a social activity. Unlike barbecue's close relative, the picnic, a barbecue's focus is both the cooking and the eating, where (usually male) guests gather around the grill, often to drink, always to talk. This book is concerned with the idea of a barbecue as a meal, as a set of foods cooked and eaten in a certain way. While the method of cooking is not a main focus in this book, the history of barbecue in America has involved two different ways of cooking of barbecue. The first is slow-cooked at a low temperature, sitting near the fire for hours before being torn or cut apart and served. This has been called "barbecue" in America for centuries, and today is often referred to as "traditional barbecue." The second type of barbecue might more appropriately be called outdoor grilling, although it, also, is usually referred to as "barbecue." This type of barbecue has only been widely popular in America for less than a hundred years, and its real popularity came in the years after World War II. This chapter is about the history of these two types of barbecue, which in many ways are quite different, and which form the history of barbecuing in America.

BARBECUING BEFORE AND JUST AFTER COLUMBUS

"Barbecue" is based on a Spanish word that came from Native American languages, so no Europeans talked about "barbecuing" before Columbus.

However, "barbecue" is often used as a synonym for grilling, and humans have been grilling food for a length of time that almost boggles the mind. Because the discovery of grilling took place so long ago, and probably at a number of different places, archeologists have only a very rough date of when humans started grilling foods: somewhere between 800,000 and 1.2 million years ago. As a comparison, the first farmers appeared about 10,000 years ago, and cattle were domesticated around 8,000 years ago. For most of the time we have been humans, dinner was grilled, and it was whatever could be caught or collected that day. Because of this, grilling shows up repeatedly in ancient manuscripts, usually when people are living away from their homes. Whether it was Greeks attacking Troy, Israelites wandering the desert, or Romans fighting in Gaul, grilling was the way to cook meals.

The cooking was done in two ways. The first method was to suspend the meat above a fire while it cooked, by using a wooden or metal skewer, a wooden or metal rack, or a rope—see the Tarzan Roast recipe in chapter 4 for an example of the later method. This essentially roasted the meat. A second method was to bury the meat in a hole with hot rocks and a damp material (like seaweed) that steamed the meat, a type of cooking resembling today's clambakes or Hawaiian Kalua Pig—there are instructions for these in chapters 2 and 4, respectively. Each of these methods was effective at cooking meat, even in cultures that had no metalworking knowledge.

In 1492, Columbus encountered the New World. Over the next few decades, Old World and New World ideas, plants, and animals moved back and forth across the Atlantic Ocean. Columbus and later explorers brought back to Europe anything they thought might be worth money, and they carried to the New World plants and animals they thought might be useful in exploring and settling the Americas. Old World foods like beef and pork headed west while New World foods like chili peppers headed east. *Barbacoa*, too, was part of this exchange.

Barbacoa was a Native American word for a wooden rack used for, among other things, cooking food. The cooking seems to have been over a low fire for an extended period, with the intention of either making food for immediate consumption or for long-term storage (essentially, they were smoking the food). The custom was fairly widespread. While the earliest explorers refer to natives in the Caribbean cooking in this manner, that is because the earliest area explored was the Caribbean. *The History of Virginia*, published in 1705, nearly a hundred years after the establishment of the first permanent English settlement in the America, explained that natives near the Virginia Colony regularly cooked meat on a raised platform of sticks over a fire, both to eat immediately and to preserve for later consumption.[1]

There is a story from Columbus's second voyage that might be the first encounter between Europeans and the cooking style that became barbecue. The explorers entered what is now Guantánamo Bay, Cuba, and saw fires on the beach but no people. Upon landing they saw that fish and rabbits were cooking on low fires, along with a number of snakes the Spanish described as "venomous and terrifying . . . covered with very hard shells, as a fish is covered with scales" (how the explorers could know that the grilling snakes were venomous is anyone's guess). It has been argued that the snakes were, in fact, iguanas, which points to the fact that, although the Europeans adopted the natives' style of cooking, they rejected some of the meats the natives barbecued. In this instance the Spanish sailors took the fish and left the rabbits and serpents to keep cooking on the barbacoas.[2]

The Spanish had a near-monopoly on New World exploration during the 1500s, conquering Mexico, Central America, and (along with the Portuguese) South America during that century. It makes sense, then, that the word barbacoa first appeared in print in 1526 in a Spanish book whose title translates as *A General and Natural History of the Indies.* The author, Gonzalo Fernandez de Oviedo y Valdés, does not use the word just once or twice; the word is peppered throughout the book, and not always in a cooking context. In looking through the text, it is apparent that, to the Spanish, the underlying meaning of a barbacoa was that it was some sort of raised platform. Early in the book Oviedo writes that the Spanish found many "barbacoas or high houses, made and constructed on posts of very strong black palm trees and almost unconquerable," partially because of their location on the posts and partially because of their sturdy construction.[3] When the Spanish attacked one of the houses they found that, yes, a barbacoa was almost unconquerable. The Indian occupiers of one house held out against an attack of over two hundred Spaniards for two days, until the defenders slipped out at night, undetected. As Oviedo writes, when the Spaniards entered the house they found enough room for all 200 of them to occupy it with extra space.[4]

The word barbacoa is used in Oviedo's book in other contexts as well. Young boys are assigned to sit on barbacoas, or platforms raised above the corn, where "they are continuously shouting, shooing away parrots and other birds that come to eat the maize fields."[5] Oviedo mentions that these sorts of platforms were familiar to the Spaniards, as similar platforms were used back in Spain "to protect hemp plants and millet and other plants from birds."[6] In describing a particular bridge, Oviedo writes that a wooden frame was sunk into the river, and then a barbacoa, or floor, was built upon the frame. Finally, he also mentions that, for cooking meat, Indians dug a hole in the ground, constructed a wooden frame over the hole, and then cooked their food over this barbacoa (which was the wooden frame).

Oviedo's usage of barbacoa was not unique in the Spanish language. The *Real Academia Española*, the group that produces the official dictionary of the Spanish language, currently includes eight definitions for barbacoa, including those that match the way Oviedo used the word. This was not always true; the word is missing from the 1884 version of the dictionary, and when the word does appear, in 1899, its only definition relates to cooking. The 1914 edition was the first to include multiple definitions.

As he describes it, Oviedo is fairly straightforward on what a barbacoa is: it is a wooden rack. The rack can be used for cooking, drying food, or storing things on, but it is a wooden rack, period. If that is so, why did the Spanish barbacoa mutate into the English barbecue, a word that *always* comes back to cooking? What happened to barbacoa's original meaning?

At this point, it is impossible to know just how or why the meaning shifted, but part of the shift probably had to do with the usefulness of the new meaning. The original meaning, that of a raised platform, was probably not especially useful for the English. Unlike the Native Americans, English villages in the New or Old Worlds were not collections of barbacoas raised above the ground out of reach of foraging animals or flooding rainwater; they were collections of houses with four solid walls to keep animals (and, hopefully, floodwater) out. The English simply did not need a new word for a raised platform (and, although it is so obvious that it barely needs to be stated, the Native Americans had different words for *everything*, but only a few words, like canoe, made the jump into European languages).

Even if they did not need a new word for a raised platform, the English apparently did need a new word for the apparatus used to slowly grill meat, or for the meat itself. While this type of cooking was known in Europe it seems to have taken an encounter with people on the other side of the ocean to have pushed home the usefulness of a single word that encapsulates that concept. As the word came off the tongues of thousands of explorers and settlers, its meaning changed, leaving behind the raised platform and developing a permanent connection to cooking.

One hundred and thirty-five years after its appearance in Spanish, the English derivative of barbacoa finally showed up in a book written in English. *Jamaica Viewed*, published in 1661, is noted by the *Oxford English Dictionary* as containing the first example of "barbecue" in print. Barbecue seems to have become popular in England in the late 1600s and early 1700s, and it seems that travelers to Jamaica brought the concept to England. The word's introduction is somewhat inauspicious, though, as the first reference in English is to cannibalism. In describing the English colony, the author included a long poem about native customs and noted that, upon the death of a head of household, the body was burned and all of his possessions were disposed of. If the man had a slave, the slave was supposed to be killed and burned along with the man, but more frequently the slave was either sold to the English or "slain, / And their Flesh forthwith Barbacu'd and eat / By them, their Wives and Children as choice meat."[7] By the time those lines were published, Jamaica's most popular method of barbecuing had long since taken root. In 1611 Jamaica's abbot mentioned that the pigs of the island, which had originally been brought by European settlers, were already being used to make jerk pork.[8]

Books such as *Jamaica Viewed* described the New World and played to an enormous European interest in newly discovered lands. Europeans were fascinated by those areas and eager to hear more about them. In this vein are a series of popular engravings of the New World made by Theodor de Bry, an illustrator who, ironically, never left Europe. De Bry mined other people's works for source materials. For example, Englishman John White traveled to what is now the Carolinas and Virginia in the 1580s as part of an expedition, about twenty years before England established its first permanent colony in the New World. He painted an image of two large fish cooking on a wooden rack over an open fire that was an example of Algonquin cooking techniques. De Bry used this image as the basis for his own picture, shown on the next page, but de Bry added a few Native Americans to the picture as well. De Bry's images of Native Americans were extremely popular, and his barbecue image was many Europeans' first sight of barbecuing. Images such as de Bry's, printed travelers' accounts, and returning explorers helped to make barbecue well known in England, at least in terms of the process of roasting an entire pig. In 1707 Edward Ward published *The Barbacue Feast: or, the Three Pigs of Peckham*, which contains a fairly complete, although fictional, account of a barbecue, including the roasting of the hogs and feeding paying guests on ramshackle tables. By the 1700s recipes for roasting pigs were appearing in English cookbooks.

BARBECUING IN THE AMERICAN COLONIES

In 1607 English settlers established a colony at Jamestown, in what later became Virginia colony. Thirteen years later settlers landed at Plymouth Rock, in what is now Massachusetts. These were the first two permanent English settlements in North America and, as other colonies developed around them, they formed the basis for the Southern and New England regions. While barbecue flourished

Einhöltzern Roost/ darauff sie die XIIII.
Fische besengen.

Ann sie eine grosse menge Fische haben gefangen/ begeben sie sich auff einen darzu verordneten Platz/ welcher die Speiß zu bereiten bequeme ist/ daselbst stecken sie vier Gabeln auff einen vierecketen Platz in die Erden hinein/ auff diese legen sie vier Höltzer/ vnd auff dieselbigen andere zwerchweise/ also/ daß es einem Roost/ der da hoch gnugsam sey/ gleichförmig werde. Wann sie die Fische auff den Roost gelegt/ machen sie ein Fewer darunter/ doch nicht nach der weise der Völcker von Florida/ welche die Fisch allein besengen/ vnnd im Rauch außtrücknen/ die sie den gantzen Winter vber behalten. Diese Völcker aber braten alles/ verzehrens/ vnd behalten nichts in vorrath/ darnach/ wann sie dessen dörfftig sind/ braten oder sieden sie frische/ wie wir hernach sehen werden. Wann aber der Roost so groß nicht ist/ daß die Fisch alle möchten darauff gelegt werden/ stecken sie kleine steck lein am Fewer in die Erden/ vnnd hencken die vbrigen Fische durch die Ohren auff/ vnd braten sie vollende so lang es gnug sey. Sie sehen aber mit fleiß zu/ daß sie nicht verbrennt werden. Wann die ersten gebraten sind/ legen sie andere/ so sie frisch herzu gebracht/ auff den Roost. Vnd also widerholen sie diß braten so lange/ biß sie der Speise gnugsam zu haben vermeynen.

Theodor de Bry's image of Native Americans barbecuing. Courtesy of the Library of Congress, LC-USZ62-53339.

for a time in both areas, it took root permanently in Virginia while fading away in New England. As it turned out, two very different types of people settled in the two colonies, and these differences had a profound effect on the popularity of barbecue in America.

The setters in New England were largely Puritan families who tried to re-create English society in the New World. They rejected some aspects of English society—most notably, the Anglican religion—but, in general, they worked to make the villages of Massachusetts or Connecticut look like the villages they left in England. One way they did this was through their food choices. The settlers tried to continue eating the same sorts of food they had consumed back in England, but unfortunately, the climate was wrong for growing wheat. Grudgingly, the settlers adopted corn as a substitute, but for baking—their predominant method of cooking—corn did not work well. Breads just did not rise with corn the way they had with wheat. The settlers had adopted corn from the Native Americans, but they often tried to cook English dishes by simply substituting corn for wheat. Even the settlers' method of growing corn pointed back to their love of English culture. The Native Americans grew corn in a haphazard fashion, planting corn seeds side by side with other crops so that as the corn grew the stalks provided shade for other crops that did not like full sun. The American settlers, in contrast, grew corn in neat rows in tidy gardens, just like they had back in England, and these gardens contained many other crops that would have been seen in gardens back in England.

The settlers in Virginia went farther in accepting and using Native American traditions. These settlers were overwhelmingly young men who had made the dangerous trip across the ocean for one purpose: to make a life in America that was better than the life offered to them in England. This meant farming, and that required land. Generally in short supply in England, land was readily available in the Southern colonies for those who could pay or work for it. Those young men were always on the lookout for a crop that would bring in cash, and the first crop to fit the bill was tobacco. Demand was high, which meant that prices were high, but raising tobacco required lots of time spent in the field checking for pests and watching for other problems. Virginia farmers did not have that much time for cooking, and they were not that choosy about what they ate. Their priority was making money.

And so they adopted more Native American traditions than their neighbors to the north. While the New Englanders raised cattle in orderly pastures, the Southerners hunted, trapped, and fished whatever game was available. Pork, now a standard barbecue meat, was seemingly made for the Southern colonists; they could let their free-roaming hogs fend for themselves, feed themselves, and then, eventually, feed the Southern colonists. The colonists had come from southern and western England, where roasting was the predominant cooking technique, and it was a short jump from roasting a piece of meat to roasting a whole hog over a fire. Barbecue fit the rough-and-ready lifestyle of the Southern colonists much more than the colonists further north.

This is not to say that barbecue was completely unheard of in the north—in fact, the first recorded instance of a colonist going to a barbecue comes from the north. No one knows just when the American colonists had their first barbecue or if the tradition came directly from the local Native Americans or from other European settlers and explorers. The first permanent English colonies in America were established in the early 1600s; over a hundred years later mentions of barbecues were regularly showing up in colonists' diaries. The first mention of a barbecue gathering in America occurred in 1733, when Benjamin Lynde, of Salem, Massachusetts, wrote "Fair and hot; Browne, Barbacue; hack overset," in his diary for August 31. The phrasing is obscure, which stands to reason: this is a note the diarist wrote to himself rather than a recording for future generations. The entry has been interpreted, though, to mean that on a fair and hot day the author went to a barbecue with Mr. Browne.[9] By the 1730s, barbecues were common occurrences among colonists.

That diary entry, from a New Englander, showed up just over forty years before the American Revolution. During that time barbecues were common in New England, when they were public events with many people in attendance. After the Revolution, though, barbecues seem to have faded away in New England as a passing fad while they continued as before in what could be called the cradle of barbecue, Virginia.

Virginia society was set up in a way that seemed to facilitate barbecues. Virginia had been settled by colonists who came to America for economic reasons, and the most successful became the richest members of society. Hosting a barbecue was an opportunity to show off wealth in a very public way.

The popularity of barbecue in Virginia brought a racial aspect to barbecue. The crops that made people rich in Virginia, like tobacco, rice, and indigo, were crops that required lots of labor. Initially, indentured servants were brought in to help with that labor. They were men and women who, in exchange for the trip to America, agreed to work for a number of years to pay off the debt. Within a generation, a problem with the system became apparent: When those people had worked off their debt, they wanted land to set themselves up as farmers, and this continual demand for land put severe pressure on colonial leaders to take land from the Indians. The most serious result of this was Bacon's Rebellion, a 1675 uprising when land-hungry colonists attacked tribes of Native Americans and then turned on the colony's leaders (luckily for the government, the head of the rebellion abruptly died). In the aftermath of this, Virginia began to shift away from using indentured servants, who were usually European, to using slaves, who were usually African, for labor (although the first slaves had been brought to America soon after colonization, the use of slaves intensified after Bacon's Rebellion). Slaves tended fields, kept up the master's house, and cooked the meals, including the barbecues.

Not only did barbecue have a racial side, but it also developed a political side in Virginia before the Revolutionary War. Candidates for office "treated" their constituency to dinners, which were often barbecues, and the eating was frequently accompanied by quite a bit of drinking, also paid for by the candidate. The idea was not to buy the election but to show that the candidate was as generous as a proper Virginia gentleman should be (and also prosperous enough to afford to pay for the meal). The political barbecue became a standard fixture of Southern culture well into the 20th century.

Colonists moved steadily into the American interior as the Revolutionary War approached, spilling over the Appalachian Mountains in defiance of British laws forbidding settlement in what was then called the Northwest Territory. As settlers from Virginia moved west and south, so did their barbecue tradition. They wanted to recreate the life they left behind, especially the rituals that marked someone as being in the upper class. Those settlers in the Carolinas and the West made lives for themselves and became successful, and then they hosted barbecues. As friends, acquaintances, and extended family streamed onto the property to observe the host's house, his fields, his generosity in terms of the food supplied for the meal, and his slaves cooking the food, they judged the host to be part of the upper class, or not. Barbecue was a part of the social life of Virginia and of those who went west or south for greener pastures.

BARBECUE IN THE EARLY UNITED STATES THROUGH THE CIVIL WAR

Americans in the late 1700s and throughout the 1800s were a social people. Europeans traveling through America often commented that Americans were more gregarious than Europeans, sometimes annoyingly so. The sociality was at least partially tied to Americans' ideas about their new country. The United States was a democracy, and democracy required participation at many different levels. Running for office, voting, and discussing the political issues of the day were all ways that citizens were actively involved with their democracy. Civic involvement, too, was the duty of citizens, and one way to be involved, especially in the South, was to have barbecues. The large public barbecues in the South required public involvement, both through the committees that planned the barbecues and from the farmers who donated the meat for the barbecues (the donations meant that meat rarely barbecued today in the South, like goat or mutton, often showed up on the tables at 19th-century barbecues).

Two accounts of Southern barbecues provide a fairly full picture of just what barbecues in the 1800s were like. The first account is from John Duncan, a Scotsman who visited America in the late 1810s and accepted an invitation to a Virginia barbecue from George Washington's nephew. Duncan's account is valuable not because he describes the cooking process—he barely mentions it, as opposed to the second account shown here—but because he does an excellent job of describing the general atmosphere of a Southern barbecue.

Duncan's barbecue was not at a plantation or other residence, but instead out in the countryside. "In a fine wood of oaks by the road side we found a whole colony of black servants," he writes, "who had made a lodgement since we passed it in the morning, and the blue smoke which was issuing here and there from among the branches, readily suggested that there was cooking going forward." Cooking was going on, indeed, done by groups of slaves. "One was preparing a fowl for the spit, another feeding a crackling fire which curled up round a large pot, others were broiling pigs, lamb, and venison, over little square pits filled with the red embers of hickory wood." Hickory was used because it gives "a much stronger heat than coals, and when completely kindled is almost without smoke." Near the crackling fires was a spring.

Leaving the cooking, he walks to the edge of the woods and finds "a rural banqueting-hall and ball room." A large dancing area was laid out in the open, along with a long table for diners, flanked by a smaller table which "groaned under numerous earthen vessels filled with various kinds of liquors, to be speedily converted" by the addition of spring water "into tubfulls of generous toddy." A crowd gathered, numbering about 30 women and 100 men—especially in the early 1800s, barbecues were a masculine affair, and the gender ratio reflects that. Eating was done in shifts, and Duncan joined the first shift, he being "too little acquainted with the tactics of a barbecue, and somewhat too well inclined to eat." The problem was that the first shift consisted of those primarily interested in dancing, and between the speed at which that shift ate—they were there for the dancing rather than the barbecue—and the fact that the men must pay attention to the women's desires, Duncan did not eat much barbecue. After rising from the table with the rest of the dancers he saw that some who ate in the second shift lingered to eat in the third shift as well. The liquor was consumed, and Duncan noted that the crowd was happy but not drunk to excess. This was a daytime barbecue that did not continue into the evening. Duncan took his leave for the ride back to Alexandria at around five o'clock, and later heard later that most others left shortly after he did.[10]

An interesting aspect of Duncan's account is the division between black labor and white leisure. He sees slaves working as soon as he approaches but their labor is in the background of his description, which focuses on the leisure enjoyed by the whites. A late lunch followed by an afternoon of dancing is what Duncan writes about. This, of course, was part of the point of the gathering: By hosting this, George Washington's nephew could show the guests that he was a man of stature, a man with enough slaves and enough time to organize a completely non-productive event. As will be discussed in chapter 5, this idea of a barbecue showing black labor and white leisure continued well into the 20th century.

A second account comes from an 1851 Georgia barbecue, and shows much more specifically what was eaten at these barbecues and how the food was prepared. The account, reprinted in a national magazine, originally appeared in the Boston *Post* and was written specifically for a Northern audience that had likely never experienced a barbecue. The article began by stating that this was a political barbecue—more on those in a moment—and featured a number of political speakers, but the point of the article was not to describe the speakers. "My particular object," the author wrote, "is to describe the dinner." The entire barbecue was prepared in the open, "upon a green lawn," and this was typical—barbecues of the 1800s were usually large affairs, involving guests numbering at least in the hundreds and sometimes up to the thousands, and the entire barbecue, from the cooking to the eating, took place outdoors in an open or shady area with non-permanent facilities. "A trench was dug about 120 feet long, 5 feet wide, and 1 1/2 feet deep. Alongside of the trench, piles of wood were burning, and the coals were thrown into the trench; forty hogs and fifteen sheep were spitted and roasting." Although it does not say so in the article, the animals were likely donated by local farmers, and this contributed to a kind of randomness in the meat: as today, hogs were a popular barbecue meat, but cows, sheep, and goats also showed up at many a barbecue, based on what could be obtained through donations. As will be described later, the current association of particular cuts of meat with certain areas—pork ribs with Memphis, beef brisket with Texas—is a 20th-century change.

After cooking over the trenches for hours, the animals at this barbecue were taken off the spits and chopped up. Six men, three white and three black, laid the animals "upon a table, and with a broad axe cut them in pieces, and then tore them into fragments with their hands. As there were neither towels nor water near them, the cooks made their mouths answer the double purpose of towels and water." The meat was put into wooden bowls which were then placed on rough pine tables. "The entire bill of fare consisted of hogs, sheep, and bread. About 400 men partook of the dinner, each man laying hold of a piece of hog with one hand and a piece of bread with the other. There was nothing to drink,

Stereographic image from approximately 1895 showing hog barbecuing. The trench and skewers are typical, the men holding the slaughtered pigs are not. Courtesy of the Library of Congress, LC-USZ62-91254.

not even water," although this was unusual, as many barbecues were intentionally sited near a stream or other water source. The writer concluded by adding, "As I had seen the cutting up process, of course I did not eat any of the dinner, but I could not help thinking that it was rather a brutal way of serving a retiring speaker of the United States House of Representatives."[11]

These two accounts came from whites who noted the black contribution to the barbecues. Long after slavery had ended, a former slave recalled his own contribution to barbecues in his area, and his memories provide a different viewpoint of slavery. His owners frequently sent him to a local store to pick up their mail, and the store had a stage nearby used for dancing during barbecues. This particular man's responsibility at barbecues was to spend the night basting the meat. "Night befo' dem barbecues, I used to stay up all night a-cooking and basting de meats wid barbecue sass (sauce)," he said. "On a long pronged stick I wraps a soft rag or cotton fer a swab, and all de night long I swabs dat meat 'till it drip into de fire. Dem drippings change de smoke into seasoned fumes dat smoke de meat. We turn de meat over and swab it dat way all night long 'till it ooze seasoning and bake all through."[12]

Barbecues were popular in the South and were an important part of Southern culture. Of course, this raises the question of just why this was. Why were barbecues so popular for public festivities, and why were they so much more popular in the South than the North? There are a couple of reasons why, in the South, barbecues were the favored type of meal for large gatherings.

One reason is that, as has been written previously, settlers whose ancestors came from the Virginia colony had a tradition of barbecuing. As those settlers spread across Kentucky and Tennessee, they took their traditions with them (and, often, retained memories of where they came from—one report about a Fourth of July barbecue in Kentucky referenced the "free, single hearted Kentuckian . . . proud of his Virginian descent").[13] The popularity of barbecues was self-sustaining: in places where barbecues were popular they were immensely popular, and in places where they were rare they were very rare. As will be discussed below, by the end of the 19th century barbecues were so rare in Boston that one newspaper mused that it might be almost impossible to get enough people to show up to consume a barbecued ox there, in spite of the fact that Boston was one of the largest cities in America.

Another reason for the popularity of barbecues in the South probably had to do with climate. The warm southern climate was much friendlier to barbecuing than the cool northern climate, and barbecues could be arranged both earlier and later in the year than in the North.

Furthermore, apart from the time involved, barbecuing for a large gathering was a relatively simple affair, as the account above illustrates. A trench was dug, its length based on how many people were to be served and therefore how much meat was to be cooked. Wood was stacked in the trench and lit, and when it had burned down to coals, metal racks were set over the hot coals and then the meat was placed upon the racks, or else the animals were placed on spits to rest above the coals. The meat was in the form of either whole animals, for goats or sheep, or sides of animals, for beef or oxen (chicken was not much used, probably because large animals were a more efficient way to feed large numbers of people). The goal was to cook at a low temperature for a long period, often starting the day before and maintaining the coals all night long. Long tables for eating were set up, often made from planks on sawhorses. Again, none of this was done in a dedicated space—accounts from the time often mention guests retiring to a cool grove, or shady glade, for the meal. Barbecuing was, essentially, a fairly simple answer to the question of how to provide for lots of guests. More guests required more hogs, sheep, or goats, and more linear feet of trenches, but the overall techniques stayed the same. Put in modern terms, barbecuing scaled nicely.

During the 1800s, there were, broadly speaking, two types of gatherings where barbecues were the norm. One type of gathering was holidays and other public festivities, particularly the Fourth of July. An example of this type of event comes from July 1847, in southern Indiana, when troops returning from the Mexican War were welcomed with a barbecue. The format for the homecoming

Posing at a barbecue in Georgia, 1916. Courtesy Georgia Archives, Vanishing Georgia Collection, COW-148.

was fairly standard for a public gathering in the 19th century. At ten o'clock in the morning a procession formed on the public square that included returned troops, "several military companies of this county; . . . citizens, and strangers; making one of the largest and most imposing processions we ever witnessed," as the local newspaper described the scene. "The whole proceeded to the beautiful grove just above town, where the ceremonies of the day were had according to previous arrangement." A local dignitary addressed the crowd, and then there were responses from several military men. "After the speaking had ceased, the company assembled around the lengthy tables near at hand, which were plentifully supplied with every substantial eatable usually seen on such occasions, 'done up' in real barbecue style—and if a single man, woman or child present left the ground with an appetite it was not because of scarcity, for there was enough left after the crowd had dispersed to feed an ordinary sized army." It was impossible to tell how many people attended the barbecue but the reporter guessed that "the number did not at least fall short of 5000."[14]

Another type of gathering that featured barbecues was political gatherings. Especially after the 1840s, these became fixtures of electioneering and had long since shifted from being demonstrations of the candidate's virtue and fitness for office to wholesale feeding frenzies. This kind of political feed had been essentially pioneered by the Democrats under Andrew Jackson at a time when democracy in America was widening. Laws requiring voters to own land were retired while the vote was extended to groups who had never voted before—recent Irish immigrants, for example. The Democrats attracted new voters by visibly working to ensure that new groups could vote (which meant, of course, that those voters would vote Democrat), and the politicians also appealed to these new voters by throwing massive barbecues complemented by large amounts of liquor. The Whig party, created in the 1830s to fight against Democratic president Andrew Jackson's policies, fully absorbed the Democrats' political tactics and took them a step further in the campaign of 1840, often called the "Log Cabin and Hard Cider" campaign. Candidate William Henry Harrison was trumpeted as a man of the people, a man born in a log cabin, and barbecues and alcohol were one way his supporters promoted him.

The political barbecues were often all-day affairs, at least partially because of the length of speeches from the time. A newspaper report on a political barbecue from 1838 stated that, after assembling at noon and being entertained by music from a band, one group of people (of "at least a thousand persons") listened to one speaker expound on the issues of the day for four solid hours before being served the meal—as the newspaper noted, his conclusion produced "the most loud and enthusiastic cheering, prolonged to the greatest extent."[15] In November 1860, when the question of secession was the foremost issue in the country, fourteen-year-old John Steele Henderson attended a barbecue in North Carolina on that topic. He and some friends went to the barbecue at seven o'clock in the morning, stayed "awhile," then traveled to a nearby town to do some shopping. They met some relatives who were on their way to the barbecue and then they themselves went back to the barbecue, where they listened to a speaker talk about the possibility of civil war. After the speaker finished the barbecue was served, "and a poor dinner it was," Henderson wrote to his father later that day (part of the problem may have been that Henderson was a Democrat and the barbecue was put together by the Whig party). Henderson complained that the meal was "composed of beef, raw pork and bread that actually wasn't fit for dogs to eat. The crowd eat up all there was there in five or ten minutes, the bread excepted." Two more politicians spoke after the meal on topics related to secession and the possibility of war.[16]

Even by the 1820s barbecue and politics had become tightly connected. In the July 31, 1829, edition, the *Hagarstown Mail* (from Pennsylvania) carried an advertisement for a barbecue for supporters of Andrew Jackson, the candidate for president in an election that was as full of mudslinging as any modern campaign. (Jackson's wife died soon after the election, and he blamed her death on the rumors spread by his opponent that she was an adulteress, she having married Jackson before her previous marriage was legally ended.) Two weeks after the barbecue the newspaper featured an editorial responding to a local doctor's opinion that barbecues were "wrong in principle—as bringing with them *broken bones and sick stomachs;* and he adds '*we saw Cholic and Cramp*.' . . . These Barbecues, the Doctor thinks, are *radically* wrong and *are got up to serve the cause of a few individuals*," which was probably an understatement; the barbecues were commonly used across the South to drum up support for candidates. "But why did he not say so last year, when Administration Barbecues [that is, barbecues for Jackson's opponent, whom the doctor presumably supported] were all the go," the editorialist asked, then listed off a number of specific barbecues that had occurred. Using a pun that played off Jackson's nickname of "Old Hickory," the writer added that "Hickory Pills will cure them—they need no other medicine—and a Hickory Pill is good for the Adams *Cramp* and the *Clay cold* Cholic," Adams and Clay being two of Jackson's main opponents in the election.[17]

In the mid-1800s two trends changed the nature of barbecues, and both of these trends involved women. The first trend was the widening democracy discussed above. Women could not yet vote in national elections (that would not come until 1920), but they were, more and more, invited to the political barbecues that had previously been testosterone-heavy affairs. As the Whigs, especially, opened barbecues to women, the drinking and carousing that had been hallmarks of barbecues began to be tamped down. The second trend, in some ways, took this idea even farther by removing what had been a major part of barbecues in the mid-1800s (and is still a big part of barbecues today): the alcohol.

Alcohol was a major part of life in the 1800s. While both wine and beer were consumed, hard liquor was also quite popular, and led to many scenes of public drunkenness. The Temperance Movement began as an effort to lessen consumption of alcohol, but as the century progressed the movement turned into a crusade to ban alcohol altogether. Alcohol and barbecues were tightly connected in the early 1800s and so, as the Temperance Movement moved from the fringe into the mainstream of American society, "cold water" barbecues (which featured no alcohol but plenty of water) became popular.

That barbecue and liquor were intimately linked in most people's minds is reflected in a popular Temperance Movement story about a cold water barbecue that showed up repeatedly in American newspapers in the 19th century. Between 1851 and 1876 the story of Paul Denton, a Methodist preacher from Texas, was repeated almost verbatim in at least six newspapers in different parts of the country, and it showed up in verse form a seventh time in 1882. The story, with quotes here from the *New York Observer and Chronicle*'s 1852 version, is this: Denton "advertised a barbecue, with better liquor than is generally furnished." When the crowd had gathered "a desperado" asked where the promised liquor was. "'There!', answered the missionary, in tones of thunder, and pointing his motionless finger at the matchless double spring gushing up in two strong columns . . . .'There!' he repeated, with a look terrible as lightning, while his enemy actually trembled at his feet; 'there is the liquor which God, the eternal, brews for all his children.'" There is much more of this speech, and one reason the story was repeated verbatim across the years is that Denton's speech is quite a good one, as he compares "the simmering still, over noxious fires, choked with poisonous gasses, surrounded with the stench of sickening odors and corruptions" with the water prepared "in the green glade, and grassy dell, where the red deer wanders, and the child loves to play, there God brews it." At the end of the story Denton asks, about the water, "'Speak out, my friends, would you exchange it for the demon's drink, alcohol?' A shout, like the roar of a tempest, answered 'NO!'"[18] This was the kind of story that put fire into the veins of Temperance supporters across the country.

THE LATE 19TH CENTURY

After the Civil War barbecues remained popular in the South, and were even used in some cases to reconcile the North and South. In 1900 the *Atlanta Constitution* announced that a massive barbecue was planned for July 19 and 20 to commemorate the Battle of Peachtree Creek, which had occurred near Atlanta on July 20, 1864. Surviving veterans of the battle from both the Union and Confederate sides were invited, and 10,000 people were expected for the dinner, served at the same place where the battle had occurred. The organizers of the event had an additional motive beyond just reconciling the two sides. There was a movement to make the battle area a national park, and in doing so to mark off the battle lines on the ground, but apparently no one could agree just where they were. As the newspaper article reported, "It was decided that the most practical way to do this would be to invite the surviving officers of the engagement to Atlanta and hold a big reunion."[19]

After the Civil War a new kind of public holiday came into vogue, and barbecues were also associated with it. Emancipation Day, also known as June-teenth, became a public holiday and was widely celebrated by blacks across the South, particularly in Texas. In 1894 the *Galveston Daily News* reported on a host of Emancipation Day barbecues across the state. At Bastrop, Texas, "The colored people . . . celebrated their Nineteenth by having an immense barbecue and speaking out at their park to-day, forming in line of procession, headed by a brass band, and marching thereto." At Brenham, Texas, "There are quite a number of barbecues and smaller celebrations in different parts of the county," while at Victoria, Texas, "A barbecue, with the usual accessories of speechmaking, games, etc., constitute the programme for the day."[20]

Although it remained popular in the South, by the late 19th century barbecue had disappeared from the North. An 1894 barbecue to raise money for a Boston church was popular enough to be repeated the next year, but barbecues were so rare in that city that a local newspaper had to go back to 1793 to find the previous example, held in honor of the French Revolution. A newspaper article on the 1895 barbecue made it clear that barbecues were a southern, not northern, tradition. "[T]he mere rumor of one [in the South] will draw a crowd from 50 miles around, just to get a smell of the roasting meat, if nothing more," the article read, adding that "No big outdoor political gathering there is complete without a barbecue." The reporter speculated on why barbecues were not popular in the North, but his theories were a little puzzling. "One reason is the great length of time it takes to properly cook an ox in this way, and another the difficulty of getting together a sufficient crowd to devour it after it is cooked." A long cooking time should not have kept crowds away—after all, only the cook and his assistants needed to be there the entire time, while the guests only needed to show up at mealtime. Finding a crowd, also, would probably not have been a problem, particularly in Boston, then one of the largest cities in the country, and the 1894 barbecue had drawn about 10,000 people. The 1895 barbecue featured not only food but also plenty of entertainment. There was "a 'playout' of the Roxbury Vets, the champions of New England . . . a kite-flying exhibition, to be given by C. B. Wong, a Nashua Chinaman . . . dancing, sports of various kinds, a balloon ascension, fire-works, and a genuine barbecue concert by Rogers' Mississippi colored troubadours, 50 in number, whose singing will add a regular flavor to the scene."[21]

THE RISE OF THE RESTAURANTS

Barbecue was a common food in the South at public gatherings. Holidays, political rallies, church dinners, and school fundraisers were all possibilities for barbecues. The meat at these barbecues was usually donated by local farmers, so beef, pork, goat, or mutton could end up on the table. The meal was usually free or, if there was a charge, the money went to a local cause. The result was that the availability of barbecue on any given date was as inconsistent as the type of meat that might be served.

24

In the late 19th century this situation began to change. Cooks began selling barbecue at definite times, often on the weekends, at a standard location along a street or road. The cost to enter the barbecue business was low since a building was not necessary, although in rainy weather it would certainly be preferable for the cook. If the business was relatively successful, though, a shack would probably be built to house the operation, although the actual barbecuing would likely still be done outside, in a pit, as was customary (even today fires are a major problem for barbecue restaurants). Customers would walk up to the shack, make their order, receive their food, and then eat it standing or sitting outside the shack, or take their food elsewhere. It was a small-time operation as evidenced by the fact that when the cook ran out of food he simply closed up shop for the weekend.

These were not proper restaurants, but as the years went on many of these shacks were replaced with more permanent buildings with tables and chairs inside. The popularity of cars, especially in the 1920s, helped barbecue restaurants as a suddenly mobile population needed to be fed, and barbecue was one of the first types of fast-food restaurants. The rise of the restaurants will be discussed in more detail in a later chapter that focuses on restaurants, but there was one interesting effect of the growth of barbecue restaurants: the growth of regional variations of barbecue.

Barbecue is strongly marked by regional variations, and barbecue aficionados will argue for hours about the superiority of one type of barbecue over another. Differences include the type of meat, the type of sauce, and the sides that accompany the meat. For comparison, eastern North Carolina style cooks the entire hog, then serves it finely chopped. The sauce is vinegar based, and one popular side dish is a very thick stew called Brunswick stew. Memphis-style barbecue focuses on pork ribs and pulled pork sandwiches, the sauce is tomato based, and a popular side dish is spaghetti in barbecue sauce, with bits of pork shoulder. Other parts of the South have their own specific types of barbecue. These differences do not seem to appear until the late 19th century, around the same time that barbecue restaurants began appearing.

This likely had to do with the restaurant business. In the days before refrigeration, chefs could not cook every type of meat; they had to pick only a few specialties and stick with them. They probably chose the meat that was most available and cheapest, and probably monitored, through sales or requests, customers' responses. The typical plan was to cook up whatever meat they could on Friday and sell it until it ran out on Saturday and Sunday. Pitmasters often learned from each other, and the apprentice system was strong in the restaurant business, so that one pitmaster would teach a number of protégés, who would later open their own barbecue joints in the same area, cooking the meat in the way they had learned. In this way the regional variations appeared in the late 19th and early 20th centuries.

BARBECUE FOR THE REST OF US: THE EARLY YEARS

By the turn of the 20th century barbecue was popular in the South, but beyond that its popularity was limited by the fact that other parts of the country had no barbecue tradition (which made it hard to learn how to cook barbecue), and it took a very long time to properly barbecue a piece of meat (which made it even harder to learn). Barbecue restaurants might have existed outside of the South, but not many people outside the South actually barbecued.

In the 20th century, though, a number of things happened to change barbecue from a marginal type of cooking associated with a particular geographical location to a major fad that never seems to have gone away. Barbecuing, in short, became mainstream.

On its way to becoming mainstream, though, it became much less well defined. In looking at newspaper and magazine accounts from the 19th century, whenever "barbecue" is mentioned it is fairly clear that it refers to a gathering where slow-cooked meats are served to many people. By the middle of the 20th century, though, the definition was much less precise. "Barbecue" referred to a type of cooking and had nothing to do with a gathering. The *Better Homes and Gardens Barbecue Book*, from 1965, provided what seems to be a fairly precise definition. On a page listing cooking terms, barbecue was defined as "To roast meat slowly on a spit over coals, in a rotisserie basket, basting occasionally with a highly seasoned sauce. Often refers to foods cooked or served with a barbecue sauce."[22] The first sentence of the definition was relatively precise, but the second sentence opened the possibilities of just what barbecue was to almost anything, so long as it was "served with barbecue sauce." By providing a formal definition, the authors of the book seemed to be at least attempting to denote what was, and therefore what was not, barbecue. However, in looking at the recipes in the book, which again had a title of *Better Homes and Gardens Barbecue Book*, it is fairly obvious that, to the authors, barbecue meant anything grilled on a grill. Flapjack Meat Loaf was essentially a regular meatloaf cooked in a skillet over the fire, Pizza Burgers had pizza toppings mixed into the ground meat, and the Shrimp-out recipe had the cook grill shrimp covered with eggs and soda cracker crumbs.[23] None of those recipes involved barbecue sauce but they all appeared in a book with "barbecue" in the title. By the middle of the 20th century, "barbecue" was synonymous to "grilling" to many people, so the rise in popularity of barbecue was really a rise in the popularity of grilling.

At this point, then, we need to leave the barbecues of the South to see what was happening in the larger American culture. The rise of barbecue in the 20th century pulled together a number of other trends from the time.

One early trend was the popularity of the outdoors and, with it, outdoor cooking. As more and more Americans moved from rural areas into the fast-growing cities, and as more and more people worked factory jobs, there was an opposing push toward the outdoors. Some of this can be seen in the increasing popularity of sports and outdoor recreation during the late 19th and early 20th centuries, when millions of Americans bought bicycles or played baseball or football. Some of it can also be seen in newly formed groups like the Boy Scouts of America, founded in 1910 to foster the development of young men through outdoor activities.

The popularity of the car, especially during and after the sales boom of the 1920s, pushed people toward the outdoors as well. While early cars were temperamental and prone to problems—blow-outs were such a problem that spare tires were often mounted on the side of the car, for quick access—there was a class of adventurers who attempted cross-country travel long before the development of the interstate system. Services for early travelers were minimal, and camping and cooking out were, in many places, the only options for those traveling across country. These situations, also, pushed people toward the outdoors. As will be discussed later, in the chapter on barbecue restaurants, barbecue was an early type of fast food in the South.

The popularity of the outdoors meant there were cookbooks that focused on outdoor cooking, but they were really about outdoor grilling and did not usually use the word *barbecue*. One example is Horace Kephart's *Camp Cookery*, from 1910. The book was written for those who were planning to camp for extended periods of time for hunting trips or just the pleasure of camping. The first sentence of the foreword nicely sums up Kephart's philosophy on camp cooking: "The less a man carries in his pack, the more he must carry in his head."[24] Simplicity was the key to Kephart's approach to cooking, as seen by how he cautioned against bringing much to season freshly caught fish or game—its freshness was seasoning enough. In a chapter on meat, he outlined numerous ways of cooking. "Meat, game, and fish may be fried, broiled, roasted, baked, boiled, stewed, or steamed," he wrote, and then differentiated between the various methods by stating that "Frying and broiling are the quickest processes; roasting, baking, and boiling take an hour or two; a stew of meat and vegetables, to be good, takes half a day, and so does soup prepared from the raw materials."[25] Slow-cooking meat over a grill was not on Kephart's list, although roasting (on a spit) was recommended. By 1910, barbecuing was not yet synonymous with grilling.

Although barbecue is usually associated with the South, the barbecue fad that started in the 1930s was associated with the West coast. *Sunset* was a West coast–oriented magazine that early on trumpeted the popularity of the barbecue, and in 1939 they published *Sunset's Barbecue Book*. "Why is it that practically everybody in the West has a barbecue, is planning to have a barbecue, or wishes he had one?" the foreword asked, then offered a number of possible reasons, including the warm western climate, the "flicker and warmth of an open-air fire" that pulls us back to pioneer days, and the "aroma of sizzling steaks."[26] By the 1960s, barbecue was still associated with westerners. In a humorous *Harper's* article from 1960 on "The Procal," "the most fanatic of local patriots" who favored southern California above all other regions, barbecue was mentioned several times as being beloved of the Californian. "His needs are not great," read the article, listing "his car, his barbecue, his sport-shirt" as being the three primary needs. "Today he is probably the most leisure- and hobby-conscious citizen in the United States," the article continued, stating that he "is dedicated to his barbecue, his swimming pool, his beaches, his deserts . . . and, above all, his television set."[27] The laid-back informality that became a hallmark of Western style would become immensely popular after World War II.

THE POSTWAR EXPLOSION

In the mid-1950s Clementine Paddleford, one of the most popular food writers of her day, took a research trip out West. Her intent was to survey the attitudes of Westerners, check out new trends, and interview cooks for her nationally syndicated newspaper column. When she returned to New York City she wrote a memo to coworkers describing what she saw.

She noted that small kitchen appliances were popular: "wash machine, ironer, dishwasher, blender, vacuum cleaner with all the gadgets. I have no statistics, but this was so in almost all the homes visited." Televisions were also popular, to the point that "the idea of inviting guests for television seems to have lost its spice as a party event," although young people still invited friends over to "to enjoy favorite shows—of course demanding refreshments." In smaller towns fewer women held jobs outside the home, and in general more men helped out with cooking.

Regarding foods, there were a few trends she observed. "The flame craze is everywhere. Flambéed items are listed on menus coast to coast, big towns, little towns." At a restaurant in Boise, Idaho, she ordered a cocktail named after the restaurant, "expecting something different but not spectacular. The drink came flaming, a sort of Martini made with lime juice and floating a half lime shell, green side turned in and this filled with dark rum, ignited!"

And, she noted,

> Everywhere the Barbecue. No longer a new thing, once a fad, now a "solid" in the way of entertaining. I doubt if ever again fried meats will be in the running. Almost every western home has an outdoor barbecue and usually a second built into the kitchen for cold weather use. Now the barbecue moves into smart dining rooms in restaurants. Charcoal broiled meats are featured served from the barbecue centered in the dining room and presided over by a chef in high hat. This trend I have noted taking hold a bit in New York, more so however, in our nearby country inns, but the west leads.[28]

This was the state of barbecue by the mid-1950s. It had moved from being a fad to a "solid," from being served in the back yard to the fanciest restaurants, from a food that was predominantly associated with the South to a food that was served across the country. In the years after World War II, a number of trends in American culture pushed barbecue into the mainstream of American cooking.

In general, the postwar years were a time of rising prosperity, when millions of Americans rose from the working class to the middle class. While there are many different ways to define the middle class, one way to think of it is in terms of disposable income. Working-class families scarcely have any money left over after buying the necessities; for them, a trip to the grocery store means always buying the cheapest item. For middle-class families, the grocery store means variety, where a chicken can be purchased whole, in parts, frozen, or canned, depending on desire. Barbecuing was certainly not a necessity, but it was often a fun activity for families.

Prosperity meant the possibility of living in a new house. Houses were in short supply coming out of World War II. During the Great Depression in the 1930s not many people could afford to build a new house, while during the war rationing meant that not many people could obtain the materials needed to build a new house. A housing boom began almost as soon as the war was over, and the new developments were often on the outskirts of cities, or outside of cities altogether, in the suburbs. Parents liked suburban houses because they had a lawn where the kids could play, and the lawn played into the barbecue craze as well, since that was where the barbecue grill could sit.

The popularity of lawns points to another postwar trend, the resurging popularity of the outdoors. In 1953, the editors of *Fortune* magazine published a series of reports, and then a book, that examined the changes in American society and culture that had taken place since 1945, the end of World War II. One set of changes involved Americans' more active role in leisure activities. Ticket sales to baseball and hockey games had dropped by 25 percent since 1947, and attendance at movies, concerts, and the theater was also down. At the same time, sales of items related to active leisure activities had increased: Stores were selling more games, toys, fishing rods, bicycles, and golf balls. Expenditures related to both domestic and international travel had increased as well.[29] With salaries rising almost across the board, and more car ownership, the 1950s and 1960 were, in some ways, the golden age of the family vacation, when millions of parents loaded the kids into the station wagon and headed west on the new interstate highway system, visiting Yellowstone or Yosemite National Park and the newly built Disneyland in California. Barbecuing offered those without time, or without a car, the ability to enjoy the great outdoors. As one prewar magazine article put it, "Outdoors is just a few steps away—actually right in your own back yard." To the question of just what someone could do in the backyard, the article's author responded, "Eat! Primitively. Gorgeously. Simply. Elaborately. But spiced with something no cordon bleu can add to food. The open sky, the good earth, the smell of smoke, the hiss of the meat, the glow of the embers. A barbecue at home!"[30]

New house designs brought the outdoors into suburban houses. The ranch-style house—described by one author as being a "simple, informal, one-story structure, [with] low-pitched eaves" was popular in the postwar years, and its informality highlighted its connection to the outdoors.[31] Picture windows and sliding glass doors were in demand; they allowed those inside the house an unobstructed view of the outdoors. The main floors of houses were built level with the outdoors, not a step or two above ground level, which made the transition between the indoors and outdoors more seamless. Old design traditions highlighting the outdoors continued as well: Over half the homes built in the first half of 1950 had front porches, and a study from 1944 indicated that that only one in forty families did not want a porch, while nearly half of them wanted several porches.[32]

Part of the new emphasis on the outdoors in house design was because of the popularity of the outdoors, but some of it was also the fact that the new suburban houses were often fairly small. The median size of new houses in 1949–1950 was 983 square feet, about a 12 percent decrease from 1940 and a tight squeeze for growing families.[33] Barbecuing was a fairly simple solution to the problems families experienced in the postwar years. Having a barbecue pushed the eating, and much of the cooking of the meal, outside. Dad cooked the meat on the grill, Mom worked on the side dishes and beverages in the kitchen, and the kids shuttled back and forth between the inside and outside.

THE BIRTH OF THE PATIO DADDY-O

As a form of cooking, barbecuing occupies a space in what has traditionally been defined as women's work. Historically, barbecuing is one of the few cooking-related tasks that men could do without fear of someone questioning their masculinity (two others are cooking pancakes for their families, especially on the weekend, and, in the days before dishwashers, drying dishes).

Barbecuing generally meant grilling outside (unless one had an indoor grill, which was unusual but not unknown in the 1950s), and postwar cookbooks often made a historical connection between barbecue chefs and Neanderthals in a way that was much less objectionable than that sounds. "Our sometime ancestors crashing through jungles, or sloshing through the marshes and soggy fields, were most enthusiastic diners-out," James Beard wrote in *Cook It Outdoors*, from 1941. "They would tear a leg off an animal, toast it over a roaring fire and toss it down the hatch accompanied by a little wild garlic, perhaps, a couple of bananas, and a few leaves from some long since forgotten tree. There was little attempt at that time to count calories or to maintain a well-balanced diet."[34]

The last sentence in Beard's quote is a counterpoint to the previous sentences as the emphasis on counting calories and watching the diet was generally associated with females, particularly the home economics movement. Essentially, the belief was that, thousands of years ago, among prehistoric peoples, the men both collected and cooked the food, albeit cooking in a very simplistic, over-the-fire sort of way. By the 20th century, though, cooking was strongly associated with women, in no small part because they did the vast majority of it in this country.

Beliefs regarding men and women cooking were a bit strange by the mid-20th century, at least as they came through in cookbooks and magazine articles. Perhaps because of the home economics movement of the early 20th century, which emphasized standardization and a scientific approach to cooking, women were seen as being both uncreative in the kitchen and sorely lacking knowledge. They read cookbooks because they had to read cookbooks, and cookbook authors constantly implored them to be creative and artistic in their cooking. Men, on the other hand, were naturally creative and had such a store of knowledge about cooking that they scarcely needed to consult a cookbook. The ability to cook came to them easily, or so the cookbooks indicated. The gender ideas that came through barbecue cookbooks will be more closely examined in chapter 5, which is on barbecuing in popular culture.

Gender beliefs were so entrenched in the 1950s that one researcher concluded that not just cooking roles but the foods themselves were gendered. Ernest Dichter was a marketing researcher who, in the 1950s, concluded that "Rice is felt as being feminine, but potatoes as masculine; tea is feminine, coffee is strongly masculine."[35] The most extreme foods were cake and meat.

Which brings us back to barbecue. While many things were roasted on the grill, the center of focus for any barbecue was the meat. In this way barbecuing was squarely a man's job. He was performing a role that, all authors seemed to agree, had been a man's job thousands of years before, and was a man's job again. In more recent history, outdoor cooking while camping was seen to be a man's responsibility, and barbecuing seems to have been something of a natural extension of outdoor cooking.

BARBECUE AND CONVENIENCE FOODS

Convenience foods exploded in popularity in the years after World War II. Many different types of products were either introduced during that time or had drastically increased sales. Frozen dinners, frozen orange juice, presweetened and vitamin-enhanced breakfast cereals, cakes mixes, and instant coffee were all big sellers in the postwar years.[36] With these products, consumers paid a bit more at the market but saved some time and effort at home. This fits with what was happening in American culture: People had more money as salaries increased at a fairly steady rate, but they had less time with all those children born in the baby boom. For many consumers, paying a bit more was a good tradeoff for more time at home.

With this in mind, the popularity of barbecuing seems somewhat strange. Barbecuing went against the two main principles of convenience foods: The foods barbecued were raw rather than heavily processed, and they took time to prepare and cook. Was the popularity of barbecuing, with the stress on its masculinity, in some way a reaction against the overly processed foods of the time, which were always targeted at women?

Perhaps. There was a type of postwar cooking that stressed using convenience foods to cook, either by simply making cake from a store-bought mix or by adding a few ingredients to the mix. In this context, barbecuing seems to be a refreshing way to cook: It not only jettisoned the mixes and packages; it also got rid of the kitchen and the female cook entirely. There was a reason so many cookbooks made at least passing reference to cavemen cooking, since barbecuing took things back to a much earlier time. In some way, barbecuing was a reaction against some of the time's predominant ideas about cooking: Scratch cooking was dead and gone, replaced by convenience foods that were quicker and easier, and tasted just the same as the foods mom used to make.

However, if barbecuing was a reaction against this idea, it was a severely limited reaction. Yes, men cooked the barbecue meal, but they usually cooked almost nothing else. The only other cooking activity men were associated with was making pancakes, and pancake mixes had been available since at least the 1880s. For most men, cooking started and stopped with barbecue.

Women were also involved with the barbecue, and here again, the reaction against convenience foods was limited. If men cooked the barbecue entrée, women were responsible for everything else, from the invitations to the side dishes to the cleanup afterward. In cookbooks and magazine articles barbecue was often pitched as a way for mom to take a night off, and if it did not quite happen that way, if mom still had to do quite a bit, manufacturers of convenience foods were there to offer anything from premade potato salad to quick cake mixes. In this way the barbecue craze worked along with the popularity of convenience foods: Convenience food manufacturers might not make money from the meat on the grill but they did make money from all the side items that went along with the meat.

THE GROWTH OF THE BARBECUE INDUSTRY

The barbecue craze really took off after World War II, and to some extent, it never let up. In 1953 the editors of *Fortune* listed some of the popular trends of the day that came from the suburbs: "hard-tops, culottes, dungarees, vodka martinis, outdoor barbecues, functional furniture, picture windows, and costume jewelry."[37] Some of these trends have faded away but the barbecue is still popular, having outlived many other food crazes of the time like flambéed drinks. Much of its initial popularity was because of cultural factors unique to the time that have already been discussed: In the midst of the baby boom it was a family activity that took much of the activity outside, during which time the man's masculinity was reinforced and the woman got a break from cooking. However, its continuing popularity is at least partially due to a new set of boosters with an active interest in keeping the barbecue craze going: the barbecue industry, which included all the companies that worked to sell fuel, grills, food, and anything else associated with backyard barbecuing.

One of the earliest of these industries was the charcoal industry. Henry Ford went into the briquette business in the 1920s as a way to maximize profits from his automobile business. Car parts were packed in wood crates, and early car frames were made from wood, so the assembly plants generated enormous amounts of scrap wood; at Ford's directive that wood was burned down into charcoal. He decided the briquette shape was easier to pack tightly, minimizing shipping costs.[38] However, it took decades for charcoal to become a fuel of choice for grillers. Until the 1950s most barbecue cooks used wood, the traditional barbecue fuel, but as the barbecue craze took off so did sales of briquettes. In 1951 Ford sold the charcoal operation to investors, and the resulting company, Kingsford, is still a major player in the charcoal industry.

Another set of companies worked to sell grills to consumers, although it took a while for that market to develop as well. The barbecue craze started before World War II in the western states, and cookbooks from that time often included instructions for building a grill. *Sunset's Barbecue Book*, produced two years before the United States entered World War II, reflected the fact that many people did not yet have grills. Much of the first part of the book is taken up with plans and instructions for constructing grills, most of which were permanent structures. The plans range from a simple grill made of two low stone walls with a grate on top all the way to a large pit made "to service approximately 350 to 600 persons."[39] The book also included instructions for a "barbecue wagon," which was essentially a trolley for trays rather than an actual grill. Women's magazines regularly had articles on constructing grills, like *McCall's* "$50.13 for an Outdoor Grill," which showed how to construct a simple grill from cinderblocks.[40] Many authors emphasized the fact that, although they could be elaborate, barbecue grills certainly did not need to be. "Your broiling facilities may be a piece of gridded iron, salvaged from an old stove and propped up on a pile of rocks, or it may be a gorgeous stainless steel cookery unit, complete with an adjustable firebox, an electric spit, and other such luxurious accouterments," wrote James Beard and Helen Evans Brown in *The Complete Book of Outdoor Cookery*, from 1955.[41]

The do-it-yourself idea was popular, but it could be taken a bit too far, and in looking through materials from the 1950s one can see ideas and recommendations that clearly show it to be a very different time from today. Regarding starting the barbecue fire, Beard and Evans recommended using "a commercial kindling fluid, tablet, flare, or jelly, but make sure it's an odorless one. Unpleasant fumes are apt to linger and add their odor to the meat. We use, and highly recommend, an odorless paint thinner which we buy by the gallon at any paint or hardware store."[42] This practice was apparently common, as *Betty Crocker's*

Outdoor Cook Book, from 1961, had the same advice using almost the same wording, although a recent reprint of the book notes at the bottom of the page that cooks should use "only a barbecue starter and never any other flammable liquid to start a fire."[43] The Incin-O-Grill was a barbecue grill that had the questionable advantage of doubling as an incinerator. A flyer for the product advertised a "colorful, handy grill that will give you years of carefree barbecuing and a wonderfully practical incinerator that will safely burn up to 5 bushels of leaves and rubbish at a time."[44] One hopes that no midcentury multitasker decided to grill some hamburgers while also disposing of some sofa cushions, but mistakes could happen. One night in June 1959, a family of four ate a meal that was probably fairly typical for the time: grilled steaks, boiled potatoes, green beans, tossed salad, soft drinks for the kids, and beer for the adults. Within an hour they were vomiting, nauseous, and complaining of headaches, all of which lasted until around midnight. Health officials investigated and found that the family had taken the do-it-yourself attitude too far. The culprit was the metal grill on the barbecue, which was "an old refrigerator shelf which was being used for this purpose for the first time." The shelf was cadmium-plated, and in the fire the cadmium seems to have melted and attached itself to the steaks, resulting in a mild case of cadmium poisoning for the family.[45]

Another option for getting a grill, of course, was simply to buy one. The 1908 Sears, Roebuck catalog, which at nearly 1,200 pages contained almost every mass-produced type of product available for purchase in the United States, did not include any portable grills for campers, most likely because campers were fine with cooking on whatever materials they could find at a campsite. By the years before World War II, though, grills were available for purchase, often from auto dealers, since they might be necessary for anyone taking an extended trip. By the 1960s there were a variety of grill choices available, as one newspaper writer described in 1962:

> There are simple round or oblong grill units with no hood. There are covered-top barbecue wagons and heavy covered porcelain-lined cauldrons on legs. There are complex units that can be built into a stone wall, and double-grill vertical broilers that broil two steaks at once. There are portable boxes that open up into barbecues, and there are Mexican bee-hive outdoor ovens, Chinese-style "smoke ovens," deep Hawaiian luau pits and Texas-style underground barbecues. Then of course there are electric rotisseries and grills.[46]

The Weber Grill, invented in 1956, was different from other grills in that, when the lid was closed, the heat was efficiently contained to cook food. Before the Weber Grill, grills were usually open so that food's proximity to the coals was an important factor in cooking—most recipes called for a rotisserie to help cook meats. Wind and rain, too, were major problems for grillers. With the Weber Grill, though, the cook could place the meat in the grill, close the lid, and be assured that the meat was cooking even though it might be many inches away from the coals.

The food industry was obviously helped by the barbecue craze. Although it did not lift sales of all food products, barbecue certainly helped sell certain products. A 1957 press release from the Grocery Manufacturers of America announced that "Frankfurters alone, a barbecue item if ever there was one, present a staggering statistic. Expectations are that a billion pounds . . . will be consumed in this country this year, meaning that each man, woman and child will average six pounds of them." The press release went on to discuss the sales opportunities involved with barbecuing: "A fortunate aspect of a barbecue is the wide variety of foods it usually presents to the backyard gourmet. Fresh salad vegetables and fruit, potato chips, pretzels, pickles, mustard, ketchup, cakes, carbonated beverages and marshmallows are only a few of the convenient foods available."[47]

The food industry had an active interest in continuing the popularity of barbecuing, and they did this in at least two ways. First, barbecue-themed advertising became a staple of spring and summer advertising, particularly in women's magazines. Advertisements for all the products that went along with barbecuing, from the meats to the side dishes to the drinks and desserts, showed those products displayed prominently in color photos of families relaxing at an outdoor table while dad stood over the grill. Because the food writers took the direction of their articles from the advertisers, articles about barbecuing ran alongside those advertisements.

A second way food companies helped perpetuate the popularity of barbecuing was through creating and publicizing recipes. By churning out a steady supply of new recipes for all the dishes that were served at barbecues, they helped to keep men's and women's interest in barbecuing alive. For example, the R. T. French Company, which produced prepared mustard and spices, issued a press release in the summer of 1958 that featured recipes for a barbecue. Although the barbecue menu "may be scoffed at by the gourmet chef, owner of secret outdoor cooking formulas . . . [t]o the average backyard, smoke-eating cook, on the other hand, this new suggested menu should be welcome." The menu featured "Frankfurter Kabobs, potato salad, pickles, olives, and hot buttered rolls. Fruit marinated in that pungent spice, cardamom seed, along with cinnamon cookies and coffee round out a toothsome outdoor repast." The press release included recipes for all of those things. The frankfurter kabobs were pieces of hot dog, processed cheese, and mushrooms alternated on sticks, although one wonders how long the processed cheese would have lasted over an open fire.[48] At any rate, by cranking out recipes that were to be used at barbecues, and that were often reprinted verbatim by newspapers and magazines, the food industry helped keep the barbecue craze alive.

Other companies supported the popularity of barbecue as well. The aluminum industry sold quite a bit of aluminum foil for use at barbecues, to the point where the Kaiser Aluminum & Chemical Corporation sponsored a barbecue contest in Hawaii. The company issued a pamphlet (which seemed to be covered in aluminum foil) announcing the contest, where twenty-five cooks would be flown to Waikiki for a cook-off. In keeping with gender ideas of the time, the contest was only open to men, although their wives would also be flown to Hawaii for the event.[49]

CONTINUATION OF SOUTHERN BARBECUE

During the 20th century barbecue in America essentially went in two directions. As discussed immediately above, for many people barbecue became synonymous with outdoor grilling. The older definition of barbecue, which featured larger cuts of meat roasted for hours over a low fire, continued as it had, though, mostly in the South. In that part of the country, a number of trends occurred during the 20th century.

One trend is simply the continuation of that type of barbecuing, particularly at political gatherings. Politicians still used barbecues as a way to draw in potential voters and get their message heard. When Franklin Delano Roosevelt visited Georgia while running for president in 1931, he was feted with a barbecue. As was the tradition, the event was held in a "grove of oaks," the crowd was filled with important politicians from Georgia, and the menu was pork, mutton, and 150 gallons of Brunswick stew.[50] With more population, and more press in attendance, the barbecues became bigger than ever. In 1923 the *New York Times* proclaimed the barbecue given in honor of Oklahoma governor John Walton's inauguration the "world's greatest barbecue," and they may have been correct. The inauguration was the occasion for festivities over several days that included a parade through Oklahoma City that featured Pawnee Bill's Wild West show and "a grand ball at the State Capitol, with four floors for dances." The barbecue itself featured "thousands of beeves [cattle], reindeer, buffalo, bear, antelope, opossums and countless numbers of sheep, hogs, rabbits, turkeys and chickens . . . cooked over a mile of trenches." Over 100,000 people partook of

President Lyndon Baines Johnson serving himself at a barbecue at his Texas ranch. LBJ Library photo by Robert Knudsen.

the meal, although they had planned for 200,000.[51] Southern political barbecues have continued into the 21st century as well. One Kentucky barbecue in 2007 fed over 5,000 people with 19,000 pounds of pork and mutton.[52]

No 20th-century president was more associated with barbecues than Lyndon Baines Johnson. Johnson made a conscious effort to project the image of a Texas cattle rancher, and giving barbecues at his ranch was one way to advance that image. Press coverage of a barbecue he hosted about a month into his first term (which began when he took the oath of office after Kennedy's assassination) shows just how tightly barbecue was wrapped up with Johnson's image, and how incongruous the combination of the presidency and a down-home barbecue could be. The White House had bused four loads of reporters to his ranch near Austin, Texas, for the occasion, and after a tour of the property, which included the house where Johnson was born and the school he attended, the crowd settled in for a barbecue dinner of beef spareribs. The *New York Times* reporter described Secretary of State Dean Rusk blinking "away tears from the acrid smoke of the hardwood fires" while McGeorge Bundy, the president's special assistant for national security affairs, juggled a briefcase and a plate of ribs. After the meal the president surprised reporters by taking questions while standing on a hay bale. In keeping with the Western theme, and

Johnson's desire to define himself as a true Westerner, at the end of the question and answer time Johnson "mounted his horse [a black Tennessee Walking Horse] and rode off into the sunset," his nervous press secretary "clutching hard at a red and white paint" at the president's side.[53] LBJ's dining preferences stood in stark contrast to Kennedy, whose French chef helped popularize French food in America. This first barbecue as president was no unusual occurrence; over the next few years there would be many barbecues at the LBJ ranch. The barbecues even followed him overseas: While visiting Australia in 1966 he "donned his ranch togs and provided his special Texas-style baked beans at a lavish barbecue . . . for Australia's leaders," and two years later, in El Salvador, he attended "a barbecue lunch by a mountain grove."[54]

Southern barbecue continued much as it had before, but by the end of the 20th century it had become self-conscious, for want of a better term. The regional cooking styles that had started at the turn of the 20th century had become an ingrained part of each region's culture, and a way of differentiating different areas. Newspaper columnists argued over which region had the best barbecue and then, more specifically, just which restaurant in a region was the best. In the 1970s the idea of celebrating Southern barbecue became popular, and it dovetailed with a number of other trends in American culture, such as the quest for "real" American traditions and the general popularity of Southern culture as seen in the increasing numbers of "born again" Christians and the election of Georgia governor (and former peanut farmer) Jimmy Carter to the presidency. Towns across the country attempted to cash in on the popularity of barbecue by hosting barbecue festivals and contests.

The development of what is called "competition barbecue" occurred during this time, and the popularity of barbecue contests is significant for a number of reasons. For one, some of the competitions are very big and very popular, for both competitors and those just there to watch. Fittingly, the two largest competitions are in cities with their own barbecue styles: Memphis in May, which began in 1978, and the American Royal, which began in 1980 in Kansas City (technically, Memphis in May and the American Royal are both much larger general events that happen to have barbecue contests attached to them). Each event draws hundreds of competitors each year. Each of these cities, in turn, has organizations that sanction these contests and many others: the Memphis Barbecue Network and the Kansas City Barbeque Society (KCBS). As the KCBS website describes it, the society was originally just a collection of people who were interested in competition barbecue and wanted to keep up on when the next contest was going to be. They started a newsletter and began hosting monthly meetings, and then, surprisingly (to them), they "began receiving calls from organizations wanting to start barbecue competitions. They wanted KCBS to sanction their event." Before this time there was no standardized scoring for competition barbecue—"each contest had its own set of rules and judging procedures."[55] The KCBS came up with a single set of rules for the competition, which included the judging. This made it easier for the organizations hosting events, since they did not need to create their own set of rules, and it also made it easier for competitors, since the rules at any KCBS (or, for that matter, Memphis Barbecue Network) sanctioned event are all the same. Of course, the standardization has another consequence as well: it makes it so that competition barbecuers cook what is in the rules, and only what is in the rules. The KCBS rules have only four meat categories, which are chicken (including Cornish game hen and Kosher chicken), pork ribs, pork (Boston butt, picnic, and/or whole shoulder), and beef brisket. Beef ribs, popular in Texas, are not on the list; nor are other cuts and meats popular in different regions, like mutton or tri-tip beef. Because the KCBS and the Memphis Barbecue Network sanction so many contests across the country, their definitions have an effect on barbecuers' perceptions of just what real barbecue is.

BARBECUING IN THE 21ST CENTURY

Barbecuing shows no sign of decreasing in popularity. Every year brings more barbecue cookbooks and more hours of television programing that features, in some way, barbecues or barbecuers. Each spring sees the return of newspaper and magazine articles devoted to barbecue recipes and techniques. There are companies like Kingsford and Weber that rely on the continuing popularity of barbecue for profits, and they are devoted to marketing charcoal, grills, and many other products that grillers can use. There are hundreds of barbecue contests across the country every year. Barbecuing is big business on television; it features prominently in cooking programs, travel programs, and reality shows (there is one reality show devoted to competition barbecuing). Barbecue is also big business to restaurants as well. All of these topics will feature in the other chapters in this book, after the next chapter, which focuses more tightly on the foods involved with typical barbecues around the country.

2

CLASSIC
BARBECUE FARE

The previous chapter looked at the history of barbecue as a way of cooking; this chapter takes a closer look at the grills, fuels, and foods involved with a barbecue. Because of the focus, this chapter is set up something like a cookbook, starting with the entrées and sauces, then going through the side dishes, beverages, and desserts that have been associated with barbecue over the years. Some of the foods, like pork ribs, are common at barbecues across the country while other foods, like Brunswick stew, are regional favorites.

A few words about the recipes. The recipes below were not chosen because they are the best tasting; they were chosen because they are representative of recipes from a certain time and a certain place. If you are looking for recipes to make at your own barbecue you should consult one of the many barbecue cookbooks on the market. Most of the recipes below have not been tested and the results can only be guessed at, and one recipe in particular (the Tartare Sandwich) should not be tried because it could put you in the hospital or, in a worst-case scenario, kill you. In short, the recipes are for looking at, not for trying (although, with that one exception, you could certainly try them). Because of issues with copyright, any recipe published before 1928 is repeated verbatim while more recent recipes are summarized.

THE GRILL, FIRE, AND EQUIPMENT

Certainly, the meat is the focus of most barbecue meals, but the grill and the fire are what make barbecuing different from other methods of preparing food. Cooks have many choices regarding the type of grill they can use. *Betty Crocker's Outdoor Cook Book*, from 1961, listed sixteen different types of grills available at that point. They ranged from a simple open trench to a large stationary barbecue, made of bricks, to the Weber-type kettle grill. Included in the list are two unusual types of grills. The vertical grill gets its name from the fact that the charcoal sits in either one or two vertical racks and the food, also in vertical racks, is placed beside the fire. One of the advantages of this type of fire is that grease will not drip onto the coals and cause a flame-up. The homemade mobile grill, as illustrated by the Betty Crocker book, was a wheelbarrow lined with aluminum foil. A four-inch layer of gravel was placed on the foil, the charcoal sat on that, and a piece of iron mesh was placed across the top of the wheelbarrow to complete the grill. As wheelbarrows can easily be tipped over while moving, one hopes that this did not happen during a barbecue party.

As a sign of the popularity of barbecuing in the 1950s, two different kinds of grills were invented during that decade, both of which are wildly popular today. The first was the Weber grill, named after the company that developed it. George Stephen was a part owner of Weber Brothers Metal, a sheet metal company based in Chicago. Stephen observed that one problem with the grills of that time was that they were open. The only way to cook food was to place it directly over the coals, which meant that cooking large pieces of meat was difficult—an electric rotisserie was a standard piece of equipment for outdoor grillers of the time, to rotate the food so that the coals warmed all sides of the meat, not just the bottom. Stephen realized that an alternative to this kind of direct heat cooking was indirect cooking, where the fire was enclosed with the meat but not directly below the meat, so that all sides of the meat were warmed at the same time. Weber-style grills are usually rounded, with a removable cover, and vents at the top and bottom of the grill to let air pass through the grill, albeit much less air than with open grilling. In 1956 Stephen designed the grill, and by 1958 it was so popular that he left Weber Brothers Metal and founded Weber-Stephen Products just to manufacture the grill. By 1964 the new company had opened another factory for the grill.[1] The other kind of grill to come out of the 1950s is the gas grill, invented (as may be guessed) by a gas company. The Arklamatic was produced by Arkla Industries, an energy company that did business in both Arkansas and Louisiana (hence the company's name).

Another type of stove gaining popularity today is the wood pellet stove, which automatically feeds small pellets into the fire as needed. Pellet stoves were originally made for heating houses, and the pellets were made from unused wood from manufacturers, ground up and pressed into small pellets. Pellet grills were then introduced and, like gas stoves, they have the advantage of automatically holding a set temperature. Today pellets made from charcoal and fruitwoods are available so that the taste of the food coming from a pellet stove is like that coming from a charcoal grill.

The two most popular choices for grilling fuel today are gas and charcoal, with electric running a very distant third. Charcoal gives a better flavor to the food but takes longer to prepare; the cook has to light the charcoal and then wait for it to burn down until it is covered with a thin sheet of ash. Gas grills can be used almost immediately after lighting but do not give any flavor to the food. As *Betty Crocker's Outdoor Cook Book* noted in 1961, using camp stoves that use propane, alcohol, or canned heat is "not suitable for grilling . . . the food they produce is no different in taste from that prepared on the range at home."[2]

In terms of grill sales, charcoal grills were most popular type until 1995, when gas grills first began outselling charcoal grills. Electric grills are also available but have never been very popular. In 2012 gas grills accounted for 57 percent of grills sold, charcoal grills were 41 percent of the market, and only 2 percent of grills sold that year were electric.

Another choice for cooks, especially for those making traditional barbecue, is which wood to use for smoking. Even electric smokers often offer the choice of using a small amount of wood for flavoring; as the electric smoker maintains a constant temperature to cook the food it also burns a very small amount of wood to give a flavor to the food. The most popular woods used in barbecue are hickory and mesquite. Mesquite gives a particular flavor to barbecue that is somewhat bitter; it is very popular in Texas. Hickory is popular for a number of reasons: The flavor is good, it is usually inexpensive because hickory's uses are otherwise limited (it cannot be used for construction, for example), and, for those going the traditional barbecue route who burn down the wood to make coals, it holds its heat and burns very slowly. Fruitwoods like apple and cherry are also popular, as is maple, but shipments of those woods are measured in the thousands of pounds sold per year, while hickory and mesquite are measured in the millions of pounds sold.[3]

Barbecue chefs can use a range of equipment while cooking. The following list comes from *Grill It!*, a 2005 barbecue book from the editors of *Good Housekeeping* magazine, and tends to be the standard pieces of equipment listed in barbecue books from the past twenty years or so.

- Grill Topper, "a perforated metal sheet or mesh screen that provides a nearly smooth surface for grilling." Used for "delicate foods such as seafood and vegetables."[4]
- Grilling Basket, which can be used for smaller pieces of foods, like vegetables or shrimp.
- Tongs and Spatula. The book notes that they should both have heatproof handles, and that the spatula should be oversized.
- Skewers. The book suggests using flat skewers rather than rounded skewers so that food does not simply spin on the skewers when turned.
- Basting brush. "Natural bristles will stand up to the heat better than synthetic ones."[5]
- Instant-read thermometer.
- Grilling mitts. Barbecue guides from the mid-20th century usually recommended asbestos grilling mitts but that advice was discontinued for obvious reasons. The editors of *Good Housekeeping* instead recommended heavy suede gloves.
- Water spray bottle, "to quash flare-ups."[6]
- Brass-bristled scrub brush, for cleaning the grill afterward.
- Chimney starter, electric starter, or liquid fire starter. One challenge of using charcoal is getting the fire started, and these three items make doing so a bit easier. A chimney starter is simply a metal cylinder, open at the top and bottom, with a metal screen inside the cylinder about a quarter of the way up. Crumpled newspaper goes in the small bottom portion, briquettes are placed on top of the screen, and the heat and fire from the lit newspapers is drawn up through the briquettes. One advantage of chimney starters is that the windier it is the better they work.

These tend to be the standard equipment recommendations in the early 21st century, and the recommendations have changed over time. *Betty Crocker's Outdoor Cook Book*, from 1961, had somewhat different recommendations. During the kid-centered baby boom, it advised using a water pistol to stop flare-ups.[7] It also listed a whole range of electrical equipment that could be used during a barbecue, to the point where the area around the grill might more closely resemble the average kitchen counter than an outdoor space: coffeepot, blender, toaster, waffle iron, and warming trays were all recommended as being useful.[8] In the days before instant-read thermometers, the book advised using a meat thermometer to check the temperature of the meat, a grill thermometer to check the temperature inside the grill, or simply using the chef's hand to check the temperature. If he could hold it above the coals for three seconds, the temperature was between 300 and 325 degrees, "right for poultry." If he could keep it there less than three seconds, the temperature was between 350 and 400 degrees, "hot enough for steak."[9] This method was quite old—it was how women had checked oven temperatures for ages, until inexpensive thermometers were available.

Another piece of equipment recommended in the Betty Crocker book, and many other books from the mid-20th century, was a rotisserie. In the days before closed grills became popular, using a rotisserie was the only way to make sure a large piece of meat cooked evenly. More expensive rotisseries had weight compensators to account for meat that was placed off-center, or that lost more fat on one side of the meat than the other. Rotisseries are rarely mentioned in barbecue cookbooks today and, if they are discussed, they are portrayed as an optional piece of equipment.

A look at the barbecue utensils offered on online retailer Amazon's website reveals nearly 5,500 items, but the vast majority of them are versions of the products listed above.[10] A company named Maverick sells different models of remote-check wireless thermometers so that the cook does not have to check the temperature constantly, and can even be away from the food while monitoring the cooking. Hamburger presses are available to quickly mold hamburgers, barbecued pizza pans are available to make pizza on the grill, and LED lights can be purchased to attach to a grill for easier grilling in the evening hours. In looking through the pages and pages of products, though, the impression one gets is that not much has changed in the world of barbecue equipment over the past several decades. Much like the act of grilling itself, the equipment needed for grilling is basic stuff. Beyond the instant-read thermometer, grilling equipment is manual-powered, low-technology equipment.

THE MEAT

The choice of meat is, of course, one of the differentiating factors involving with barbecuing. Pork and beef are both traditional favorites, lamb and the occasional goat grace many American barbecues, and then there is also chicken, turkey, and various game birds. Historical accounts from before about 1900 report that beef, pork, mutton, and goat all showed up at barbecues while poultry almost never did, mainly because the older barbecues were focused on feeding lots of people and so used larger animals. Furthermore, the meat for those barbecues often came from donations from local farmers so the meat that was cooked was somewhat randomly chosen. Since 1900, though, three trends have made it so that the type of meat has become a major focus of barbecues.

The first trend was the rise of barbecue restaurants. Restaurateurs could not simply cook all the meat available to them and hope to sell it all; they had to a make conscious choice of just which meat to focus on. Frequently, this choice was guided by what was available locally at an inexpensive price. Beef barbecue became popular in Texas while pork became the choice in the Carolinas, and even today those states are major cattle and pork producers, respectively.

A second trend was the continuing development of the meat-processing industry. By 1900 the industry had already centralized its slaughterhouses in places like Chicago and Kansas City, and during the 20th century its operations became increasingly sophisticated. An ongoing problem for the industry is the nature of its raw materials: Although chicken breasts may be popular, a slaughtered chicken produces a breast and quite a few other pieces of meat which, if not sold, are waste (in this way Russia and China are veritable gold mines for the poultry industry since items like chicken feet are still widely eaten in those areas). Rather than taking the passive approach of just pricing items cheaply in order to get rid of them, during the 20th century the meat-processing industry took an active approach to developing markets for cuts of meat that had relatively little demand. An example of this is Memphis dry ribs. They were created at the Rendezvous, a Memphis restaurant that in the 1950s was looking for a new dish to add to the menu. They had previously tried smoked chicken and smoked oysters, neither of which sold well. Then their meat vendor suggested that they try pork ribs. They experimented with different ways of quickly cooking the ribs and in the process created a barbecue favorite. Today the meatpacking industry spends a considerable amount of money marketing different products to consumers, and a big part of that advertising is for cuts to barbecue.

A third trend was the redefinition of "barbecue" from cooking over a low, slow fire to its being a synonym for outdoor grilling. Backyard barbecuing is usually a small-scale affair where the choice of meat becomes a major choice. Chicken does not taste like pork, which does not taste like beef, and all three of those popular meats have cuts that do not taste like each other. Cooking for only a few people makes the type of meat the central choice.

Pork

Pork has been popular for centuries in America. It was well liked in Europe, and many immigrants brought with them a love of pork. Pork remained a popular barbecue meat, and a popular meat in general, because hogs were so easy to raise.

In the years before barbed wire, when fences were few and far between (and easy for hogs to get through), the animals could generally take care of themselves. They foraged for their food and, with their aggressive personalities, could defend themselves from predators. Even city dwellers had access to live hogs since, up until the end of the 19th century, hogs roamed the streets of every town and city in America from the smallest country cluster of houses to New York and Boston. As one might expect, they functioned as garbage patrol. When Frances Trollope, mother of English novelist Anthony Trollope, visited America in the 1820s, a landlord told her to throw all her trash into the street, but not the edge of the street, "they must just all be cast right into the middle, and the pigs soon takes them off."[11] Trollope complained that the hogs made it impossible for her to cross the street and keep her dress clean, since they kept rubbing against her, but women like her eventually had their revenge on the hogs, helping to pass laws later that century to remove all hogs from American streets.

Another reason pork is popular is because of the wide variety of cuts of meat that come from a hog. A few hundred years ago, "whole hog" barbecuing was the main way of cooking pork, since barbecues were generally held for many people, and chopped whole hog is still popular at restaurants and large barbecues in eastern North Carolina. Pork shoulder and ribs are also traditional favorites. Shifting to more modern favorites (that is, the smaller cuts of meat used for quick outdoor grilling rather than slower traditional barbecuing) pork chops are always popular, as are the variations on meat in a casing: sausage, hot dogs, and bratwurst.

To Barbecue Shoat

Shoat is a young pig, especially one that has recently been weaned. Lettice Bryan's *The Kentucky Housewife* was published in 1839 and contains a very early recipe for something that would be recognized as barbecue today. This is long before barbecue sauce existed, which can be seen by the fact that she recommends basting with salt water and pepper and serving the dish "without a garnish." The recipe for bread sauce follows this recipe, and her recipes for "slaugh" are included in the section below on coleslaw recipes.

> Take either a hind or fore quarter, rub it well with salt, pepper, and a small portion of molasses, and if practicable, let it lie for a few hours; then rinse it clean, and wipe it dry with a cloth, and place it on a large gridiron, over a bed of clear coals. Do not barbecue it hastily, but let it cook slowly for several hours, turning it over occasionally, and basting it with nothing but a little salt-water and pepper,

merely to season and moisten it a little. When it is well done, serve it without a garnish, and having the skin taken off, which should be done before it is put down to roast, squeeze over it a little lemon juice, and accompany it with melted butter and wine, bread sauce, raw sallad, slaugh, or cucumbers, and stewed fruit. Beef may be barbecued in the same manner.[12]

Bread Sauce for a Pig

While there is a section below on barbecue sauces, this sauce, from *The Kentucky Housewife*, is different enough that it is included here with the barbecued pig recipe rather than mixed in with the other sauces. All of the popular barbecue sauces of today are based on either tomatoes, vinegar, or mustard, but none of those ingredients makes an appearance here. With its inclusion of drippings from the pig, this is essentially a kind of gravy for the meat.

> Cut several slices from a fine loaf of bread, put them in a sauce-pan, and having skimmed the drippings from a roasted pig, pour it over the bread. Let it set for a few minutes, till the bread is completely saturated with the drippings; then add a table-spoonful of powdered sage, a tea-spoonful of kitchen pepper, one of grated lemon, four ounces of butter, and enough sweet cream or madeira wine to liquify it sufficiently; boil it up, and serve it in a boat.[13]

Technically Not Barbecued Pig

Vince Staten and Greg Johnson's *Real Barbecue* is a guide to the best barbecue restaurants in the country, but it also includes quite a bit of information on barbecuing in general. In one chapter they outline the various types of barbecue grills, and while discussing how to cook in a covered pit they give a recipe for whole hog barbecue that combines the two extremes of traditional barbecue: the backbreaking work of barbecuing heavy animals and the long hours of watching the fire burn. At the end of the recipe they state that this is not, in fact, traditional barbecue because it was "cooked in moist heat and not a steam of hot smoke."[14]

The recipe is combined with instructions for making the pit; the size of the pit is based on the size of the hog. They recommend an eighty-pound hog, dressed by a butcher but not skinned. The pit should be a few inches wider than the hog, and twice as deep. Cover the bottom of the pit with heavy rocks, which will absorb the heat from the fire and maintain the temperature during cooking. Build a "healthy fire of wood" in the pit and let it burn down to coals.

The hog will need to be lowered into the pit when it is time, and the easy way to do this is with chicken wire. Lay a long enough piece of chicken wire on the ground so that it will extend above the pit when the hog is lowered. Put a layer of aluminum foil over the chicken wire, which will protect the hog from the coals.

The hog now needs to be prepared. Wrap the hog in gunnysacks that have been soaked in either "water and a mixture of spices—like sage, thyme, garlic, bay, salt, and pepper" or else in barbecue sauce. Lay the wrapped hog on the aluminum foil, and lower the entire package into the pit. Cover the hog with a layer of rocks, and build another fire on top of the rocks to cook the hog from the top side as well.

The cooking will take about eight hours, during which time nothing needs to be done other than feeding the fire. At the end of the cooking time, move the rocks off the hog using a shovel or rack, and (wearing protective gloves and clothing) bring the hog up from the pit.

Snoots

Snoots are barbecued pig snouts. They are neither popular nor well known, but that seems to give them a certain mystique among foodies. In the book *Smokestack Lightning*, Lolis Eric Elie went looking for snoots, having heard of them but never eaten one. He found that they were popular in East St. Louis, an area that used to have many packinghouses, where the snouts, and other unpopular parts of the pig, were often given away free. As one of the locals related to him, to make snoots the cook needs to remove most of the fat on the meat as well as a vein that runs through it, and then score one side of the snoot so it does not curl up during cooking. For Elie, snoots turned out to be an acquired taste and difficult to eat. When he and his photographer found a restaurant that sold snoots, they ordered a sandwich, which is simply the snoot between white bread with some barbecue sauce. "They are . . . like cracklins with their combination of crisply fried fat on one side and the hard, crunchy skin on the other," Elie writes. "It's the skin that gives you the most trouble. It seems that no matter what angle you take the snoot from, it's hard to bite into."[15] The two later ordered a second set of snoot sandwiches from another barbecue place and found those to be much more edible, although the two were unable to finish a complete sandwich between them.

Beef

Beef has been a favorite barbecue meat for centuries partially because, when many people need to be fed at once, barbecuing an entire ox or side of beef results in lots of food (and it also means more hours of cooking for the cook). In the past hundred years, as barbecue cooks have focused on smaller cuts of meat, certain cuts of beef have become popular. Texas and Kansas are both centers of beef production, and Texas- and Kansas City–style barbecue includes beef brisket as a traditional cut of meat. Steak has been popular in the United States for decades, both on the grill and off. And hamburger is a type of meat that became popular during the 20th century.

Salt Crusted Steak

A 1947 Gallup Poll asked Americans what their perfect meal would consist of, and most people chose an entrée of steak.[16] A few years later *McCall's* magazine printed an article titled "The Dinner I'd Love to Come Home To" in which famous men talked about their favorite meals, and a steak dinner was a favorite for both then president Dwight Eisenhower and athlete Jackie Robinson. Before the 1950s cookbooks usually included recipes for making steaks but grilling was certainly not the only method they recommended; frying and broiling were also popular. During and after that period, though, grilling became the preferred way to make steaks in America.

One very old way of cooking meat is to pack a layer of wet salt around it. The salt has the effect of keeping the meat moist while also making a nice crust on the outside of the meat. Although it is not often done, this method of cooking can also be used on the grill, and is impressive for guests, especially when the salt crust is cracked, revealing a perfectly cooked steak. A wire basket will be needed, since the salt crust can be fragile.

To make salt-crusted steak, put a few cups of kosher salt in a bowl. Add enough water to make a thick paste.

Next, put the wire basket on a table and lay a few thicknesses of wet paper towels on the basket. Spread half the salt paste on the towels, and lay the steaks on the salt paste. Cover the steaks with the rest of the salt paste and a few more damp paper towels. Close the basket.

Cook the steaks near the coals as you normally would. Use an instant-read thermometer to check for doneness.

Burgers with Herb Butter

Hamburger had an unsavory reputation at the start of the 20th century as a meat that was filled with the ground-up odds and ends of the butchering process. The bits of meat were so small that almost anything could be in it, although the

USDA worked to minimize the number of things that could possibly be in it by declaring that anything sold as hamburger had to be 100 percent beef. White Castle, the first big hamburger chain in the country, made sure to include in its name a color that indicated cleanliness, they placed their grill in full view of customers, and they publicized that their meat was delivered twice a day.[17] The Great Depression increased hamburger's reputation since it was an inexpensive meat and because filler such as oatmeal or cornflakes could easily be added to it by the cook to extend the amount of food.

This recipe is simple but results in burgers that have different, but excellent, flavors in each bite. You'll have to work hard to get the butter to stay in the burger, but the herbs that remain are quite tasty.

Makes four burgers
1 pound hamburger
4 tablespoons unsalted butter at room temperature
1 tablespoon minced fresh parsley
1 tablespoon minced fresh basil or oregano
Salt and pepper

Mix the butter and herbs and form into four pats of herbed butter. Chill until solid. Form four patties with the hamburger, and place one pat of herbed butter in each burger (it may be easier to form eight patties and sandwich a pat of butter between two patties, sealing the sides together). Season the burgers with salt and pepper and grill as you normally would.

Tartare Sandwich[18]

The Complete Book of Outdoor Cookery, by Helen Evans Brown and James Beard, was published in the mid-1950s and is very much of that period. In spite of the fact that it includes a recipe for Kentucky Burgoo, most of the recipes are heavily influenced by French cooking. The book includes a recipe for a tartare sandwich. When Beard and Evans related the recipe, the slaughterhouse industry was not nearly as centralized as it is today, and the dangers of foodborne illness were minimal. Today, you are risking serious harm or death if you make the recipe from store-bought beef.

Their recipe was simple: for one serving, take two pieces of thinly sliced bread (they recommend pumpernickel or rye). Spread a quarter pound of hamburger between the two slices, about half an inch thick. Lay the sandwich on the grill just long enough to toast the bread and warm the hamburger.

Poultry

Poultry rarely shows up in mentions of the big barbecues held before about 1900 because, compared to cattle or hogs, the birds are so small and because they take so much work to butcher and prepare for cooking. In the 20th century, two changes occurred to make chicken take center stage on the grill. There was the shift to smaller barbecues, so that a few pounds of chicken could feed all the guests, and there were also major changes in the poultry industry to make chicken both inexpensive and convenient. Poultry production became centralized and focused on only a few locations in this country, which minimized the cost of chicken. The industry also concentrated on raising and processing a distinct breed of chicken, which further reduced the cost. Furthermore, over the course of the 20th century, as America shifted from being a rural to an urban country, fewer and fewer people raised their own poultry (which could have been a wide variety of birds) and fewer people went hunting for game birds. The packaged chicken at the grocery store is now the default choice for poultry.

This transition can be seen in cookbooks. The *Better Homes and Gardens Barbecue Book*, from 1965, includes only four chicken recipes in its poultry section, and three of them call for either a broiler-fryer or a broiler, terms that are not used today (they refer to a younger bird, which is why they are out of use today—all birds processed by the big slaughterhouses today are young birds). Seven recipes call for either a Rock Cornish game hen or capon, five call for turkey, and two call for duck.[19] In contrast, the *Kingsford Complete Grilling Cookbook*, from 2007, includes eight chicken recipes in its poultry section, along with three turkey recipes and only one each for duck and Cornish game hen.[20]

Beer Can Chicken

Within the past few decades the idea of using beer in a can to moisten the inside of a grilled chicken has become popular enough that consumers can buy products to make it easier to balance the chicken as it sits atop the can (or to completely replace the beer can). A few disposable pie pans can do the same job. The advantage to this kind of grilling is that the skin of the chicken becomes crispy while the inside of the bird stays moist.

1 4-pound chicken
Salt and pepper
Garlic powder
Seasoning salt
1 12-ounce can beer

Rinse the chicken and pat dry. Mix some of the salt, pepper, and garlic powder, and rub onto the outside of the chicken. Repeat with the seasoning salt.

Start a fire for indirect grilling. When the coals are ready, open the can of beer and drain some off (or simply drink some) so that the beer does not foam up while grilling. Insert the top of the can into the cavity of the chicken, and sit the chicken, standing up, atop two disposable pie pans placed inside each other. Put the chicken on the pans into the grill, away from coals. Grill for about 70 minutes, until the chicken reaches 165 degrees.

Barbecued Chicken

As has been discussed elsewhere in the book, just what constitutes barbecued food varies tremendously among between different people. For many people, particularly American Southerners, barbecue is food that has been cooked for hours in a cooker. For some corporate marketers, it is anything with barbecue sauce on it.

A sample of how the definition of barbecue has grown to encompass almost anything comes from a microwave cookbook from the 1980s, which came free with a new Quasar microwave. The recipe is something of a cultural artifact from a time when many people believed that microwave ovens would replace conventional ovens in the kitchen since microwaves could cook foods quickly. It took a few years before those people realized that speed is not the only criteria for making good food; this can be seen in the book's recipe for barbecued chicken. The cook was to put a two and a half to three pound chicken, cut up, in a microwave-safe dish, pour a cup of barbecue sauce over the chicken, and cover the bird with wax paper. Ten to thirteen minutes of high-power microwaving then resulted in a barbecued chicken with a very different sort of texture from a grilled chicken although, of course, the chicken is cooked much more quickly than it would be done on the grill.[21]

Mutton and Everything Else

Pork, beef, and chicken are the three big grilling meats, but that does not mean they are the only grilling meats. Before the 20th century, donated goats and sheep made an appearance at many a barbecue, and mutton is still popular in some parts of Kentucky.

Barbecued Lamb

Martha McCulloch-Williams's *Dishes and Beverages of the Old South*, from 1913, provides a host of memories and recipes dating to before the Civil War,

Factory farming made chicken cheap enough to barbecue easily. Agricultural Extension and Research Services (UA023.007), ua023_007-003-bx0007-005-019, Special Collections Research Center, North Carolina State University Libraries.

and the book includes a recipe for "barbecued lamb." The quotes are around it here because it is actually a roasted, not barbecued, lamb, which the author acknowledges at the end of the recipe: "This is as near an approach to a real barbecue, which is cooked over live coals in the bottom of a trench, as a civilized kitchen can supply."[22] She was writing to an audience of women, and outdoor cooking, then as often now, was men's work. In spite of that, the recipe is interesting to examine because of the cut of meat and seasoning she recommends for her "barbecued" lamb.

She calls for using the middle of the lamb—the "bracelet" was how butchers referred to it then. "Have it split down the backbone, and the rib-ends neatly trimmed, also the ribs proper, broken about midway, but not quite through."

After washing the meat, the cook was to rub it with salt, prick it all over with a knife point, and then rub it with black pepper, paprika, a little dry mustard, and a dash of Tabasco. The lamb was roasted in a hot oven, with a cupful of water in the pan but not touching the meat; the lamb was to be arranged "in a sort of Gothic arch," with the backbone and rib ends supporting the rest of the meat. "Roast till the fat is crisped and brown throughout, the lean very tender." She suggested serving it "with a sauce, of melted butter, mixed with equal quantity of strong vinegar, boiling hot, made thick with red and black pepper, minced cucumber pickle, and a bare dash of onion juice." Quite different from today's barbecue sauces, but that is the point: It is a throwback to earlier ways of making barbecue.

Barbecued Sheep

Buckeye Cookery and Practical Housekeeping, published in 1877, is an all-purpose guide for young housewives that, along with recipes, included tips on washing clothes, taking care of the infirm, and storing fruits and vegetables in an icehouse. The book also describes how to barbecue a sheep, and, although the recipe does not give measurements, advises using the type of mustard-based barbecue sauce popular today in South Carolina.

> Dig a hole in ground, in it build a wood fire, and drive four stakes or posts just far enough away so they will not burn; on these build a rack of poles to support the carcass. These should be of a kind of wood that will not flavor the meat. When the wood in the pit has burned to coals, lay sheep on rack, have a bent stick with a large sponge tied on one end, and the other fastened on one corner of the rack, and turn so that it will hang over the mutton; make a mixture of ground mustard and vinegar, salt and pepper, add sufficient water to fill the sponge the necessary number of times, and let it drip over the meat until done; have another fire burning near from which to add coals as they are needed.[23]

Planked Fish

Planking is an old method for cooking meat, particularly fish, where the meat is nailed to a plank of wood and then propped in front of the fire. A good example of the technique comes from Horace Kephart's *Camp Cookery*, from 1910.

> [Planking is] More expeditious than baking, and better flavored. Split and smooth a slab of sweet hardwood two or three inches thick, two feet long, and somewhat wider than the opened fish. Prop it in front of a bed of coals till it is sizzling hot. Split the fish down the back its entire length, but do not cut through the belly skin.

Clean and wipe it quite dry. When plank is hot, spread fish out like an opened book, tack it, skin side down, to the plank and prop before fire. Baste continuously with a bit of pork on a switch held above it. Reverse ends of plank from time to time. If the flesh is flaky when pierced with a fork, it is done. Sprinkle salt and pepper over the fish, moisten with drippings, and serve on the hot plank. No better dish ever was set before an epicure. Plenty of butter improves it at table.[24]

Canned Luncheon Meat

When people think about Spam today they are probably more likely to think about unwanted e-mail than they are to think about something that can be eaten, but it was not always that way. Canned luncheon meat, of which Spam is the most popular example, was quite a popular food in the mid-20th century, popular enough to show up in numerous barbecue books.

In a section on cooking with skewers, James Beard and Helen Evans Brown offered this suggestion for shish-kebabing: "Cubes of canned luncheon meat, with sections of banana, well buttered."[25] The *Better Homes and Gardens Barbecue Book* included Cheese-frosted Luncheon Meat in its section of skewered recipes, a recipe that obviously comes from the 1950s. That recipe required the cook to skewer cubes of luncheon meat, then cover the cubes with a mixture of purchased cheese sauce and mustard. The skewers were to be browned on the grill, then served on buns.[26]

Barbecued Armadillo

Although some of the most typical barbecue meats, like beef and pork, come from larger animals, there is a long history of grilling smaller animals as well. Armadillos range throughout the American Southwest and have appeared on many dinner tables, particularly in their grilled form. The authors of *The Texas Cookbook*, published in 1949, wrote that armadillo "tastes considerably like a pig," and advised using a dry rub (that is, a blend of seasonings) to cook the animal. [27] Their method used a dressed armadillo that was first seared on the grill, then seasoned a few times while cooking. Warm ketchup accompanied the armadillo meat on the plate, but any barbecue sauce would probably provide an appropriate accompaniment as well.

Barbecued "Beef" Sandwiches

Barbecue is popular enough that recipes for it are showing up in vegan cookbooks. Vegans not only do not eat meat, but they also do not eat anything derived from a meat source, like cheese, eggs, or beef broth, so barbecue is a bit hard to do for a vegan. Nevertheless, an example of a barbecue recipe appears in Celine Steen and Joni Marie Newman's *500 Vegan Recipes*, published in 2009. The recipe for barbecued "beef" is a bit complicated. The first part of the recipe has the cook make large dough dumplings from flour, yeast, and some flavorings like steak sauce and mustard. Those dumplings are then dropped into a boiling liquid made from vegetable broth and seasonings, including cayenne pepper and liquid smoke. The dumplings are removed after simmering for twenty minutes and pulled apart with a fork (something like pulled pork). As is sometimes seen with real barbecued sandwiches, the authors recommend serving this barbecue on crusty French rolls, with a dollop of coleslaw on top of the barbecue.[28]

Grilled Pizza

True to the American love of barbecue, barbecued pizza was invented in the 1980s at the restaurant Al Forno in Providence, Rhode Island. The technique for making the pizza is a little tricky as the crust needs to be flipped a few minutes into grilling, but otherwise, this is just like making a regular pizza. The recipe here is not from any book in particular but is more a set of guidelines for making barbecued pizza, since any recipe for pizza can be used for making barbecued pizza. Since the grill is hot anyway you may want to consider adding grilled versions of your normal toppings, such as onions, peppers, and mushrooms, to your pizza. The recipe below assumes the cook is using enough dough, either fresh or frozen, for a twelve-inch pizza.

To make the pizza, prepare the grill for grilling. If using a gas grill, set the flame at medium. If using charcoal, let the coals burn down until covered with ash and spread the coals out.

Prepare the dough by rolling it into a twelve-inch round. If the dough retracts, reroll until it stays. Do not make a lip around the edge of the dough since you will be flipping the dough during cooking. Use enough flour so that no part of the dough, top or bottom, is sticky. Put the dough on a pizza peel or rimless baking sheet, in order to slide it onto the grill quickly.

Prepare all toppings. You will be applying the toppings at the grill, not before grilling, so everything should be cut and ready to apply quickly.

The grill is ready when you can hold your hand over it for three to four seconds. Using a brush or a tongs and a paper towel, wipe the grill with olive oil and put the dough on the grill. Close the lid for about two minutes.

Check the bottom of the dough to see if it is lightly brown. If it is, skip to the next paragraph. If it is brown in spots, rotate it ninety degrees and let it cook for another minute. If it is not brown at all, close the lid and let it cook for another two minutes. Continue until the bottom of the dough is lightly browned.

If you are using many pizza toppings that will take a few minutes to add (sauce, meat, vegetables, cheese, etc.), flip the dough onto a flat baking pan. If you are adding only a few toppings (like only oil, cheese, and basil), flip the dough on the grill.

Add the toppings to the browned side of the pizza and return the dough to the grill, if necessary. Close the cover and grill another few minutes, until the cheese is melted and the dough is cooked all the way through.

New England Clambake

Barbecuing disappeared from New England during the 19th century, but a similar tradition that continues to this day is the clambake. In a clambake the foods are steamed rather than roasted or smoked, but the same can also be said for pork cooked in a deep, or closed, pit.

The basic process for having a clambake is simple, but it requires a fair amount of work. The process described here comes from *The Art of Barbecue and Outdoor Cooking*, from 1971, a rare mass-market cookbook that includes detailed instructions for making traditional barbecue and a clambake.

As with pit barbecuing, the first step is to dig a hole. For a crowd of fifty, the book recommends a hole about two and a half feet square and a foot deep (the hole digging and the later use of water is one reason the beach is a traditional location for a clam bake). The bottom of the hole should be lined with stones "the size of a small head of cabbage or lettuce."[29] Many more stones will be used here, and the point of them is to hold the heat since no hot coals will be used in cooking the food. Cover the stones with a layer of hardwood firewood, and light the firewood. While that is starting to burn, cover it with alternating layers of stones and firewood until the pile is about three feet high. This will take two to three hours to burn down; when it has burned to ash, rake away the embers and begin constructing the layers for the clambake. The bottom layer, on top of the hot stones, is fresh seaweed—it needs to be wet, or at least damp, because this is where the water to steam the food comes from. The book recommends a total of three bushels of seaweed for fifty people. A layer of clams goes on top of the seaweed, then another layer of seaweed. On top of this place "one lobster for each guest, then sweet corn, potatoes and onions, enough for everyone, with a final layer of seaweed. Finally over the top, put a wet canvas or tarpaulin."[30] This should be covered with rocks, to keep steam from escaping. Cooking time is about an hour, and can be checked by pulling out a lobster that is near one edge. When the lobster is done, the food is done. Peel back the canvas and seaweed and let guests serve themselves. Melted butter should be supplied for the lobster, clams, and corn.

SAUCES AND RUBS

Sauces and rubs are both applied to meat. Sauces are often applied during cooking, to keep the meat from drying out, although sauces with sugar (which most purchased barbecue sauces contain) can only be applied toward the end of the process because of their tendency to burn. Sauces are frequently added after cooking as well. Rubs are blends of dry ingredients that are rubbed (hence the name) on the meat before cooking to give it additional flavor.

Barbecue sauces come in a number of different varieties. Tomato-based sauce is by far the most popular; this type fills most grocery store shelves across the country. Tomato-based sauce can simply be sweet, like the sauce popular in Kansas City. The sweetness is a function of the fact that the sauce is closely related to ketchup—in the early 20th century American ketchup became much sweeter than previously because of changes in the manufacturing process. Molasses can be added to the tomato base, resulting in the darker sauce popular in Memphis and Georgia, or peppers can be added, resulting in a spicy sauce popular in Alabama. Vinegar-based sauce omits the tomato entirely and results in the sauce popular in eastern North Carolina. Finally, the sauce popular in South Carolina is mustard based, resulting in a very different-tasting barbecue sauce.

Daddy's Sauce

Dishes and Beverages of the Old South, from 1913, is part cookbook and part memoir. Martha McCulloch-Williams was born on a southern plantation before the Civil War and was clearly a part of the privileged class. In her introduction, she writes with fond memories of her mammy's cooking—a mammy being the slave who was both cook and nanny for a plantation (Aunt Jemima's advertising originally described her as being a mammy). Typical of her station, McCulloch-Williams does not relate her mammy's name in the book. The book contains vivid remembrances of prewar barbecues, both of the political and dancing kinds, and McCulloch-Williams also relates her father's sauce recipe, so much as she knew: As she writes, he kept some of it secret. His was a spicy vinegar-based sauce.

Daddy made it thus: Two pounds sweet lard, melted in a brass kettle, with one pound beaten, not ground, black pepper, a pint of small fiery red peppers, nubbed and stewed soft in water to barely cover, a spoonful of herbs in powder—he would never tell what they were,—and a quart and pint of the strongest apple vinegar, with a little salt. These were simmered together for half an hour, as the barbecue was getting done. Then a fresh, clean mop was dabbed lightly in the mixture, and as lightly smeared over the upper sides of the carcasses. Not a drop was permitted to fall on the coals—it would have sent up smoke, and films of light ashes.[31]

Note the addition of "a pint of small fiery red peppers." Just after relating the recipe McCulloch-Williams wrote, "Hot! After eating it one wanted to lie down at the spring-side and let the water of it flow down the mouth. But of a flavor, a savor, a tastiness, nothing else earthly approaches. Not food for the gods, perhaps, but certainly meat for men."[32]

A variation of the vinegar-based sauce that was sweet and not spicy was remembered by Wesley Jones, a former slave who was later interviewed about his life as a slave. He was responsible for basting the meat during the long hours of barbecue cooking. While he did not relate a particular recipe he did discuss the ingredients in the sauce he used. It was "made of vinegar, black and red pepper, salt, butter, a little sage, coriander, basil, onion, and garlic. Some folks drop a little sugar in it."[33]

South Carolina–Style Mustard Sauce

While most sauces are tomato based, South Carolina–style sauce is mustard based. Plenty of recipes exist on the Internet and in cookbooks that make the process of making mustard sauce, and barbecue sauce in general, seem an exacting one, but the fact is that making barbecue sauce is a process wide open to experimentation and rule-breaking.

There are three basic ingredients in mustard sauce: mustard, vinegar, and a sweetener. The mustard is always a prepared mustard, bought from the store, but it can be any sort of mustard, and yellow or Dijon-style are fine to use. Many recipes call for white vinegar, which has the bite of vinegar without much additional taste, but some call for cider vinegar, which adds a slightly different flavor to the finished product. Most recipes call for a sweetener that adds something to the taste of the sauce, along with sweetness. White sugar and corn syrup both add sweetness without flavor, and appear sometimes along with sweeteners that do add flavor, such as brown sugar or molasses (which is used sparingly, a tablespoon at a time, because it can easily overpower a sauce).

The ratios of those three ingredients vary, depending on just which flavor a cook wants to emphasize. It is a mustard sauce, so the dominant ingredient is always mustard, but the vinegar can approach that amount, while the sweetener is often about a third or fourth of the amount of the mustard. Recipes can vary tremendously.

Mustard sauces almost always contain another set of ingredients, in much smaller amounts (measured in teaspoons and tablespoons, rather than half or full cups), that add more flavors to the sauce. These are usually spices, like cayenne or black pepper; salt; chopped vegetables like onion or jalapenos; or other flavorings like Worcestershire sauce, lemon juice, or soy sauce.

The difficult part of mustard sauce seems to be deciding just what to add. To make mustard sauce, all the cook needs to do is simmer the ingredients for ten minutes or so in a saucepan and store, cooled, in the refrigerator.

Alabama White Sauce

A unique type of barbecue sauce is popular in Alabama. Unlike most other sauces it is not tomato based, and its color, or lack of it, comes from its prime ingredient being mayonnaise. Writing about the sauce in the *New York Times*, barbecue expert Steven Raichlen commented that "It sounds weird, and it is in fact weird. But sometimes weird is best when it comes to barbecue."[34] In that article, Raichlen provided a recipe that called for one cup of mayonnaise, just less than a cup of white vinegar, and some white horseradish, black pepper, and salt.

Texas-Style Barbecue Sauce

It is hard to find a sauce recipe more Texan than that from Walter Jetton, who became famous as Lyndon Johnson's pitmaster while Johnson was president. When Jetton published his cookbook in the 1960s he included two sauce recipes, one for use at the table and another to use while cooking. The table sauce was for "beef, chicken, pork or almost anything else. Don't cook things in it."[35] That recipe required a cup and a half of water, a cup of ketchup, and half a cup of cider vinegar, along with flavorings like chili powder, chopped onion and celery, and Worcestershire sauce. The use of that much ketchup resulted in a fairly sweet sauce, and the water meant that it was relatively runny as well.

Mop for All Barbecue Meats

Most people are familiar with the idea of spreading barbecue sauce on cooking meats as a way to add flavor to the cooking meats, in addition to simply

Walter Jetton, left, with President Johnson, second from right. LBJ Library photo by Navy Photographer.

pouring sauce on the meat as it is being served or eaten. That idea of flavoring cooking meat can be taken a step further by basting the meat in a liquid that is never intended to be poured on the finished product (this is usually referred to as a "mop," since using a clean cotton mop is an ideal way to apply the liquid). Walter Jetton printed his favorite mop recipe in his cookbook.[36] His recipe used a gallon of meat stock, two pints of Worcestershire sauce, and a pint each of vinegar and oil. Spices such as paprika and garlic powder helped to round out the flavor, as did the addition of hot sauce and MSG. To make the sauce, the cook only had to mix the ingredients and let them sit overnight. As Jetton pointed out, the flavor of the mop would change with use, since the instrument used to apply the mop would both move the mop to the meat and move juices from the meat back into the mop.

Black Coffee–Molasses BBQ Sauce

Barbecue sauces can be made from as few as three or four ingredients, with a process as simple as boiling the ingredients in a saucepan for five minutes. Sauce making can also be an elaborate procedure, resulting in something with many complex flavors. This latter type of recipe shows up in Robb Walsh's *Texas*

Cowboy Cookbook, which includes a recipe for black coffee–molasses BBQ sauce, inspired by the type of sauce cowboys might have used (they did love their coffee).[37] The sauce is interesting because instead of having one or two ingredients that form the basis of the sauce, there are many ingredients that contribute distinct flavors. The recipe requires one cup each of strong black coffee, ketchup, and chili sauce, a half cup of molasses, and a quarter cup each of Worcestershire sauce, cider vinegar, and fresh lemon juice. Additionally, sautéed onions and garlic show up in the recipe, as do salt and mustard. The ingredients are simmered for thirty minutes in total, and pureed in a blender. The result is a sauce that has a mixture of flavors unlike that seen in most other barbecue sauces.

Barbecue Honey

In *Real Barbecue*, Vince Staten and Greg Johnson briefly discuss barbecue honey, a type of sauce they observed in the Kansas City area that has a tendency to burn (because of the sugar content) but that offers a unique taste. Staten and Johnson do not offer so much a recipe as general guidelines for how to make it, starting with a jar of honey. "Add pinches of cayenne pepper or hot Hungarian paprika, even prepared horseradish. The combination of hot, sweet, and burnt is intriguing and unusual, the sort of thing that can set your barbecue apart from the pack."[38] The sauce should be applied at the end of the cooking process, or on the finished meat.

Rubs

Rubs are mixtures of dried seasonings that get their name from the fact that they are rubbed on the meat before cooking—unlike barbecue sauce, rubs are not intended to be put on cooked meat. Rubs have two types of ingredients. One type is sugar, most often brown sugar. Obviously, the sugar makes the rub sweet, and it also turns the rub into a glaze during cooking. The amount of sugar in rubs varies tremendously; some rubs are half brown sugar, while other rubs have only a tablespoon of sugar in a cup of rub. The other type of ingredient is spices, and the list of spices in different rubs runs the gamut from onion and garlic powder to oregano and thyme to chili powder or paprika (paprika is a very popular rub ingredient). Rich Davis, the creator of KC Masterpiece barbecue sauce, published his dry rub recipe in a cookbook; his ingredients were brown sugar, black pepper, paprika, chili powder, salt, and garlic powder. As he wrote in the book, his recipe was nothing more than a general guide: "you could take the salt away . . . cut ingredients in half, or add seasoned garlic, celery or onion salts."[39]

SIDE DISHES, BEVERAGES, AND DESSERTS

There are a plethora of side dishes that go along with barbecue; baked beans, potato salad, and coleslaw are just a few of the typical dishes. However, if one looks very far back in history, those dishes tend to fall away in favor of much simpler fare. Many of the political barbecues of the 1800s featured nothing but meat and bread. As early 20th-century author Martha McCulloch-Williams wrote about the meals she remembered from before the Civil War, "The proper accompaniments to barbecue are sliced cucumbers in strong vinegar, sliced tomatoes, a great plenty of salt-rising light bread—and a greater plenty of cool ripe watermelons, by way of dessert."[40]

Baked Beans

Baked beans are as American as, well, lots of things. Both the Native Americans and Europeans who colonized America commonly ate beans, and that love of beans stayed with later Americans. Nutritional analysis of beans had to wait until the 20th century, but even early American settlers realized that, with the right companion ingredients, beans could make a filling meal.

William Bircher was one American who loved his beans. He kept a diary while fighting in the Civil War; one of the most amusing passages in the book occurs after a camp-mate says, "Come around to our tent to-morrow morning; we're going to have baked beans for breakfast." Bircher shows up for breakfast, but he also stops by about fifteen hours before to watch the entire process. By three o'clock the afternoon before the meal his friends had dug a hole "about three feet square and two deep," and they had prepared "an enormous camp-kettle about two-thirds full of parboiled beans." Into the hole went kindling and wood, and at dusk the wood was set ablaze. When the fire had burned down to coals, the kettle was placed in the coals, a few pounds of fat pork were placed on the beans, and an inverted mess pan made a lid for the kettle. Coals were shoveled over the kettle and the camp guards, while making their rounds, occasionally threw another log onto the fire "to keep matters going." As Bircher wrote,

> Early the next morning some one shook me roughly as I lay sleeping soundly in my tent: "Get up, Billy! breakfast is ready. Come to our tent. If you never ate baked beans before, you never ate anything worth eating." I found three or four of the boys seated around the camp-kettle, each with a tin plate on his knee and a spoon in his hand, doing their very best to establish the truth of the old adage,

"The proof of the pudding is in the eating." Now, it is a far more difficult matter to describe the experience of the palate than of either the eye or the ear, and therefore I shall not attempt to tell how very good baked beans are.[41]

Bircher added that "The only trouble with a camp-kettle full of the delicious food was that it was gone too soon."[42]

Bircher did not relate the recipe his camp-mates used but a recipe that is surely similar to it appears in *One Big Table: A Portrait of American Cooking*, a modern book that includes a recipe for Beanhole Beans for 100 people. That recipe calls for ten pounds of beans and five pounds of salt pork, both molasses and maple syrup for sweetening, five onions, and assorted spices such as cloves, mustard, and cinnamon. The beans are soaked overnight, then simmered for forty minutes to add to their tenderness. At that point the recipe becomes very similar to other recipes that call for underground cooking. A pit is dug, lined with rocks, filled with wood, and the wood is set alight. A few hours later a pot, filled with the ingredients and covered in a tightly-fitting lid, is lowered onto the hot coals. Additional coals are raked over the pot, dirt is shoveled onto the coals, and then the beans cook for ten hours, undisturbed in the pot, resulting in tender, old-fashioned baked beans.[43]

Green Beans

Green beans, especially when in season, are also a traditional barbecue favorite, partially because they are delicious and partially because the simplicity of cooking green beans matches the simplicity of making barbecue. The beans go well with ham, so chunks of ham are sometimes added to cooked green beans.

Coleslaw

Coleslaw has graced the table of many a barbecue over the years, and its appearance at barbecues dates from at least the early 1800s. The dish itself is of Dutch origin, where it was *kool sla*; *cole* is the old English word for cabbage, the main ingredient in the dish (and the plant today called kale is a close relative). The following two recipes come from Lettice Bryan's *The Kentucky Housewife*, from 1839. In her recipe for barbecued pig, reprinted above, she recommends "slaugh" as an accompaniment, and includes recipes for both cold and warm slaw (strangely, "slaw" is how it is spelled in the index). The recipes date from long before the popularity of mayonnaise so this is a vinegar-based slaw.

Cold Slaugh

Select firm fragile heads of cabbage (no other sort being fit for slaugh); having stripped off the outer leaves cleave the top part of the head into four equal parts, leaving the lower part whole, so that they may not be separated till shaved or cut fine from the stalk. Take a very sharp knife, shave off the cabbage roundwise, cutting it very smoothly and evenly, and at no rate more than a quarter of an inch in width. Put the shavings or slaugh in a deep china dish, pile it high, and make it smooth; mix with enough good vinegar to nearly fill the dish, a sufficient quantity of salt and pepper to season the slaugh; add a spoonful of whole white mustard seeds, and pour it over the slaugh, garnish it round on the edge of the dish with pickled eggs, cut in ringlets. Never put butter on cabbage that is to be eaten cold, as it is by no means pleasant to the taste or sight.[44]

Warm Slaugh

Cut them as for cold slaugh; having put in a skillet enough butter, salt, pepper, and vinegar to season the slaugh very well, put it into the seasonings; stir it fast, that it all may warm equally, and as soon as it gets hot, serve it in a deep china dish; make it smooth, and disseminate over it hard boiled yolks of eggs, that are minced fine.[45]

Barbecue Cole Slaw

At some Southern barbecue restaurants the coleslaw is red because it has either ketchup or barbecue sauce added to it. That version of coleslaw obviously carries a barbecue theme, but it also omits the mayonnaise, meaning that refrigeration is not as critical as it is with mayonnaise-based slaw, which in turn drastically simplifies the selling of coleslaw at a restaurant. Recipes for barbecue coleslaw are not too different from regular coleslaw recipes except for the substitution of slightly less barbecue sauce or ketchup for the mayonnaise, and a possible substitution of apple cider vinegar for the white vinegar (the taste of apple cider vinegar complements the barbecue sauce).

Potato Salad

Potato salad tends to come in two versions, one that uses mayonnaise and one that does not. The mayonnaise version is always served cold and includes a number of spices. The other version, often referred as German potato salad, usually includes bacon, onions, and vinegar, and can be served hot or cold. Recipes for the two versions have not changed much over the years, as seen by a recipe for cold potato salad from 1906: "Use fresh boiled potatoes. Quarter them and cut slices across the grain. Season some cooked mayonnaise. Add a little minced parsley and grated onions; some whipped cream to make it light. Mix with the potatoes and garnish with hard boiled eggs cut in strips or parsley."[46]

Candied Sweet Potatoes

Sweet potatoes as a side dish for barbecues reflect the Southern influence on barbecue, as sweet potatoes tend to be more popular in the South than the North. Some of that is because of the African, and African American, influences on Southern cooking, and some of that is also because Southerners seem to have an affinity for sweets. In this recipe, from Martha McCulloch-Williams's 1913 cookbook *Dishes and Beverages of the Old South*, the sweet potatoes essentially function as carriers for syrup.

> Boil medium potatoes of even size, till a fork will pierce—steaming is better though a bit more trouble—throw in cold water for a minute, peel, and brush over with soft butter, then lay separately in a wide skillet, with an inch of very rich syrup over the bottom and set over slow fire. Turn the potatoes often in the syrup, letting it coat all sides. Keep turning them until candied and a little brown. If wanted very rich put butter and lemon juice in the syrup when making it. Blade mace also flavors it very well.[47]

Grilled Corn

Corn on the cob can easily be grilled; there are two popular ways of going about it: either leaving the husks on or first removing them. Grilling corn with the husks on technically steams the corn, since the husks trap the moisture as it heats up.

To grill corn with the husks on, first soak the ears of corn in cold water for about fifteen minutes. This will add quite a bit of water to the ears, which will help with the steaming. Next, pull the husks back without removing them. Do remove all the silk, though, and then put the husks back in their place. Grill the ears over indirect heat for about fifteen minutes. Some recipes call for additional ingredients to be added to the corn in the husk. For example, the *Better Homes and Gardens Barbecue Book* from the 1960s suggested spreading a spoonful of peanut butter on each ear, and then wrapping the ear with a slice of bacon, before replacing the husk.

To grill corn directly on the grill, remove the husks and the silk. Place the ears over the coals and brush with butter. The downward-facing portion of the ear will brown within about five minutes, so every five minutes or so rotate the ears slightly to brown a new section. The corn will need to cook about twenty minutes total.

Brunswick Stew

Brunswick stew is an old Southern dish often served at barbecues. Squirrel meat was traditionally used in the stew, a reflection of the fact that it was probably created by hunters using whatever ingredients they had on hand. Brunswick stew's importance to Southerners can be seen in its inclusion in *Recipes Out of Bilibid*, a cookbook compiled by residents of a World War II prisoner of war

Making stew at a 60th birthday barbecue, 1948. Courtesy Georgia Archives, Vanishing Georgia Collection, CAR-56.

camp in the Philippines. The recipes in that cookbook came from the memories of men who may have been away from their homes for years, but the Brunswick stew entry is not that different from Brunswick stew recipes in other cookbooks (the book also included four different barbecue sauces "given because each contributor was convinced that his concoction was superior to the others").[48]

Common Sense in the Household, from 1873, is a cookbook written by an older woman for young women who may be starting their own household. The book has a Southern flavor to it and includes a section on cooking with squirrels, and in that section is the following recipe for Brunswick stew. The recipe is marked with a symbol indicating that it is an easier recipe for beginning cooks, although there are not that many cooks these days who would want to handle chopping up squirrels. The author does, however, indicate that the squirrels can be replaced by chickens. This recipe has been modified slightly from the original by putting the ingredients in their proper order, and by specifically saying that the cayenne should be added with the butter; the original recipe does not indicate when the cayenne should be added.

Brunswick Stew

1 gallon water
1 tablespoon salt
1 onion, minced small
1 pint butter or Lima beans
6 ears of green corn cut from the cob
1/2 pound salt pork or bacon, cut in shreds
6 potatoes, parboiled and sliced
1 teaspoonful ground black pepper
2 squirrels—3, if small
1 quart of tomatoes—peeled and sliced
2 teaspoons white sugar
1/2 pound butter
1/2 teaspoon cayenne

Put on the water with the salt in it, and boil five minutes. Put in the onion, beans, corn, pork or bacon, potatoes, pepper, and the squirrels, which must first be cut into joints and laid in cold salt and water to draw out the blood. Cover closely and stew two and a half hours very slowly, stirring frequently from the bottom. Then add the tomatoes and sugar, and stew an hour longer. Ten minutes before you take it from the fire add the butter, cut into bits the size of a walnut, rolled in flour, and also add the cayenne. Give a final boil, taste to see that it is seasoned to your liking, and turn into a soup-tureen.[49]

Burgoo

Burgoo is a stew which is often served along with barbecue in Kentucky. An 1897 *New York Times* article on an immense Kentucky barbecue speculated that burgoo was descended from a Welsh stew. That article focused on Gustave Jaubert, the man in charge of the barbecue, and also a man who was famous for his burgoo. Jaubert gave the reporter his recipe for cooking enough burgoo to serve between 5,000 and 7,000 people.

Burgoo for a Very Large Crowd

For this barbecue I made 1,000 gallons of burgoo. Its ingredients are 400 pounds of beef, six dozen chickens, four dozen rabbits, thirty cans of tomatoes, twenty dozen cans of corn, fifteen bushels of potatoes, and five bushels of onions. It takes burgoo ten or twelve hours to cook, and it requires constant stirring. I was up all of last night. First, I filled up the two big kettles—one containing 700, and the other 300, gallons—with water; then I put in the beef and the chickens, and let them boil until daybreak, when we skimmed off the froth of grease that had formed on the surface and took out all the bones. The vegetables and the seasoning, including a quantity of red pepper, were then put in and allowed to cook for five hours, and the burgoo is ready to be served.[50]

The *Times* article reported that the 1,000 gallons of burgoo "failed to hold out."

John Egerton recounted a more manageable recipe in his book *Southern Food: At Home, on the Road, in History*. He traced the recipe to one published in the 1940s which had "since appeared in print enough times to be thought of as a public trust and a standard by which modern burgoo is made."[51] While his recipe does not include the squirrel or game meat burgoo traditionally included, it does require a very long cooking time typical of burgoo—the recipe can be cooked in seven hours, but Egerton recommends ten to twelve hours to really get the job done.

In his recipe, two hours are required to boil the beef, chicken, and lamb or mutton that constitute the meats used in the recipe. The chicken is deboned and then added back to the pot, followed by potatoes, onions, green bell peppers, carrots, corn kernels, and butter or baby lima beans, all of which simmers for three more hours. At different points thereafter other ingredients, including garlic, cayenne pepper, tomatoes, and okra are added, resulting in a thick, well-cooked stew that can take longer to cook than the barbecue it accompanies.

Barbecue Salad

Beginning in the early 20th century, food companies hired home economists to develop recipes that featured the food the companies produced. These recipes ended up on food boxes, in advertisements, in cookbooks, and in press releases sent to food writers throughout the 20th and 21st centuries. Vast numbers of recipes were produced, and not all of them had the success of, say, Nestlé's Toll House Cookie recipe, which was the first chocolate chip cookie recipe. Many of the recipes were not very good, and some attempted to take a popular concept and push it a bit too far.

An example of a recipe that attempted to connect to a popular trend but perhaps went too far is the barbecue salad recipe from the mid-1960s edition of *The Joys of Jell-O*. Barbecue salad does appear today on the menus of some barbecue restaurants where, as may be expected, the dish is made of barbecued meat on a bed of greens, with barbecue sauce as the dressing. Not so in *The Joys of Jell-O* cookbook. The salad referred to in that title is not a green salad but a gelatin salad (over some greens), and the resulting dish is a bit odd. The recipe has the cook dissolve a package of lemon, orange, or orange-pineapple gelatin in boiling water, then add tomato sauce, vinegar, salt, and a dash of pepper to the liquid. The hot liquid is poured into four small molds, chilled, and then dropped onto greens, one mold for each guest. Although the recipe does not call for barbecue sauce, the combination of vinegar and tomato sauce could be said to make an imitation of it, albeit a fairly poor one.[52]

Barbecue Nachos

Barbecue nachos have begun appearing at barbecue restaurants across the country, and the recipe for them has also begun appearing in cookbooks. In *Smokin' with Myron Mixon*, Mixon (famous for winning many barbecue competitions) calls barbecue nachos "the best damn appetizer in the world, especially good for things like Super Bowl parties and poker games."[53] It is also good for getting rid of excess barbecue meat.

The recipe for barbecue nachos is simple. A bag of nacho chips is laid out on a baking sheet, and then covered with about a pound of any type of barbecue meat, cut or pulled into small pieces. Shredded cheese goes on top of this, as well as jalapeno slices, if desired. The nachos are baked in a 350° oven for five minutes or so, until the cheese has melted and the chips are hot. Salsa and sour cream can be served on the side.

Round-up Coffee

Coffee has almost disappeared from today's barbecues, but in the mid-20th century it was a standard beverage. Part of the fun of barbecuing was the primitive cooking conditions, and this fun seemed to have extended to making coffee as well. Even though electric coffee makers existed, some mid-century cookbooks gave instructions for making coffee on the grill. The *Big Boy Barbecue Book*, from 1956, gave instructions for a fairly old technique for making coffee that involved a large pot and layers of cheesecloth, a method that veterans of World War II surely were familiar with.

The basic technique was to wrap coffee grounds in four layers of cheesecloth. The amount of grounds varied depending on how much coffee was to be made, but it was around three-quarters of a cup of grounds per five cups of coffee. This would have produced some very strong coffee relative to today's coffee; this recommendation is far more than today's one spoonful per cup recommendation, and the grounds sat in the water for much longer than with today's coffeemakers. The four layers of cheesecloth should be laid out flat, the grounds should go on a pile at the middle of the cheesecloth, the edges of the cheesecloth should be gathered up to form a bag, and the top should be secured shut. This bag, then, went into a pot of cold water, enough water for the amount of coffee being made. The water was brought to a boil, being stirred every few minutes, and when the water boiled, the coffee was done.

Lemonade

Lemonade is a fine beverage for a summer barbecue. It is not that difficult to make lemonade from fresh lemons, and fresh lemonade tastes much better than lemonade made from a mix. This recipe is from the *Kentucky Housewife*, from 1839.

> Take ripe lemons, roll them under your fingers on a table till they appear like they are full of juice; then squeeze the juice into a bowl, to each pint of which allow three pints of water, or if in summer, allow two and a half pints of water and a lump of ice equal to the other half pint. Sweeten it to your taste with loaf sugar, and serve it up in small glasses.[54]

Bonfire "Big Apples"

The 1939 edition of *Sunset's Barbecue Book* is quite early for a book devoted entirely to barbecue, and it contains a simple but delicious-sounding recipe for candied apples, one that was probably originally used for cooking around a bonfire. To make the apples, each person spears an apple with a stick and then roasts the apple directly over the hot coals until the skin peels off easily. The skin should then be removed and the apple rolled in brown sugar and then returned briefly to the coals, just until the brown sugar has melted. The recipe ends by telling the cook that, once the brown sugar has melted to candy, "You'll know what to do next."[55]

Powow Sundae

It is difficult to know just where this recipe got its name from, since there seems to be no connection to Native Americans, but this dish makes good use of the hot coals left over from a fire to make a delicious ice cream topping (the recipe originally appeared in the *Better Homes and Gardens Barbecue Book* in 1965). The instructions are simple: Toast a number of marshmallows on sticks over hot coals, and when the marshmallows are good and soft, plunge them immediately into about a cup of chocolate syrup. Stir just to get a marble texture, then pour this warm topping over vanilla ice cream.

PUTTING IT ALL TOGETHER: THE BARBECUE PARTY

As was discussed in the previous chapter, in the 19th-century barbecue made its appearance at two broad types of occasions: at political rallies and at other social occasions. Especially in the South, barbecue was the default food for political rallies because it was culturally accepted and because roasting large parts of animals was an easy way to provide food for large numbers of people. At social gatherings, like Fourth of July celebrations or dances, barbecue might have been the main food served, or it could be one of many foods served. One woman who wrote about the pre–Civil War outdoor dances she remembered from her early life described potlucks at the dances that included "Broiled chicken, fried chicken, in quantity, whole hams simply entreating to be sliced, barbecue, pickles in great variety . . . beaten biscuit, soda biscuit, egg bread, salt-rising bread, or rolls raised with hop-yeast . . . every manner of pie, tart, and tartlet."[56] In the 19th century, barbecue was a popular food, but at both political rallies and other social occasions it was not the focus of the occasion but merely a food to be eaten.

In the 20th century, as barbecuing became a mainstream activity, and as its definition shifted to be equated with outdoor grilling, the food, and socializing, became the focus of barbecues. Especially in the 1950s and afterward, backyard barbecues were opportunities to spend time with friends and family. As the popularity of barbecues spread across the country, the idea of just what constituted a barbecue was reflected in cookbooks and newspaper and magazine articles.

Sunset's Barbecue Book, from 1939, was an early barbecue cookbook, so early that over half the book consists of construction plans for building a grill and grill-related furniture. The last chapter of the book, after the barbecue recipes, is a guide to "Successful Barbecue Parties" that outlined three "frequently-mentioned reasons for possible party imperfection."[57] Potential problems were that guests did not have anything to do before the food was served, food service did not go smoothly, and guests did not have anything to do after the meal was over. That all of these things were seen as problems points to the fact that, by 1939, barbecues were seen primarily as social gatherings where guests expected to be entertained. To combat boredom before the meal *Sunset* recommended setting up a card table topped with paper plates, jars of paint, and paintbrushes. Each guest would be asked to paint a plate in whatever way they wanted, and the plates would be displayed on a wall behind the barbecue. There were also active games that could be played, such as "Tennis, badminton, ping pong, archery, darts, croquet, horseshoes, shuffleboard, [and] bean bags."[58] *Sunset* portrayed the barbecue as an evening meal, and so the after-meal games, described below, were quieter, non-active games, compared with the active before-meal games. For guests who wanted some sustenance before the meal, the book recommended "a chilled fruit juice cocktail or a cup of steaming bouillon"—while bouillon seems an odd drink today, in the 1930s it was seen as a filling, nutritious drink. To correct the second common problem in barbecues, that food service did not go smoothly, the book advised planning things down to almost the minute. "Have everything possible ready and laid out in advance. From past experience, know the cooking time for every dish, and plan definitely so that everything finishes at once. Give your guests jobs as helpers if you can. It's fun for everybody if you can parcel out definite, tidy jobs."[59] After the meal, the book suggested keeping the party outside, which meant having previously set up outdoor floodlights so guests could play "cards, checkers, or dominoes on small card tables placed in the lighted area." If there was no artificial lighting, the book recommended that the host "just throw another log on the fire and start off some old-fashioned guessing games or singing. Games that can be played sitting around the fire—such as 'Who am I?,' '20 Questions,' 'Coffeepot,' 'Geography,' etc.—are often amazingly successful."[60]

In 1959, the *General Foods Kitchens Cookbook* outlined an idea for a California barbecue. The suggested menu mixed two different sets of ideas popular

Young people at a barbecue in west Texas in the 1950s. Standard Oil of New Jersey Collection, SONJ 53409_M_16, Archives and Special Collections, University of Louisville.

among food writers of the time: the idea that "barbecue" was another word for outdoor grilling and the conception of California as a place where people ate healthy, somewhat exotic foods. Here, there was no connection between barbecue and the South; instead, this was a newer-style barbecue from the West. The menu began with avocado-grapefruit salad, then moved on to charcoal-broiled steak, baked potatoes, broccoli, and pineapple fruit bowls. As was typical for mid-century barbecues, coffee finished off the meal. The authors of the cookbook included instructions on setting things up for the meal. "[S]et out your table on the porch or lawn, near the grill. A table covering of fresh fern and leaves would look beautiful, and a centerpiece of a small white birdcage with ivy twining from it, or a shallow pottery bowl with pink geraniums or hollyhocks afloat. Hurricane lamps for the candles will look handsome and protect the candles from the wind."[61]

A few years later, Walter Jetton, President Lyndon Johnson's pitmaster, furnished his own description of a good barbecue in a cookbook he published in 1965. Jetton was Texan and believed that barbecues descended from cowboy traditions, so his idea of a barbecue was Western themed, something that would have dovetailed nicely with the popularity of the countless Western movies and television shows of the 1950s and 1960s. He advised the potential barbecue host or hostess to "go to some good hotel dining room or another elegant eating place, see what they do for atmosphere and serving—and then do just the opposite, or as near to it as you can come." Rather than serving food on the table, service should be from a "chow-line" or buffet. "The best chairs and tables, I would say, are fallen down logs or maybe some bales of hay under a shady tree." If tables were to be used, they should be covered with checkered tablecloths, and lanterns or candles were the preferred light sources. Food and drink should be served on tin plates and tin cups, and twigs should be used for stirring coffee (although he did allow that "You've got to have some kind of knife and fork for people to eat with").[62]

In 1947 *Vogue* published its own ideas for a Texas-style barbecue party. "At a typical barbecue, guests sit at a long table, under the trees, and eat the meats that have been roasting over the deep barbecues since the night before. There are chickens, pigs, and baby goats, burning with pepper, sweet with herbs."[63] After the meal comes blacks singing spirituals—this idea may be eyebrow-raising, but this portion of the article was recycled from a *Vogue* article from five years previously, when the author visited a Texas barbecue where there were, in fact, blacks singing spirituals after the meal (that article will be examined in detail in chapter 5). This article is interesting in that it goes into a considerable amount of detail regarding how to make Texas-style barbecue, beginning with the pit: "First dig a pit about two and a half feet deep and five to six feet long. Cover the top with thick wire netting, held in place by iron rods."[64] The next step is to "Gather a supply of hickory wood sufficient to burn for at least twenty-four hours."[65] It continues with instructions on building the fire, tending to the meat, and basting the meat with barbecue sauce, which *Vogue* helpfully printed a recipe for. It is difficult to imagine any *Vogue* reader, today or back then, going through these steps to have a barbecue, but the *Vogue* editors certainly provided the instructions for a barbecue, just in case their readers were interested in having one.

In the early 1960s *Better Homes & Gardens* magazine had an idea for a barbecue party that solved two perennial problems with barbecues: the cost involved for the host, and the fact that not everyone always got what they wanted. "Here's the idea: Neighbors barbecue together, but each guy buys his own meat to suit his pocketbook and family, then chefs it on his own grill. The wives go potluck on the rest of the meal—the salad, vegetables, dessert and beverages. All the joys of a big shindig, yet nobody is dealt a budget blow!" A photo with the article showed four men standing at four grills, each cooking his own family's meal, as wives and children looked on.[66] Of course, this was a bit of an extreme suggestion as hauling a grill across town could take quite a bit of effort. Interestingly, the same magazine made nearly the same suggestion eighteen years earlier, during World War II, but the solution was then pitched as a rationing issue. Various types of foods, including meat and coffee, were rationed, and by having guests bring their own meat and coffee the hosts of the barbecue could save their rationing points for themselves. Another alternative suggested in the article was to serve chicken or fish, meats that were not rationed.[67]

BREAKFAST

The barbecue craze of the 1950s was strong enough that some cookbook writers advocated using the barbecue in not just the afternoon or evening but in the morning hours. There are some drawbacks to the idea of having a breakfast barbecue, of course, including the difficulty of getting guests together early in the morning and the fact that, unless it is a gas grill, starting the grill adds an additional forty-five minutes of prep time to the meal. These drawbacks probably contribute to the fact that the vast majority of barbecue cookbooks make no mention of breakfast barbecues. There are two examples from the past, though.

Sunset's Barbecue Book, from 1939, is from a time when barbecue grills were still new and exciting, and so the book let the reader know that "If you've never used your barbecue for outdoor breakfasts, you've missed a good part of its charm."[68] The book lists two menus for breakfast barbecues. The first features "Chilled Melon Wedges, Grilled Ham, Fried Eggs, Hot Coffee Cake, Doughnuts, [and] Coffee." The second consists of "Prepared Cereal with Fresh Berries, Little Sausages, Griddle Cakes, [and] Coffee." The coffee could be prepared in a tin over the fire, the ham could be made on the grill, and the eggs, little sausages, and griddle cakes could all be made on a frying pan over the fire.

Twenty years later, the *General Foods Kitchens Cookbook* suggested a chuck wagon breakfast, during the heyday of the cowboy in American culture. The suggested menu was similar to *Sunset's*: "Spiced tomato juice, Buttermilk pancakes, Creamed chipped beef, Maple-orange sauce, Link sausage, Coffee, [and] Milk."[69] While this was an outdoor meal, the authors advised readers to stay away from using the grill to cook all of this. "This is a cook-it-outdoors occasion, that *can* be accomplished on an outdoor barbecue, but will go a lot faster if you use an electric fry pan (sausages), griddles (pancakes), and a couple of candle warmers (for fruit syrup and chipped beef, which you'll make in the house earlier)." Of course, this advice raises the question of just why the cooking should be done outside at all, since quite a bit of stuff would need to be hauled out to the patio—it could just be the excitement of eating breakfast outdoors.

3

BARBECUE
EATEN OUT

The kitchen and the backyard are not the only places one can find barbecue, of course. Restaurants have offered barbecue since the late 1800s, and in the past few decades more and more barbecue restaurants have appeared throughout America. The earliest places to buy barbecue were nothing more than a shack alongside the road with a pit out back, and sometimes there was only the pit. Consumers were expected to either eat the barbecue while standing or sitting near the shack, or else to take the barbecue away with them. Over time, many of the shacks became sit-down restaurants, although the food they served often did not change much—in fact, barbecue purists often prefer restaurants that look the same as they did decades before. In the context of restaurants, though, the use of the word "barbecue" is somewhat different than in other contexts. When most restaurants describe something as being barbecued, they usually mean it was cooked at a low temperature for a long period of time. The use of "barbecue" as a synonym for grilling is very rare in the restaurant industry. However, when it comes to barbecue served in non-barbecue restaurants, "barbecue" is often shorthand for food served with barbecue sauce on it (e.g., the Carolina BBQ Whopper that sometimes appears at Burger King). In this way there may be some confusion over just what the definition of barbecue is, when served at a restaurant.

THE BIRTH OF THE BARBECUE RESTAURANT

As has been discussed previously, the modern barbecue restaurant was created over a period of decades in different places, and not all at once. Until the late 19th century, barbecue was usually given away, whether at a political rally, public festivity, or social occasion. In the late 19th century, though, cooks began selling barbecue at some of those public festivities. From there it was a short jump to setting up shop at a standard location during a standard time. Most often, the location was simply a spot along the road during the weekend. The barbecue cook usually had a regular job he worked during the week, and barbecuing was just a way to make extra money on the side. He prepared a certain amount of food at the beginning of the weekend and stayed open until he sold out, at which point he closed up shop until the following weekend.

A few things need to be noted here about these early barbecue joints—"restaurant" is too proper a word to use for what was usually just a small shack perched alongside the road, and these early places had a very strong connection to the road. All businesses rely on roads for traffic, but the early barbecue shacks relied on them especially, since they were usually either outside of town or on the outskirts. Being open only on the weekends meant that these places generated far too little revenue to be able to rent a building or lot in town. There was also the problem of the low-burning fire that smoked all of Thursday night and most of Friday—this would result in quite a few complaints from neighbors. The barbecue shacks were away from population centers and so relied on traffic and, as will be explored below, the popularity of the automobile helped the businesses considerably.

These early barbecue places were responsible for the development of different meats being popular in different places. The older-style barbecues were free to the public and used whatever meat was donated by local farmers for the festivity or rally. The newer barbecue places had to pay for their meat, and to maximize profits they had to sell everything they cooked. They likely chose the cheapest meat possible, which was usually whatever was plentiful in their area: pork in most places, beef in Texas, and goat or mutton in a very few locations. Eastern North Carolina barbecue joints retained the tradition of cooking and serving the entire hog, but in other locations, barbecuers made a conscious choice of which cut of meat to prepare. In most places, pork shoulder or pork ribs became standard, but beef brisket also became popular in some areas. Brisket is a tough, inexpensive cut of meat; because of its toughness it is ideal for barbecuing. The long hours of cooking result in tender meat.

Exterior of a barbecue restaurant from Corpus Christi, Texas. Courtesy of the Library of Congress, cph 3c29918.

The developments described here proceeded in different ways in different places. In central Texas, the standard location to buy barbecue was not a roadside shack but the local meat market. In the days before refrigeration and a centralized slaughterhouse industry, butchers slaughtered animals to sell at their store, which resulted in meat that was either unsold or sold extremely cheaply. In central Texas, that meat was turned into barbecue, which was then sold for a higher price than the raw meat. The German immigrants who often operated meat markets there brought with them a tradition of making "hot sausage," the "hot" referring not to spice or temperature but to the fact that the meat had been cooked before being added to the sausage (and, therefore, the hot sausage could easily be made up of the previous day's leftover scraps). Another example of a different path to development was locations with a reliable, steady supply of barbecue consumers, such as a local factory. Barbecue is both a slow and fast food: It takes hours to cook a pork shoulder, but when it is done the entire shoulder can be quickly carved and sold. This sort of food was ideal for factory workers who needed to be served quickly during a lunch hour or shift change, and those workers in turn helped local barbecue shacks become full-fledged restaurants quickly.

Czech grocers in central Texas pose with some of their meat. General Photograph Collection MS 362: 098-076-0388, UTSA Libraries Special Collections.

As the shacks perched alongside the road slowly turned into sit-down restaurants, the question of a name for the restaurant came up. Often, the restaurant was simply given the owner's name, either his or her given name or a nickname. This can be seen in some of the most famous barbecue restaurants in this country, such as Arthur Bryant's in Kansas City; Kreuz Market in Lockhart, Texas; or Stamey's in Greensboro, North Carolina. There are other naming conventions as well. Vince Staten and Greg Johnson, who crisscrossed the country doing research for *Real Barbecue*, their guide to the best barbecue restaurants in America, reported that Old Hickory, or variations using the word hickory, was the most popular name they encountered. Names using the word "Bubba" were also popular, mainly because that was the owner's nickname. They also noted some names that seemed strikingly wrong for barbecue restaurants, like the Swiss Chalet Barbecue in Miami, or Mama Rosa's in Philadelphia.[1]

Early barbecue places flourished in locations with an existing barbecue culture, both because the population was already acquainted with barbecue and because that was where most of the barbecue cooks lived, although many cooks who went west or north were able to start viable businesses on the strength of their cooking. As the roadside shacks did more and more business, many of them shifted to being open during the week as well as during the weekend (although it should be noted that it is still very possible to find roadside shacks open only during the weekend throughout the country). In the early 20th century, another development helped these businesses to flourish: the growing use of the automobile.

Increasing ownership of automobiles went hand in hand with the increasing miles of paved roads in America. Railroads remained an important method of passenger transportation well into the middle portion of the 20th century, but the automobile allowed drivers the opportunity to go almost anywhere, at any time. Early drivers had to put up with quite a bit for the opportunity to explore the country with their car, since cars were plagued with mechanical problems, roads were usually unpaved, and services such as gas stations and restaurants could be few and far between (in fact, the popularity of outdoor grilling in the 1950s can be traced to car owners grilling on long trips in the decades before).

As motorists pushed their way into the South, they came in contact with barbecue, sometimes for the first time, often sold from shacks along the road. As magazines began printing articles about traveling across the country, "barbecue stand" became the default phrase used to describe any roadside eatery, not necessarily one that sold barbecue.[2] Barbecue worked perfectly for these motorists because it could be served quickly and because the stands were already conveniently positioned along the road. The barbecue might be messy to eat but it was certainly a quick meal for motorists wanting to get from one town to another.

In this way barbecue functioned as some of the first fast food. Its position as an early fast-food star declined over time, though, because of the complications in preparing barbecue. The McDonald brothers, the creators of the archetypical fast-food restaurant, learned this at their first restaurant. A McDonald's menu from 1943 proudly proclaims that "We barbecue all meats in our own barbecue pit." The pit was behind the restaurant, which allowed the brothers to also print on the menu, "Don't be misled. Other places advertise their meat as 'barbecued,' when it is merely cooked in a stove. . . . You are welcome to see our meat while it is actually being barbecued in our own Barbecue Pit."[3] McDonald's, of course, later became famous for its hamburgers, not its barbecue, and the fame did not come until after the McDonald brothers intentionally dropped barbecue from the menu to focus on hamburgers. As it turned out, barbecue had some big problems.

THE TROUBLE WITH BARBECUE RESTAURANTS

In a very simplistic way, American restaurants can be divided into two large groups: fast-food restaurants and "sit-down" restaurants. Fast-food restaurants are intended to be cheaper, and so they put more work on the customer. The customer orders his or her own food at a counter, carries it to the table, and cleans the table afterward. Sit-down restaurants are more expensive, since wait-staff take orders, carry the food to the table, and clean up afterward, and the experience takes longer, since the food preparation takes longer than at a fast-food restaurant. Barbecue originally seemed to work well for fast-food restaurants but, as it turns out, has mostly appeared in sit-down restaurants.

Regarding fast-food restaurants, there are at least two ways to define "fast food." One way is to simply take the words at face value: fast food is food that can be offered to the customer quickly. In this, barbecue succeeded admirably. Pulled pork or beef brisket could be quickly assembled into sandwiches or plates and given to the customer who, before the development of sit-down restaurants, would either eat the food near the barbecue stand (possibly in his car), or take it to eat somewhere else. Barbecue places began offering curbside service where customers stopped along the road and were serviced by busboys who were often paid solely by tips from customers. Those early restaurants will be looked at in more depth below.

However, the more typical definition of fast food flows from the operations of the big franchised restaurants, particularly McDonald's. Fast food involves a host of business concepts that, in the 1950s, moved from the manufacturing industry to the restaurant business. In the same way that Ford cranked out Model Ts in the early 20th century, McDonald's cranked out hamburgers, using standardized ingredients and an assembly-line approach. Most of the fast-food chain restaurants were not owned by the originating company but by franchisees who followed explicit directions on how to run their business. All of this is what is usually meant by "fast food," and in this sense of the phrase, barbecue failed miserably.

Barbecue has two basic problems when it comes to fast food. Its first problem is cooking time. Barbecue can be served very quickly, but it takes hours to cook brisket or pork shoulder, and this cooking time adds up to labor costs that go against the basic tenets of a fast-food restaurant. There are two reasons why the hamburger is the archetypical fast food: The meat is cheap and it cooks in a few minutes. Barbecue meat, too, has traditionally been cheap, since the cuts of meat favored for barbecue are too tough for quick cooking, but it takes a very long time to cook.

The second problem with barbecue is the fact that the creation of good barbecue takes skill and, again, this results in higher labor costs. Fast-food restaurants hire workers with only basic skills and make the cooking process as simple as possible (customers at fast-food restaurants can sometimes see the pictorial instructions of how to make a hamburger taped to a wall in the cooking area). Making good barbecue takes experience and knowledge; those things contribute to higher labor costs than fast-food restaurants can handle. Standardization is a priority in the fast-food business, where a hamburger purchased in Seattle should taste exactly the same as a hamburger purchased in Miami. With the complexities of barbecue, though, it can be difficult for the same restaurant chain to produce similar results at two restaurants that are ten blocks apart, rather than two thousand miles apart. As one restaurant owner in Chapel Hill, North Carolina, said, "They tried to class barbecue as a fast food, but it's not a fast food. You can't rubber-stamp barbecue and have good quality. You can put it out there, but that don't mean it's good."[4]

Barbecue works better in a sit-down restaurant, and the vast majority of barbecue restaurants in this country are of the sit-down variety. However, as the quote above indicates when it refers to rubber-stamping a product, barbecue restaurants have had a very hard time developing chains that covered more than a relatively small geographical area. This area often extends to only how far can be driven in a few hours' time, since beyond that a single person (an owner) cannot easily keep track of quality control at each restaurant.

Running a successful barbecue restaurant, like running any restaurant, is a difficult proposition. Vince Staten and Greg Johnson, writing in *Real Barbecue*, point out that all the restaurants they include are good ones, for a simple reason. "[T]here is no low end of the scale, no barbecue equivalent of a one-star restaurant. They just don't survive."[5]

If running a successful restaurant is difficult, making the transition to a chain seems to be almost impossible; as John Shelton Reed wrote, "Expansion is not good for barbecue joints. That's a rule almost as reliable as Vince Staten's maxim that a place without flies is no good."[6] (There seems to be a strange flip side to that rule: many, if not most, chain restaurants such as Chili's and Applebee's offer at least one barbecue item on their menus, giving the impression that the big chains have to at least try to do something with barbecue.) The history of barbecue restaurants is littered with barbecue chains that tried to become big, expanded too far and too fast, and then collapsed back to only a few remaining restaurants. One early example is the Pig Stand, which opened its first restaurant in Dallas in 1921. As its name implies, the Pig Stand became not a chain of restaurants but a chain of barbecue stands where customers either took their food elsewhere or ate it outside. The Pig Stand may have been the first chain to offer curbside service where unpaid waitstaff, who survived on tips, ran orders, food, and money back and forth between the cars that parked along the curb and the barbecue stand. Supposedly, the Pig Stand's owner added the service because, in his words, "People with cars are so lazy they don't want to get out of them to eat!"[7] By 1934 there were over 120 Pig Stands across the southern United States but the chain was in decline by World War II, even as the nationwide craze for barbecue (that is, outdoor grilling) was heating up.[8] A second barbecue chain to boom and then bust was Luther's, a Houston-based chain with sixty-three stores by the mid-1980s, including one in Dover, Delaware. Ten years later, though, it was down to only twenty restaurants.[9]

A more famous collapse, because of its well-known name, is KC Masterpiece, which currently has no restaurants. The story of KC Masterpiece began in 1977 when Rich Davis, a Kansas City–area physician and child psychologist, began selling bottles of a barbecue sauce he had developed to local grocery stores. After some name changes, Davis settled on "KC Masterpiece" as the name of the sauce. In 1980 sauce sales were helped by Davis winning the inaugural American Royal Barbecue competition in Kansas City, which was held with the existing American Royal Livestock Show. Davis was extremely good at salesmanship, and sauce sales climbed and climbed. As popular as his sauce was, though, his company was not a major player in the food industry, and in the mid-1980s Davis realized that, in order to push his brand to the next level, he would need to either partner with a much larger company or simply sell out to a larger company. He chose the latter route and sold KC Masterpiece to Clorox in 1986 for between $8 and $10 million.[10] As part of the deal, though, he retained the ability to open his own restaurants with the KC Masterpiece name. The first KC Masterpiece restaurant opened in 1987 in Overland Park, Kansas, a suburb of Kansas City and a place with no shortage of quality barbecue restaurants. Two years later the company expanded into the St. Louis area, and Charlie Davis, Rich's son, talked about expanding to be a nationwide chain. KC Masterpiece eventually grew to have two restaurants each in the areas around Kansas City, St. Louis, and Chicago. This was the chain at its peak, and the problems in running the company were becoming apparent. As the first manager of the first restaurant explained it to a reporter (in an article titled "KC Disasterpiece," published after the chain had closed most of its restaurants), the problems existed at many levels. The chain was very spread out geographically, making it hard to manage. The Davis family did not at first grasp the complexity of running a restaurant—as the manager told the founder, "Dr. Davis, you know there's a little bit of difference between putting two briskets on the grill in the backyard and putting 60 briskets in a smoker so that you could produce them for customers the next day." There was also infighting within the family, as Dr. Davis's sons, Rich and Charlie, who were both involved in running the business, struggled with each other and with their father as they all tried to run the restaurants.[11] By the year 2000 the Chicago restaurants had closed and Dr. Davis's sons had left the business. Famous Dave's, the second largest barbecue chain in the country, expressed interest in acquiring the four remaining restaurants but dropped out of the deal after examining the company's financial statements. By 2005 the company was mired in litigation for not paying vendors, and all of the restaurants eventually closed.

The KC Masterpiece story shows the impact of poor business decisions on a restaurant chain. There are other factors inherent to barbecue that seem to have made it difficult to build a restaurant chain based on barbecue. There is the fact that consumers in different parts of the country have fairly fixed ideas of just what "real" barbecue is. A chain that does not offer brisket in Texas, or chopped pork in eastern North Carolina, will probably not do very well. However, as will be discussed below, ideas about barbecue seem to be changing, and the regional differences that have marked barbecue since early in the 20th century seem to be lessening.

Another reason that barbecue chains have not done well over time is that the restaurant industry as a whole is very cyclical. Trends peak and then subside, and the restaurants that expanded too much when they were popular suddenly find themselves with too many empty tables when their popularity wanes. An example of this is Boston Market, a chain that specializes in meat-and-potatoes comfort food. Boston Market prospered during a comfort food boom in the early 1990s, opened hundreds of stores across the country, and then declared bankruptcy in 1998 after customer tastes shifted to healthier foods. A similar cycle of expansion and contraction occurred with Smokey Bones, a barbecue chain owned by Darden Restaurants, the same company that owns Red Lobster and Olive Garden. Smokey Bones started in 1999 and, by 2007, had grown to 127 restaurants in the eastern part of the United States. Business slowed at the chain, as it did for all restaurants, during the economic downturn of the late 2000s, and in 2007 Darden closed fifty-four Smokey Bones restaurants and sold the remaining seventy-three to an investment company, getting itself out of the barbecue business.[12]

Consumer tastes are notoriously fickle, and a barbecue restaurant is, in a way, a one-dimensional restaurant: It specializes in meat. Over the past few decades there have been trends that helped barbecue restaurants considerably. The Atkins diet, which was very popular in the early 2000s, focuses on eating protein at the exclusion of carbohydrates, and a barbecue restaurant would be a good choice for someone on that diet. But that diet subsided, and health officials have repeatedly warned Americans of the danger of eating too much pork and beef, the two main foods served at barbecue restaurants.

It is, of course, possible to find barbecue at national chains. Chili's is known for its baby back ribs, and Tony Roma's is also known for its ribs. However, these are not chains that advertise themselves as barbecue restaurants. They are restaurants that offer some barbecue items, and in this way are able to ride out fickle consumer tastes. When high-protein diets are popular they promote their barbecue items, but when the trends are for lighter foods they publicize their salads, while still offering barbecue on their menu.

There are a few things about barbecue restaurants that are very attractive to potential restaurant owners, especially the franchisees who own the vast majority of chain restaurants in the United States. The bigger franchisees own and operate several different restaurant chains at the same time; they might own a few McDonald's, a few KFCs, and a few Pizza Huts. The restaurant landscape is crowded with established concepts, and a franchisee who owns some McDonald's restaurants is probably not going to want to own a few Burger Kings as well. However, there are very few barbecue chains, so a franchisee who wants to expand might look at barbecue as a way to do that without competing with their existing restaurants. Siting a new barbecue restaurant could be easier as well. Restaurant tenants in locations like shopping malls often have non-compete clauses in their rental contracts that forbid the mall from letting another, similar restaurant open on the same property; an Applebee's would not want a Chili's opening right next door. Again, since there are so few barbecue restaurants, and since barbecue restaurants are not perceived to be direct competition for most other restaurants, barbecue restaurants can avoid problems with locating the restaurant.

BARBECUE RESTAURANTS AND RACE

The South was heavily segregated well into the civil rights era, and that segregation extended to restaurants. The segregation existed in the restaurant at different levels. In terms of patrons, some restaurants were whites only, some (in black sections of town) were blacks only, and some served both but kept the races physically separated, either by having different seating areas or by seating whites inside the building and blacks out back. The segregation extended to workers as well. The kitchen staff was often black because they could be paid less, and the waitstaff might be black or white. However, there was at least one type of restaurant that always had black waitstaff: the Southern-style restaurant that harkened back to the past and that used black labor as a type of window dressing. For example, a postcard from the 1960s advertising the Plantation

Inn in Florida shows black waiters in Colonial-style garb setting tables, with a caption proclaiming that "The Inn radiates contentment and hospitality of a bygone day."[13] A mid-century menu from the Old Southern Tea Room in Vicksburg, Mississippi, described "Colored waitresses in bright 'Mammy' costumes, bandannas and hoop earrings" who brought customers their food.[14]

Barbecue's relationship with race was more complicated than for other restaurants because barbecue had a long tradition of being associated with blacks. Blacks had been the traditional barbecue cooks on pre–Civil War plantations, and that tradition continued through the late 19th and early 20th centuries. Because blacks were known and accepted as barbecue cooks, black-owned barbecue restaurants attracted both black and white patrons. For many whites, a trip to the best barbecue restaurant in the area meant a trip into the black section of town. Calvin Trillin wrote that Arthur Bryant's barbecue restaurant was the only integrated restaurant in Kansas City when Trillin was growing up simply "because it was a black restaurant that white people couldn't stay out of."[15] This crossing of racial barriers can be looked at in two ways. As food historian John T. Edge has pointed out, the traditional interpretation of this is that the mixing was a positive thing, a chance for whites to mingle with blacks in their own culture. But Edge goes on to observe that this can also be seen as simplistic cultural slumming, "an ephemeral indulgence, entered into lightly, exited from easily."[16] For some of the white barbecue aficionados who ventured into the black sections of town, Edge's analysis is probably right, especially for those who made only one or two trips. However, long-term patrons would surely have felt a closer connection to black culture as a result of long-term patronage of a black-owned barbecue restaurant.

As segregation ended in the 1960s, most barbecue restaurants quickly shifted to serving both black and white patrons. However, two important court cases, both involving segregation at barbecue restaurants, helped establish the fact that all restaurants were required to be desegregated. Both cases came about in response to the Civil Rights Act of 1964, which ended discrimination in public accommodations, including restaurants. Because the law existed at the federal level, it included language relating to interstate commerce, since the federal government regulates movement between states, and both court cases directly attacked the interstate commerce portion of the law. In the first case to come to court, Ollie's Barbecue, in Birmingham, Alabama, claimed that it should not have to desegregate because it did not serve customers who were traveling from state to state: It was located away from interstate highways, bus stations, and other places where travelers might congregate. At that point the federal government had not, in fact, approached the restaurant regarding its segregation policies, where whites ate inside the restaurant while blacks ordered from a take-out window. Instead, the restaurant wanted an early injunction from the court to stop the federal government from ever approaching the restaurant. The court originally agreed with Ollie McClung, the owner of Ollie's, but when the case made it to the U.S. Supreme Court, that court looked at the interstate commerce issue from a different direction. While the restaurant may not have served travelers, a large portion of the meat it sold was shipped in from out of state, and therefore was interstate commerce. The owner of Ollie's accepted the ruling and desegregated his business within two days of the ruling.[17]

A second case regarding segregation in a barbecue restaurant also focused on the interstate commerce portion of the law. Maurice Bessinger owned a barbecue restaurant and a chain of Piggy Park barbecue drive-ins in Columbia, South Carolina. A few days after the Civil Rights Act was signed into law, a black minister filed a complaint against one of the restaurants, saying he was refused service. In court, Bessinger argued that his restaurants should not be required to desegregate because, unlike Ollie's, he did not serve out-of-state meat in his restaurants. Furthermore, he did not serve out-of-state travelers because their tastes would be different from the barbecue he sold. Again, the courts ruled against him. The district court disagreed with Bessinger's arguments regarding interstate commerce but then ruled that, because the law explicitly applied to establishments where food was eaten on the premises, the order to desegregate only applied to his sit-down restaurant and he was not required to desegregate his drive-in restaurants. An appeals court later widened the ruling to also apply to the drive-in restaurants, reasoning that the law's language describing on-site consumption was to differentiate places where prepared food was sold (restaurants) from places where food was sold to be taken and prepared elsewhere (grocery stores). A drive-in was a restaurant, albeit with no seating, but the law was clearly intended to apply to drive-ins as well as sit-down restaurants.[18]

In 2000 Bessinger was again in the news, this time for raising the Confederate flag over his Piggy Park restaurants. The flag had flown over the South Carolina Statehouse for decades but was removed after protests over the symbolism behind the flag. In response, Bessinger raised it over his restaurants. The public response was swift. Sam's Club, Wal-Mart, and a number of other major supermarket chains pulled his sauce from their shelves. A year later, a bottling factory Bessinger had built for the operation sat idle. At that point he estimated that he had lost $20 million because of the controversy, but he refused to take down the flags. As a *New York Times* reporter observed, the flag controversy, and the resulting boycotts, essentially brought Bessinger's restaurants full circle.

"Of course, blacks now avoid Maurice's altogether. The old segregation of the Piggie Park days has reconstituted itself for a new age."[19]

BARBECUE RESTAURANTS AND AUTHENTICITY

At some point in the development of barbecue restaurants, questions of authenticity arose. If there is one source for barbecue in an area, there is no question about authenticity—the barbecue restaurant is the barbecue restaurant. However, if there are two restaurants the question of which one is better inevitably arises. And from there it is only a short jump to which one is more authentic.

Choosing a good barbecue restaurant, like choosing any restaurant, can be a difficult thing: It is hard to tell a good book by its cover. Over the years, many authors have offered up advice on how to tell a great barbecue restaurant from the rest. Quoting "an old hand" at barbecue, food historian Stephen Smith writes that the restaurant parking lot should contain a mix of old and new cars: "Too many expensive new cars and the joint is likely to be fake; too many pickups and it's liable to be a dive. Balance is the key word." Inside, everything "including the help, should be old."[20] Smith also quotes a *Southern Living* article that instructed consumers to watch for "torn screen doors, scratched and dented furniture, cough syrup calendars, potato chip racks, sometimes a jukebox, and always a counter, producing an ambience similar to a county-line beer joint."[21] Barbecue expert John Shelton Reed wrote that when he has "a choice I prefer the local product, ideally served up in a cinder-block building with a dancing pig sign out front."[22] After looking through quite a few barbecue books and articles to prepare for a cross-country barbecue tasting, Lolis Eric Elie summed up the advice he had absorbed: "the place must be small and out of the way; the silverware must be made of plastic, the china of cardboard, and the fine wine of barley and hops. The clientele must be pure and bucolic and have been coming to the place for years, and the proprietor must be old and innocently amused that outsiders find his food so exceptional."[23]

Sometimes the reality of a place matches the expectation. Barbecue expert Steven Raichlen described Louie Mueller's, a meat market that sells barbecue in Taylor, Texas, as a place where the "menu and decor have remained pretty much the same since the 1940s: mismatched wood tables are lined up under bare fluorescent lights, and the once-green walls have darkened to an indeterminate shade of brown. Decades worth of business cards flake off a bulletin board like paint off the side of an old barn."[24] Of course, barbecue restaurants are not the only eateries that have expected attributes. In the book *Fast Food*, geographer

John Jakle and historian Keith Sculle survey the writings of a number of authors to describe the expected attributes of diners, which include a Rotary Club sign near the door, glass sugar containers on the tables, and numerous calendars displayed on the walls.[25] Mexican restaurants often have interiors with rough or broken plaster, while Chinese restaurants often have piano music softly playing.

According to the experts, then, the perfect barbecue restaurant looks exactly like it did when it opened (preferably at least twenty years previously), except with a coating of dust and grime that is, to many barbecue aficionados, the perfect patina of age. There are probably a number of reasons for this emphasis on age. One is the dedication to tradition that this lack of change supposedly shows. If both the exterior and interior of the restaurant have barely changed over the years, the thinking seems to be, the food will also be exactly like it was when the restaurant opened. Of course, the barbecue of today, and of fifty years ago, is largely an invented tradition that has been around for less than 150 years, but for many aficionados, change in the world of barbecue is not a good thing. A second reason for the emphasis on a lack of change has to do with the perceived emphasis of the restaurant owner. If the owner has put almost no attention into keeping up the restaurant, the belief seems to be, he or she will have put a maximum amount of time into keeping up the food. There is also a more realistic reason for looking for age in a barbecue restaurant: The restaurant business is a difficult one, and a place that has survived four or five decades is probably at least passably good.

In reality, of course, there is no way to tell from looking at a barbecue restaurant if it offers good food or not, or if it offers traditional barbecue or not. Traveling in search of good barbecue out west, barbecue expert Lolis Eric Elie wrote that he "soon learned you are just as likely to find bad food at fly-infested restaurants with fat chefs and diverse clientele as you are to find it anywhere else."[26]

An example of the difficulty in matching a restaurant's furnishings with the quality of its food comes from a tasting tour I experienced in Memphis in April, 2013, and which will be discussed more in chapter 5. The tasting tour, which was composed of five guests and a local guide, stopped at six restaurants in the Memphis area over three hours. Two of the restaurants, Central BBQ and the Cozy Corner, provide contrasts in terms of expectations and the reality of the food.

Central BBQ came out of competition barbecuing. Craig Blondis and Roger Sapp competed for years on the barbecue circuit and then went into the restaurant business together. By 2013 they had opened three locations in Memphis, and the tasting tour stopped at the third location, on Butler Avenue, with an outdoor patio that faces the National Civil Rights Museum. This location followed none of the assumptions of what a good barbecue restaurant should be. Most of the restaurant consists of one very large room, professionally decorated, with high-quality furniture. It has "funky" accents like a long, porcelain, industrial-style sink behind the bar, with beer taps replacing the faucets. The menu has non-traditional foods such as barbecue nachos, which the tasting group tried and which were very good. But the group also tried the ribs, and they were as good as any ribs in Memphis: They tasted wonderful, fell off the bone, and had the "bark" that develops from long, slow cooking. Because Central BBQ comes out of competition barbecue there is a heavy emphasis on making food that looks and tastes like "traditional" barbecue, or at least an emphasis on following the rules of competition barbecue, and of standardized quality. This brings out something of an irony in restaurants like Central BBQ: With their professionally decorated restaurants, they look completely unlike what a good barbecue restaurant "should" look like, but their food tastes like the kind of food any barbecue aficionado would love. As a sign of how well known Central Barbecue has become, while the tasting tour sampled barbecue nachos and ribs on the patio, chef Mario Batali, who was visiting town, sat munching barbecue in one corner of the patio.

Another restaurant the tour visited was the Cozy Corner restaurant. It looks *precisely* the way a "good" barbecue restaurant should look. The restaurant is located in a strip mall in a run-down section of Memphis and, from looking at the outdoor structure, only a bare minimum has been spent on decorations. In fact, there is little outside that indicates just how good the restaurant is other than the completely full parking lot. The same is true of the interior, which has surely not changed much since it opened more than twenty-five years ago. The ceilings are low, the rooms feel cramped and full of tables, and while the interior is clean it is definitely not professionally decorated. The restaurant is family owned and operated, and several generations are involved with running the operation. The menu is the same as most other barbecue restaurants, with one exception: barbecued Cornish hen, which one can dimly see through the glass of the barbecue cooker at the front of the restaurant. At this restaurant the tasting group again tried the ribs, and they were surprising: They were nothing like any other ribs in Memphis. The barbecue cooker the restaurant uses introduces steam into the cooking process, resulting in ribs that are very solid and do not fall off the bone in any way. The ribs were delicious and obviously had fans throughout Memphis, but these were not traditional barbecued ribs. Much like Central BBQ's interior said nothing about the quality of the food served there, the Cozy Corner's exterior and interior revealed nothing about how non-traditional their ribs were.

THE THREE ORIGINS OF TODAY'S
BARBECUE RESTAURANTS

It is possible to divide barbecue restaurants into three groups, based on the circumstance of how the restaurant started. There are restaurants that started as barbecue restaurants, whose founders came from a barbecue tradition outside the world of competition barbecue; there are restaurants whose owners came from a background in the restaurant business and knew little about barbecue, and who decided to either open a barbecue restaurant or convert an existing restaurant into one with a focus on barbecue; and there are restaurants whose owners participated in competition barbecue, and then decided to open a restaurant.

An example of a barbecue cook who "bootstrapped" himself into a barbecue restaurant comes from Off the Bone, a Nashville restaurant that opened in 2013. Three years before one of the co-owners, Edward Miller, began selling smoked turkey legs from an unlicensed shop in a grassy lot near Fisk University. He also sold the legs at the Elks Lodge on Saturday nights. "I remember he would stand down there with that dirty white T-shirt," one of his long-time customers later said. "He was working hard. He had all that grease on him, tired as all get out, trying to figure out how he was going to get those turkey legs out."[27] He soon moved to a rented trailer, where his family helped out, and then he opened Off the Bone, a sit-down restaurant, in a renovated storefront.

Many of the original barbecue restaurants of the late 19th and early 20th centuries were opened by people with experience in barbecuing who had an entrepreneurial bent. They may have had a shack along the road where they sold barbecue, and that evolved into an actual restaurant, or they may have become known locally for cooking barbecue for family or friends, and then decided to open a restaurant. They might also have gotten their start at another barbecue restaurant. As the restaurants became established, they trained new generations of barbecue chefs, who eventually left and started their own restaurants. This was very common in parts of the country with a strong barbecue tradition. The connections between restaurants are so complicated that the book *Holy Smoke: The Big Book of North Carolina Barbecue* contains a two-page graphic that illustrates the connections, and instead of calling the picture a tree it is called a "briarpatch." At the bottom of the page are three "trunks" indicating the three founders of Lexington barbecue from back in the early 20th century, and branches from these three lead to twenty-seven different restaurants.[28]

A specific example of restaurants coming from smaller enterprises, and of those restaurants leading to other restaurants, comes from the early history of Kansas City barbecue. Henry Perry, born in 1875 in Tennessee, is widely credited with beginning the tradition of selling barbecue in Kansas City (barbecue was already popular in Kansas City before Perry arrived, but his seems to have been the first popular barbecue stand). Perry was drawn to the Mississippi River and worked as a cook on steamboats by the time he was fifteen, and by his early thirties was living in Kansas City, working as a porter at a saloon. He was unhappy with the job, though, and opened a stand where he sold barbecue. The stand was so popular that he eventually moved into a restaurant, and over time opened two more in Kansas City, which were also very popular. His restaurant functioned as a training ground for other African American barbecue cooks. Brothers Arthur and Charlie Bryant both worked in his restaurants before going off and starting their own, and Arthur Bryant's restaurant is usually seen as offering the epitome of Kansas City–style barbecue.[29]

A second type of barbecue restaurant is one started by people whose background is in the restaurant industry and who have little, if any, knowledge of barbecue. Sometimes these entrepreneurs have a good opportunity to buy a barbecue restaurant, and sometimes they own an existing restaurant that transitions into cooking barbecue. An example of the former situation can be seen in the Gates barbecue chain in Kansas City. In 1946, George Gates bought the Ol' Kentucky Bar-B-Q (the fact that a restaurant referring to Kentucky barbecue existed in Kansas City points to the fact that, by the 1940s, Kansas City was not nearly the barbecue town it would later become). The restaurant was not doing well and Gates knew nothing about making barbecue, but one employee who came with the restaurant was Arthur Pinkard. Pinkard had previously worked for Henry Perry, and he taught Gates what he knew about barbecue, which was apparently quite a bit. As of this writing there are six Gates's restaurants in Kansas City. A second example of a restaurateur who moved into barbecue is Charles Vergos, who ran a sandwich shop named the Rendezvous in Memphis, Tennessee. The building had an unused elevator shaft in the basement, and Vergos decided to turn it into a smoker. He smoked a number of different types of meat without finding anything that appealed to his customers and then, at his meat supplier's suggestion, tried smoking pork ribs. Vergos did not know anything about barbecuing pork ribs but one of his employees did, and together they created the style of dry ribs Memphis is famous for.[30]

A third type of barbecue restaurant is one started by competition barbecuers. These are the most recent types of restaurants, since competition barbecue has only been around since the 1970s. There are some similarities between competition barbecuing and running a restaurant that may aid those cooks who make the transition. Both activities place a heavy emphasis on providing a standardized

**Some restaurants have come out of local church efforts
to raise money. Penny De Los Santos.**

product, since both judges and customers have certain expectations for barbecued
food, not only in the cooking but in the presentation of the plated food.
Competitors know that almost anything can happen during a competition, from
heavy rainstorms to problems with cooking thermometers, and this is also certainly
true of running a restaurant. Both activities also require a considerable amount of
logistical and organizational expertise. Teams competing at the highest levels may
spend most weekends of the year competing, in addition to holding full-time jobs,
and the time and expense involved in this requires competitors to pay attention
to logistical and organizational details. All of these skills can transfer to running
a successful restaurant. As is discussed above, Central BBQ, in Memphis, is an
example of a restaurant started by competition barbecuers that has done well.

BARBECUE BECOMES RESPECTABLE

Barbecue restaurants have been around, in certain parts of the country, since at least the early 20th century. While they were locally popular, they were usually not considered to be "respectable." They could be a good place for workers to eat lunch or a nice place for someone (usually a male) to celebrate a birthday, but a barbecue restaurant would certainly not be a place for a local patron to take an out-of-town visitor. A more proper destination for visiting guests might be a steak house or a restaurant serving European-based dishes, the type of restaurant writer Calvin Trillin was often directed to when traveling and that he referred to, with disdain, as "La Maison de la Casa House, Continental Cuisine."

At some point in the late 20th century, though, barbecue's reputation in America began to shift, and to become much more respectable. Locals began taking out-of-town visitors to the best barbecue restaurant in town, and local chambers of commerce began not only touting barbecue restaurants but also using newly created barbecue competitions as a way to draw visitors, and out-of-town money, into town.

Calvin Trillin wrote about the shift in attitudes in a 1983 *New Yorker* article on the annual American Royal livestock show in Kansas City, which had recently added competition barbecue to the list of events. According to Trillin, in the early 1970s many local boosters had been upset with his naming Arthur Bryant's barbecue restaurant the best restaurant in the city. Their irritation likely came from a number of sources: The restaurant was in the black section of the city, it was not a glamorous or showy restaurant, and, during the 1976 Republican National Convention and a 1974 Democratic mini-convention, both in Kansas City, the popularity of the restaurant resulted in a considerable amount of press coverage for the restaurant instead of other locations on which white civic boosters would have preferred the focus.

In the late 1970s, though, attitudes about barbecue restaurants changed as part of a larger reevaluation of certain parts of American culture—as Trillin writes, the shift involved boosters "coming around to an appreciation of what was local and regional rather than simply whatever could be called the Fourth Largest in the Country or the Third Highest West of the Mississippi. They decided that local customs like playing bluegrass music and eating enchiladas were not as shameful as they had once been led to believe."[31] Trillin lists several events that may have contributed to the change, including the Bicentennial celebrations in 1976, the move toward preserving older buildings rather than tearing them down to make room for new structures, and "a sort of drawing in, in the years after the Vietnam War and the first energy crunch, to concerns that were local or regional rather than national or international."[32] Ideas from the counterculture, which often celebrated older ways of living and cooking, had also likely permeated into the wider American culture. The shift had gone so far that when Arthur Bryant died, in 1982, the Kansas City *Star* devoted four columns on its front page to his life and death.

THE TEMPLATE-BASED BARBECUE RESTAURANT MENU

Barbecue, especially in the South, is a highly regional type of cooking. Different areas focus on different meats and cuts of meat: beef in Texas, ribs in Memphis, pork in the Carolinas, and mutton around Lexington, Kentucky. One would assume, then, that these preferences should be reflected in restaurant menus in those different areas. There should be major differences in what is served at restaurants across the country. The truth of the matter is that while there are regional differences, barbecue restaurants in disparate parts of the country tend to have very similar menus. Barbecue restaurant menus seem to be based on a common template, with individual restaurants adding items based on local and personal preference (that is, the preference of the restaurant owner).

The sections of a menu are the same for barbecue restaurants as they are for most American restaurants. Appetizers, salads, sides, stews, entrees, desserts, and drinks are the components of the barbecue restaurant template. In looking through a sampling of barbecue menus, the appetizer, salad, and soup sections have the greatest variation from restaurant to restaurant; the dessert section tends to have a limited number of items pulled from a large number of possible choices; and the entrée and side items both are the most standardized and have the most regional variation.

Appetizers, Salads, and Stews

The appetizer, salad, and soup sections of menus have the most variation, and are frequently omitted entirely from barbecue restaurants' menus. Appetizers often show up for restaurants that are more upscale, and the appetizers frequently have little connection to barbecue, with the exception of barbecue nachos, which usually include barbecued meat and sauce, and wings, which include sauce. Some regional items show up in the appetizer section. For example, barbecue restaurants in the Memphis area often include tamales as an appetizer while tamales never show up in other areas as appetizers.

A typical barbecue plate with ribs, sausage, brisket, beans, potato salad, and pickles. Penny De Los Santos.

While barbecue restaurants have a reputation for serving only artery-clogging meat, many restaurant menus include at least a side salad, and some include a salad topped with barbecued meat. Soups appear on barbecue menus infrequently, although Brunswick stew and burgoo are regional soups that appear on menus in areas where those soups are a part of barbecue culture.

Entrées

Obviously, the meat is the focus of a barbecue restaurant. In looking at the meats served at restaurants across the country, it is clear that the selection of meats is wider than it was at the beginning of the 20th century. Although Texas is known for beef brisket, beef brisket appears on restaurant menus across the country, from Texas to Los Angeles to the Carolinas. This is where the idea of a template for barbecue restaurants comes through most strongly. The vast majority of barbecue restaurants do not serve only one or two types of meat; they may advertise that a certain type of meat is their specialty, but they serve a number of types. The most common meats and cuts of meat served (in no particular order) are pork shoulder (which is either pulled or chopped), pork ribs, sausage, chicken (most often a portion of the bird, rather than chopped or pulled), and beef brisket; turkey shows up slightly less often. These six meats and cuts of meat seem to be the default choices for a restaurant. Regional favorites also figure in the entrée sections of barbecue menus. Bologna is a popular addition in the Memphis area, while burnt ends seem to only be popular around Kansas City. Barbecue restaurants in Fayetteville, North Carolina, offer more than just barbecue. Both the Barbecue Hut and Cape Fear Bar-B-Que & Chicken in Fayetteville feature fried chicken prominently on their menus, and Fuller's Old Fashioned BBQ is a buffet restaurant that also offers fried chicken and seafood (including shrimp, scallops, and crab).

The fact that brisket, which was formerly seen as being only a regional specialty in Texas, shows up on so many restaurant menus across the country could be an indication that the older preferences for meats in certain parts of the country are breaking down. It should be noted that, most often, the brisket served outside of Texas tastes different from most of that served in Texas because the wood used to smoke the brisket is different. In Texas, mesquite is most often used since it is plentiful locally and gives the brisket something of a bitter taste. Outside of Texas other woods are used, usually hickory, oak, and fruitwoods like apple. These woods give the brisket a very different flavor (often, it is sweeter) that may make it more palatable for local tastes.

Barbecue Sauce

Barbecue sauce is generally not included on the menu of barbecue restaurants, except when it is for sale in bottles, but it is still an important part of the restaurant experience. Even restaurants where the owner swears his or her meat does not need sauce are likely to still make some sauces available because of customer demand. Most restaurants include at least two sauces, usually differentiated by whether they are hot or mild, but some restaurants feature many different sauces for consumers to use. The type of sauce available can vary considerably even within a small geographic area. While sampling barbecue throughout Tennessee, Lolis Eric Elie noted that sauces from rural restaurants differed from urban restaurants. In Memphis, the sauces were sweet and thick while in the rural areas they were thin, with a "consistency . . . more like low-fat milk" and were much less sweet.[33]

Side Items

The most variation in barbecue restaurants' menus appears in the side items area. Some restaurants serve only a few sides while others have a wide selection.

Interstate Barbecue, in Memphis, serves a wide variety of meat entrées, including beef links and rib tips, but only offers beans, coleslaw, and potato salad as sides. Zarda's, a small chain in Kansas City, offers seventeen sides, including non-traditional items like fried pickles and fried mushrooms (the addition of a deep fryer seems to drastically widen the options for restaurants). The most common side items are baked beans, potato salad, french fries, and coleslaw, followed closely by onion rings. Macaroni and cheese and green beans were also fairly common on restaurant menus. Again, there were regional variations. Serving hush puppies as a side item with barbecue seems to have originated with Warner Stamey, a North Carolina restaurant owner who trained many other restaurateurs, and today hush puppies are common on barbecue menus in North Carolina but show up almost nowhere else. There are also some items that are unique to only one restaurant. The Barbecue Sundae appears on the menu of the Q Company, in Leesburg, Virginia, and is layers of pulled pork, baked beans, and coleslaw, which can then be topped with one of several sauces the restaurant features.[34]

Catering and Shipping

A significant percentage of many restaurants' revenues come from catering for local events and shipping food nationwide. Dickey's, the largest barbecue chain in America, derives about 15 percent of its overall business from catering, which is about four times what other sit-down restaurants get from catering.[35] Dickey's is mostly franchised, which means that most Dickey's restaurants are owned and operated by a local company, and catering is such a big part of the business that the corporate owners of the chain created a catering hotline to handle orders to all Dickey's restaurants, even those that are franchised. Customers calling the hotline speak with corporate employees, who then route the orders to local, franchised restaurants, in this way attempting to keep customers happy who may be calling during a busy time at the restaurant.

Smaller restaurants also do catering, and some will ship their barbecue, even though that fact is often not advertised. Charles Vergo's Rendezvous, a well-known barbecue restaurant in Memphis, advertises on its web page that it will ship its barbecue anywhere in the United States. Their chopped pork shoulder or pork ribs are sent overnight via FedEx, which is based in Memphis. Customers pay quite a price for having relatively fresh barbecue shipped to their doorstep, though: As of mid-2013, four pounds of pork shoulder or two racks of ribs cost $105, shipping included (just for comparison, two large orders of ribs picked up at the restaurant would cost $37.50). Allen & Son, a barbecue restaurant located in Chapel Hill, North Carolina, has catered events as far away as Baltimore, Maryland (over 300 miles away) and the Outer Banks (at least 200 miles away). Chapel Hill is a college town, and many alumni take their love of barbecue with them when they leave town. Allen & Son have shipped their meat across the country, with the meat arriving two days after it has been cooked. As Keith Allen described it, "I cook it today, freeze it tonight, and ship it tomorrow, UPS guaranteed by ten thirty the next day."[36]

Ancillary Items

Some barbecue restaurants also include items that are not meant to be eaten immediately, or that are not food at all. T-shirts show up on some menus, particularly for those restaurants that have more of a marketing bent; for example, Central BBQ in Memphis, which has often appeared on television cooking shows, sells T-shirts in both solid and tie-dyed colors. Barbecue sauces and spices are also popular sales items for restaurants. As mentioned above, before the Confederate flag–raising controversy, Maurice Bessinger's barbecue sauce was stocked in Wal-Mart and Sam's Club stores. Some restaurants with only a marginal connection to barbecue still manage to sell their own sauces. In 2013 Boston Market, a chain that specializes in comfort food, put ribs on its menu nationwide for the first time, and at the same time also stocked bottles of barbecue sauce for customers to purchase.[37]

BARBECUE'S ENCROACHMENT INTO UPSCALE RESTAURANTS

In the late 1800s, the definition of an upscale restaurant in America was fairly simple: It was a restaurant that served expensive French food. Beyond tasting good, French food worked well for upscale restaurants for a number of reasons, all having to do with exclusivity: Only a limited number of chefs in America could cook the food, reading the menu required a knowledge of the French language, and the multiple courses involved in a meal served to increase its price.

The growing middle class of the early 20th century put pressure on the concept of what an upscale restaurant served. Middle-class diners could generally not read French, they could not afford the expensive prices of the upscale restaurants, and they were irritated by the snobbish waiters. As food historian Andrew Haley has written, middle-class diners responded by frequenting urban ethnic restaurants, celebrating the diversity of their cities. By the 1950s, French food was still the epitome of upscale dining, but "fine dining" restaurants could also be found that offered Chinese, German, or Italian foods. The interest in the foods of these other cultures only increased in the years after World War II, as many Americans took advantage of regular passenger air service to visit Europe.

In the context of the upscale dining in the 1950s, barbecue did not exist. Barbecue had a number of perceived characteristics that kept it out of the finest restaurants. It was an American food, it was a rural food, and it had a strong association with African Americans. That was in the 1950s. Twenty years later, some of those same attributes would make it much more attractive.

The countercultural movement, which began on a large scale in the 1960s, had an enormous impact on American society, and it remade ideas about food just as it did with almost everything else. To a large extent, the ideas and values that came out of the counterculture were the larger culture's values turned upside down. Blacks were equal to whites, women were equal to men, and the Vietnam War was wrong. Ideas about food, too, were inverted. Heavily processed foods were bad, raw foods were good, and foods containing living organisms (like yeast bread or yogurt) were especially good. Young people went "back to the land," started communes, and began growing their own food and making their own bread. They also became interested in older ways of living and cooking.

A number of ideas from the counterculture gradually percolated into the cooking culture surrounding upscale restaurants. Today there is an emphasis on locally sourced, high-quality ingredients that come directly from a farm instead of a food vendor. Not only is the food locally sourced, but many upscale restaurants also feature foods with a historic connection to the area. For example, they might use an ingredient that was locally harvested on a large scale a hundred years previously but which, because it was not easy to ship or store, gradually fell out of use during the 20th century. Many upscale restaurants also make dishes and use cooking techniques that have fallen from favor over the past century.

In this new context of upscale cooking, barbecue does have at least a foothold. Barbecue's connection to a specific region of the country and its perception as a food with a connection to the past are both positive characteristics. While there are not many upscale barbecue restaurants, there are some. An example is Lambert's Downtown Barbecue, located in Austin, Texas. The restaurant has typical barbecue food like pulled pork, smoked chicken, and hot links, and also serves various grilled foods. The food's descriptions in the menu make it clear that local connections are important. The chicken is described as being local; the quail is "Lockhart Quail," Lockhart being a nearby town; and the Jalapeño Hot Links are made on site.

Early BBQ take out: Employees at a Georgia kaolin company enjoy some barbecue in the 1950s. Courtesy of Georgia Archives, Vanishing Georgia Collection, WKS-24.

Those ideas of local connections, and of highlighting a food that is prepared slowly, are moving their way to restaurants that are more mainstream. Jim 'N Nick's Bar-B-Q, a chain with thirty-two restaurants, mostly in the deep South, emphasizes its connections with the past, and with local farms, on its menu. Everything is made from scratch: "No short cuts. No freezers," as the menu reads.[38] The seal of the Southern Foodways Alliance, a group dedicated to preserving older ways of cooking, is on the front of the menu, and the last page of the menu says that "Jim 'N Nick's supports family farms whenever and wherever possible."

BARBECUE AWAY FROM THE BARBECUE RESTAURANT

To purchase barbecue one does not necessarily have to go to a barbecue restaurant. There are non-barbecue restaurants that sell barbecue, and there are places that sell barbecue that don't qualify as restaurants.

An example of the latter can be found in parking lots and grassy fields across the country. In early 2013 the *Santa Fe Reporter* (New Mexico) profiled Steve

Schmidt, a barbecuer who sells meat directly from his smoker, parked in one of various lots around Santa Fe. Schmidt had previously owned a cigar shop but decided that barbecue was more his style and, for the past three years, had been selling barbecue two or three times a week from the smoker attached to his truck. His method of business recalls the barbecuers of a century ago, who also sold barbecue at somewhat random locations on somewhat random days, although Schmidt has a web page where he lists his schedule. On a typical day he sold about "40 baby back ribs, 45 turkey legs, 25 pounds of brisket, 20 pounds of pork and around a dozen sausages." He put in around fifteen or sixteen hours a day, and only took cash.[39] Schmidt's operation is certainly not unique; especially in the South, there are many small-time barbecuers who sell barbecue for only a few days a week in an empty lot.

Benefit sales are another type of operation that sells barbecue. These can be seen in cities and towns across the country on Saturdays and Sundays, where a large barbecue grill has been set up in a parking lot. As the name implies, the benefit sales are set up to make money for a particular purpose, often for a sports team, some sort of youth group (such as Boy Scouts), or an individual or family that needs help. People driving by can stop and buy a meal featuring meat that has been cooked on the grill. The selection of meat, and the meals, are sometimes regionally standardized. For example, in central California what is known as Santa Maria–style barbecue is often sold, which is beef tri-tip served with pinquito beans, salsa, salad, and French bread. In southern Texas the meals are usually sirloin steak with borracho beans, while in northern Indiana barbecued chicken is sold.

On the other side of the spectrum are non-barbecue restaurants that sell some barbecue items. The definition of "barbecue" here is quite loose; often, the item simply has some barbecue sauce on it. In June 2012, Burger King announced a number of new "Regional BBQ Sandwiches" that, as one might expect, played fast and loose with definitions. The only part of the Carolina BBQ Whopper or the Texas BBQ Whopper that had anything to do with barbecue was the Bull's-Eye Carolina Style BBQ sauce or the Bull's Eye Texas Style BBQ sauce added to the sandwiches. The Memphis Pulled Pork BBQ sandwich did, however, feature pulled pork in Sweet Baby Ray's Sweet n' Spicy BBQ sauce, so it was at least somewhat closer to being "real" barbecue.[40] In 2012, also, the Hard Rock Café chain of restaurants added a number of menu items with the word "smokehouse" in their name, calling attention to the fact that they had, in fact, been prepared in the restaurants' onsite smokers (all of the restaurants added oak-wood smokers in 2006). Commenting on the Hard Rock Café's new menu items, one food industry consultant said that *smokehouse* "strongly suggests authenticity, connects with Southern comfort and conjures an image of an artisanal approach to [food] prep."[41] While the Hard Rock did not use the word "barbecue" in the names of the dishes, they did have a South Carolina Smokehouse Sandwich and a Texas Smokehouse Sandwich, which were similar in names to the Burger King sandwiches (Hard Rock announced their sandwich names a month before Burger King).

Of the top ten restaurant chains in the United States, ranked by sales, half of them (McDonald's, Burger King, Pizza Hut, KFC, and Applebee's) have menu items that refer to barbecue in some way.[42] For Pizza Hut, KFC, and Applebee's, the items were chicken wings with barbecue sauce; for Burger King they were the previously mentioned sandwiches; and for McDonald's they were a Chipotle BBQ Snack Wrap and the McRib sandwich. These were menu items as of early June 2013; sometimes these restaurants have temporary menu items that also have "BBQ" in the name. It should also be noted that another connection can be made between KFC and typical barbecue menus in that the side items available are almost exactly the same as those served at barbecue restaurants, such as green beans, baked beans, coleslaw, potato salad, and macaroni and cheese.

Barbecue seems to be showing up on more and more menus of non-barbecue restaurants. In 2012 Technomic, Inc., a food industry consulting company, released a report that found that barbecue appeared in some way on 63 percent of menus from the 500 largest restaurant chains in the country, either as a way of preparing food, an ingredient, or a flavor. Mentions of barbecue sauce increased 5 percent from the previous year.[43]

THE NATIONALLY RECOGNIZED
BARBECUE RESTAURANTS

There are thousands of barbecue restaurants across the country. None of these are household names, but many are well known, particularly in barbecue circles. There tends to be two kinds of well-known restaurants: those that have many locations, and those that are recognized as being prime examples of barbecue from a certain location.

Dickey's Barbecue Pit: National

Dickey's Barbecue Pit is one of those restaurants with many locations—over 300 in June 2013, with another twenty-seven slated to open by the end of 2013. It has national reach, with restaurants in thirty-eight of the forty-eight continental states, missing only Kentucky and Tennessee in the South, New Mexico in the West, and a number of New England states. There are no international locations. The chain began in 1941 in Dallas, Texas, as a bar with a brick barbecue in the back, and over time the focus of the operation shifted from selling beer to selling barbecue. Dickey's grew slowly over the next few decades, and did not begin franchising until 1995. Franchising is a tricky thing for restaurants. On the one hand, franchising means more money for a chain since, under most contracts, the franchisees pay a percentage of sales to the original company, along with a set dollar amount yearly, and it also means the chain becomes much more visible, with more locations. On the other hand, franchising means a loss of control, since the franchised restaurants are owned and operated by a completely different company, and the relationship between the franchisees and the original company is not always entirely positive. Barbecue can be a difficult thing to make, a product that requires quite a bit of knowledge and expertise. Dickey's began expanding through franchising in 1995 and the franchising does not seem to have caused many problems, although the company tries to simplify and standardize its product as much as possible. New franchisees attend a three-week "Barbecue U" course at its Dallas headquarters, and the menu at restaurants is quite simple. Restaurants serve only nine meats, twelve appetizers, three types of salad and four types of baked potato.

Dickey's Barbecue Pit is one of the few barbecue chains with truly national coverage. According to Roland Dickey Jr. (chief executive and part of the third generation to run the company), regional variations in barbecue preferences have caused only minimal issues. The mix of food sold is different in different places. As Dickey said in a 2012 interview, "Texas is two-to-one beef to pork. In North Carolina it's two-to-one pulled pork over beef brisket. The product mix changes, but our core menu doesn't change."[44] The Texas-based company has even made solid inroads into barbecue states like North Carolina, where, in mid-2013, they had fourteen restaurants. Carolina sauces are usually mustard or vinegar based, but the local sauces proved to be unpopular in the restaurants. "We offered the mustard and vinegar sauces," Dickey said, "but the tomato-based [sauce] drove it out of the stores." This could be interpreted in two ways. It could mean that regional differences are falling away as the tomato-based sauce, which is popular in most of the country, is overwhelming the mustard and vinegar sauces. It could also simply mean that, in an area thick with barbecue restaurants, those who prefer the mustard and vinegar sauces are going to other barbecue restaurants.

Famous Dave's: National

Famous Dave's is the second largest barbecue chain in the United States with, in mid-2013, 188 restaurants in thirty-four states and one Canadian province. It is big enough to be the only barbecue chain to appear in the *Nation's Restaurant News* lists of the top 100 chains in the country (while Dickey's has more restaurants it does less business overall). In mid-2013 Famous Dave's was number 80 in terms of sales, number 92 in terms of number of restaurants, and, significantly, number 25 in estimated sales per restaurant, appearing just above McDonald's.[45] Its menu features pork, ribs, brisket, and chicken, along with catfish and salmon, and does not include sausage, which is somewhat unusual for a national barbecue chain.

The chain is large enough that it is experimenting with a smaller version of its typical restaurant design aimed to attract customers who want a quicker meal than they might get at a traditional Famous Dave's (the new version of the restaurants are named "Famous Dave's BBQ Shack"). The original restaurants cater to customers going out for an important meal, such as a celebration, and they tend to be located in major retail areas, such as near Best Buy stores or busy shopping malls. The newer restaurants, which are about two-thirds the size of the original restaurants, are designed to be more neighborhood focused and to appeal specifically to women, since they make most of the dining decisions for a family.[46]

Being chains with nationwide coverage, Dickey's and Famous Dave's do not have a deep connection to a particular region. The other nationally known restaurants are either single locations or fairly small chains with a definite connection to a place. In looking at the history of some of the famous places it becomes difficult to judge whether the restaurants became famous because of the quality of their food or because of their sheer longevity (one is reminded of John Huston's comment in the movie Chinatown that "Politicians, ugly buildings, and whores all get respectable if they last long enough"—perhaps barbecue restaurants should be added to the list as well).

Stamey's: Greensboro, North Carolina

Stamey's, with two locations in Greensboro, is often cited as a prime example of a Piedmont-style barbecue restaurant. The menu is quite simple. Pork and chicken are the only two meats served, and there are only seven side dishes: hush puppies, french fries, slaw, baked beans, chicken tenders, Brunswick stew, and a roll. The desserts are old-fashioned and simple as well: cobblers, ice cream, milkshakes (only at one of the locations), and floats.

Part of the reason for Stamey's fame, along with the quality of the food, is the founder's influence on North Carolina barbecue. Stamey's is named after C. Warner Stamey, who learned the barbecue business in the early 20th century when working with two men, Jess Swicegood and Sid Weaver. Swicegood and Weaver sold barbecue from tents across from the local courthouse, and Stamey started working with them while still in high school. After high school Stamey continued in the business in a nearby town and then, in 1938, moved back to Lexington to buy Swicegood's Barbecue and rename it Stamey's.

In the course of his life, Stamey trained many pitmasters who went on to open their own restaurants in the region, and so Warner Stamey was influential beyond the confines of his restaurant. Warner appears to have been the first to add hush puppies as a side item to barbecue, and the barbecuers he trained took that idea with them; hush puppies are a common side item in North Carolina barbecue restaurants. Warner's grandson Chip runs Stamey's today, and Chip has said the hush puppies were almost taken off the menu by his father, who wanted to sell barbecue meat and nothing else. According to Chip, his father would have been more comfortable running something like a Texas meat market–style barbecue restaurant, rather than an actual restaurant. "He was always trying to take stuff away [from the menu,] and I was always adding it back," Chip Stamey said. "My father was a student of keeping it simple."[47]

Charles Vergo's Rendezvous: Memphis, Tennessee

As is noted above, Charles Vergo's Rendezvous was not originally a barbecue restaurant. Just after World War II, Vergos, whose parents immigrated from Greece, opened a diner with his brother-in-law in downtown Memphis. The two men soon realized that a diner could not support both men and their families but, unfortunately, they were locked into a long-term lease on the property. Vergos cleaned out the basement and opened the Rendezvous while his brother-in-law ran the diner upstairs. As Charles Vergos's son, John, has said, the Rendezvous in those days "was just a tavern. He just served beer, ham and cheese sandwiches and he had little appetizer plates of cheese and pickles."[48] There was, however, an unused elevator shaft in the back, and Vergos seized the opportunity to turn it into a chimney for a smoker. After smoking a number of different types of meats, none of it catching on with his patrons, he finally began smoking pork ribs at the urging of his meat supplier. The recipe he and a cook came up with was different from that for traditional ribs. The cooking time was shorter and the heat was more intense—only an hour and fifteen minutes cooked close to the flame—and the spices in the rub were based on those he had used in making Greek chili. From this recipe Memphis style "dry rub" ribs were born.

Kreuz Market and Smitty's: Lockhart, Texas

Texas barbecue comes from two traditions. The older tradition dates back to settlers from the American South who brought their taste for barbecue, both as slave owners and as slaves, with them from states like Virginia and Tennessee. They settled mostly in the wetter, eastern part of Texas, near Houston and Galveston. The newer tradition comes from German settlers at around the turn of the 20th century, many of whom settled toward the center of Texas (within a hundred or so miles of Austin) and who opened butcher shops. Some parts of the hogs and cattle they butchered did not sell quickly, so in the days before refrigeration the butcher shops barbecued the unsold portions and then sold the barbecue. Kreuz Market and Smitty's come out of that tradition.

Charlie Kreuz opened the original Kreuz Market more than a hundred years ago. It was a grocery store and butcher shop that sold barbecue as well, and for many years it stayed just like that. Charlie sold the place to his sons, they sold it to a brother-in-law, and in 1948 the Schmidt family bought it (Charlie Schmidt was a worker at Kreuz Market). Again, the store was passed through the family, as sons Don and Rick bought it from their father. However, the ownership became a bit complicated, as daughter Nina was willed the building the business was housed in while the sons got the business. In 1999 came the big feud: Rick Schmidt felt his sister was charging too much rent on the building, so he moved the business to a new building blocks away, and dragged a brazier full of coals from the old building to the new building. This symbolized the continuation of the tradition, with Kreuz Market moving to a new building. A few weeks later Nina Schmidt opened her own barbecue restaurant, Smitty's, in the old Kreuz Market building. Today, both restaurants lay some claim to the Kreuz Market tradition. Smitty's has the original building and the original fire pits, while Kreuz Market has the name.[49]

Before the split, Lolis Eric Elie traveled to Kreuz Market and described the experience. Again, the restaurant is often seen as the classic example of a Texas barbecue restaurant. At Kreuz Market "you order the meat right in front of the pit and you order it by the pound. It is pulled off brick barbecue pits whose doors are made of metal and opened with the assistance of the counterweights attached to them."[50] In the large dining room "are rows of plain tables and chairs, no forks or spoons, and no barbecue sauce. There are, however, knives chained to the tables to cut the meat, little paper trays full of a mixture of salt and coarse-ground black pepper to be scooped out with fingers and sprinkled on the meat if you want, and hot sauce."[51] Originally, there was no sauce whatsoever; customers who wanted sauce went to the grocery side of the business, bought a bottle of hot sauce, and left the bottle on the table when they were done. Other customers then used that hot sauce. Eventually, customers assumed that the market was supplying the bottles and demanded that they be refilled by the market when the bottles were empty.

The biggest change with Kreuz Market has obviously been the split into two competing businesses (chapter 5, which looks at barbecue's depictions in popular culture, examines an episode of the television series *Food Wars* that focuses on the Kreuz Market/Smitty's split, and also has a more recent description of the old Kreuz Market building). When visiting Kreuz Market before the split, Lolis Eric Elie talked to owner Rick Schmidt and asked him about the criticism over the years from people who wanted the restaurant to change in one way or another. Schmidt's reply is true of the criticism of every successful business, and is ironic in the context of what was to happen to Kreuz Market: "The hardest thing about running this place is not to change things."[52]

The split happened back in 1999, and in the years since, the family seems to have patched things up. In fact, in 2012 members of both parts of the family opened a new barbecue restaurant near Austin named Schmidt Family Barbecue, a name that emphasizes the family connections. The owners, who are all cousins, were Keith Schmidt, the owner of Kreuz Market; John Fullilove, the pitmaster at Smitty's; and Susie Schmidt-Franks, another member of the family. The pitmaster of the new restaurant was trained by both the pitmasters of Kreuz Market and Smitty's, and, while the new business was obviously going to barbecue its own meat, the owners were also planning on buying their sausages from both Kreuz Market and Smitty's.[53]

Arthur Bryant's: Kansas City

Arthur Bryant's is generally considered to be one of the best barbecue restaurants in Kansas City, and is also the most famous. The restaurant traces its lineage back to Henry Perry, the first successful barbecue restaurateur in Kansas City, and a man who taught a generation of pitmasters. Brothers Charlie and Arthur Bryant took over one of Perry's restaurants and, as is typical of the famous barbecue restaurants, not much has changed over the years, although the spiciness of the sauce was toned down considerably. According to writer Calvin

Trillin, Perry's sauce was extremely hot, and Perry took delight in watching new customers take their first bite of barbecue. Arthur Bryant called Perry "the greatest barbecue man in the world," but also "a mean outfit."[54]

Henry Perry likely originated a barbecue entrée common in Kansas City but hard to find elsewhere: burnt ends. These are the charred ends of the brisket. Years ago, as the pitmaster sliced the brisket he pushed the burnt ends to the side of the counter to be given away to anyone who wanted them. People who ate them developed a taste for them, demand increased, and today burnt ends are on the menu of many Kansas City barbecue restaurants, like Arthur Bryant's, alongside ribs, sausage, and the rest of the meats.

4

BARBECUE AROUND
THE WORLD

B arbecue is a phenomenon that does not pay much attention to geopolitical borders. Within the United States, for example, are a number of different kinds of barbecuing traditions. Barbecue styles do a much better job of following cultural borders, though: Again, in the United States, traditional slow-cooked barbecue has tended to be more popular in the South than elsewhere.

Worldwide, there are a number of large-scale cultural traditions that have affected barbecue's spread into various countries. One primary factor has been colonization, particularly the global colonization of the 1500s and 1600s by the Spanish and Portuguese. Unlike Britain, where baking and roasting in the oven were the most popular cooking methods, Spain and Portugal had an existing tradition of grilling, and this tradition followed the path of colonization into the wider world. Thus, countries like Argentina, which also developed an enormous cattle export industry, today are known for grilling large amounts of meat—one leading Argentinian chef recommends cooking four pounds of meat per guest for a barbecue.[1] Spanish and Portuguese colonization did not just affect South America; the Portuguese also colonized large parts of Africa and the Pacific, and the grilling tradition survives there as well today. Of course, British colonization did result in three cultures where barbecue is not simply a way of cooking but also a type of gathering: the United States, Australia (home of the Barbie), and South Africa, where Braai Day, named after their version of barbecue, is quickly becoming a national holiday.

Regarding the precise definition of "barbecue" in this chapter, most of the barbecuing done around the world is outdoor grilling. A few cultures have traditions of cooking large pieces of meat for hours over a fire or underground, but, for most people around the world, their version of barbecue is cooking smaller pieces of meat over an open fire.

GRILLED MEAT ON A STICK

Probably the most widespread type of barbecue worldwide is the various versions of grilled meat on a stick. This dish can be seen across Eurasia, where it goes by many names, such as kebabs (throughout central Asia), souvlaki (in Greece), yakitori (in Japan), and satay (in Thailand and Indonesia). This style of cooking has a number of advantages. Since the meat is cut into small pieces, it can be grilled quickly, reducing the need for much fuel (American-style "low and slow" barbecuing assumes the existence of lots of wood, a questionable assumption in most parts of the world). The skewer serves several functions. It keeps the food in place, which makes cooking easier, and makes the gridiron optional, since the cook can just rest the ends of the skewer on the edges of the grill. Using skewers also helps define portion size, which makes it easy for roadside barbecue stands to quickly serve a customer—all they need to do is grab a single skewer for one customer. Meat grilled in this way is usually marinated beforehand. Marinating adds a considerable amount of flavor and helps tenderize the meat in cases where tougher meat is used (this is why marinades often call for acidic fruit juice, which breaks down the meat). Traditional American-style barbecue achieves tenderness through a long cooking time, which again assumes a nearly unlimited amount of fuel.

That this type of cooking is both old and widespread can be seen in the roots of the name "shish kebab." In Turkic languages (those spoken both in Turkey and many former Soviet Republics) "shish" means "skewer," while "kebab" probably comes from the Arabic *kabab*, referring to small pieces of cooked food. Thus, shish kebab has roots in two different languages, though the concept is more widespread through Eurasia than the phrase "shish kebab."

Three different recipes from *The Art of Uzbek Cooking*, by Lynn Visson, illustrate different kinds of kebabs (or shashlyk, as they are called in Uzbekistan). The first recipe is for lamb kebabs—the skewered meat recipes of Eurasia all use whatever meat is popular in a given region, and lamb is the favored meat of Uzbekistan, a former republic of the Soviet Union. The second recipe uses ground lamb, showing that it is possible to make kebabs from ground meat, and the last recipe is for fish kebabs, although those kebabs take a bit of preparation beforehand. The recipes do not include vegetables grilled on the same skewers as the meat. This is because the two types of food have very different cooking times, and combining them means either eating well cooked vegetables and very rare meat or well cooked meat and mushy, overdone vegetables. Vegetables can be delicious when grilled but it is best to cook them on separate skewers, toward the end of the cooking time for the meat.

Visson's lamb kebab recipe begins with a few pounds of lamb, with the fat removed, cut into small cubes.[2] The lamb is placed in a large dish and crushed cumin seeds, sweet paprika, salt and pepper, and minced onions are sprinkled over the meat. Enough seltzer water to cover the meat is added to the dish and then a large plate, with heavy cans of food on top of it, is placed on the dish, to press down on the lamb while it marinates. The lamb then marinates in the refrigerator for anywhere from two hours to overnight. To cook, the lamb is simply placed on skewers, grilled for five to seven minutes per side, and served with sliced onion.

The ground meat kebab recipe takes a different approach to flavoring the meat.[3] Instead of marinating the ground lamb, which would be something of a mess to drain, spices are added to the meat and then left to infuse the meat. To a few pounds of ground lamb Visson adds finely chopped onion, cumin, coriander, a few tablespoons of red wine vinegar, and salt and pepper. The cook kneads the ground meat to mix everything together and then chills it for thirty minutes. To put the meat on the skewers the cook first forms the meat into thin, long, sausage-like patties and then threads them onto the skewers, rather than forming the meat around the skewers, which does not ultimately work well. The kebabs are then grilled for ten to fifteen minutes, and the meat served with quartered tomatoes and sliced scallions.

Finally, Visson includes a recipe for fish kebabs, showing that not just land animals can be used for kebabs.[4] Fish is delicate, though, so the meat needs some preparation. Visson recommends using a few pounds of fish steaks for the kebabs, such as sturgeon, swordfish, or halibut, cut into inch and a half cubes. The cubes are carefully dropped into boiling water for precisely thirty seconds to get them to a correct consistency for going on a kebab, then removed and allowed to cool slightly. Each piece is then rubbed with softened butter, sprinkled with cayenne and black pepper, and threaded onto flat skewers. The fish is grilled about eight to ten minutes and served hot.

COUNTRIES AND REGIONS

Germany

Technically speaking, Germany does not have an extensive barbecue tradition. As food researcher Ursula Heinzelmann has pointed out, outdoor grilling is popular today in Germany in much the same way it is popular in many places around the world. "Younger Germans and Turkish citizens flock to public parks for this occasion, loaded down with grill, table, and chairs as well as victuals," she writes. "However, the majority of Germans prefer to retreat to their private yards." In their yards they cook something of a subset of the foods Americans grill, mainly "sausages and marinated pork, lamb, and beef steaks or *schaschlik* (shish kebab, that is, meat on skewers with onions and bell peppers)." The Germans and Turks keep much the same gender roles as Americans: "The men rule over the fire, be it charcoal or gas, whereas the women do the background work, making salads and sauces to go with the meat."[5]

While their barbecues are much the same as many American barbecues, the Germans have made a considerable contribution to worldwide barbecue in their development of a wide variety of sausages. The sausages use either uncooked or cooked meat, and this latter type, which they called "hot sausage," is what German immigrants began selling at Texas meat markets in the early 20th century to use up unsold barbecue meat. Germans produce a dizzying array of sausages, mostly made from pork, but from almost every imaginable part of the pig (as the saying goes, everything but the oink), such as liver sausage, tongue sausage, and blood sausage. Other ingredients are added, as well, to make cheese sausage, beer sausage, and sausage that includes truffles and herbs.[6] True, in their native land these sausages are usually boiled, steamed, or eaten cold, but barbecue lovers worldwide have realized the enjoyment that comes from grilling sausages.

Portugal

Being a coastal country means that Portugal has access to many different types of seafood, some of which has been used for kebabs. Mussel and Vegetable Kebabs is a dish that supposedly originated centuries ago in a fishing village just west of Lisbon. A typical version of that dish is prepared by first sautéing the mussels, in shells, in a frying pan with oil, garlic, salt, and pepper. As each shell opens it is removed from the pan and the mussel is removed from the shell (shells that do not open are assumed to be bad). Each mussel is wrapped in half a slice of bacon and then placed on a skewer, alternated between tomato quarters and thick slices of green peppers. The skewers are grilled, then served with a sauce made from onions, white vinegar, garlic, olive oil, and hard-boiled eggs.

Russia and Central Asia

Many of the countries of central Asia (such as the former Soviet Republics) have a tradition of open fire cooking in the tandoor, a type of stove that is in widespread use there (see the entry below for India for more information on the tandoor). Additionally, the Russians and Central Asians have a tradition of cooking outside in terms of picnicking and barbecuing as social activities. As a rule, in those countries men do not cook except when it is outdoor cooking, and then, as in America, men are generally in charge. The outdoor cooking there, though, is different from outdoor cooking in America in a few significant ways. Most of the grilled food is meat, as in America, usually in the form of kebabs, but pilaf is also cooked on the fire. Pilaf, a rice dish, is an important food in this area, central enough to the culture that it can be cooked by a man over the fire (while a rice dish like pilaf may appear at an American barbecue, it would usually be one of the side dishes prepared in the kitchen by a woman). As food researchers Glenn R. Mack and Asele Surina have observed, the ingredients required for cooking pilaf for a crowd are expensive enough that only someone very experienced with the process would do this: the patriarch of the family (if cooked inside, it would be the matriarch). Indeed, the researchers take this idea a step further and point out that, when the next generation begins cooking pilaf, either inside or outside, it is a major change in the family that signifies a new matriarch and patriarch have taken over. In this way, cooking pilaf over a fire has a significance for Central Asians that goes far beyond what open fire cooking signifies for Americans.[7]

The Middle East

In general, the Middle East does not have a tradition of grilled meat, with one exception: döner-kebabs (*shawarma*, in Arabic, and also known as gyros in Greece), which are different from the kebabs discussed above. To make döner-kebabs, thin layers of marinated meat are wrapped around a long metal skewer. The skewer is placed in a cooker that is vertically oriented. Rather than sit above the fire, the meat slowly spins beside the fire so that the drippings from the meat run down the length of the meat, to be captured in a pan below. Most of the cookers use gas or electric heat. To assemble a döner-kebab, the cook holds a knife in one hand and cuts in a downward motion against the meat while slices of meat fall onto a special shovel-like utensil the cook holds with a second hand. With this setup the meat does not have to be fully cooked to serve, since only the outside layers of the meat (which are the warmest) will be served at any one time. Döner-kebabs are then served on different breads in different regions, such as pita bread in Greece.

Another type of restaurant serving grilled food that has appeared in the Middle East over the past several decades is one that serves grilled chicken. From the Western point of view the restaurants are very basic: Most of them serve only grilled chicken. As one writer reported of the restaurants, "Often there is no bread or rice, no soup, no vegetables, and no sweets. Sometimes it is even hard to get something to drink apart from cool water."[8] The only serving sizes are a whole or half chicken, and the food is served on a cardboard plate, with a paper napkin.

Mozambique

The grilling culture of Mozambique is influenced by both the country's Portuguese colonization and its location in Africa. Grilled Chicken African Style, a dish from the cookbook *Cuisines of Portuguese Encounters*, shows both influences.[9] That recipe has the cook make a paste, in a food processor, from garlic, salt, pepper flakes, and lemon juice, and spread it on a chicken, inside and out. The chicken then marinates in the refrigerator for a few hours. A distinctly non-European taste comes in when the chicken is on the grill, with a basting liquid made from olive oil and coconut milk.

South Africa

In the United States, some summer holidays, like July 4, are associated with barbecue because barbecuing is an enjoyable activity on a warm day off. The South Africans have taken this a step further and have an unofficial holiday named "Braai Day," braai being their version of the barbecue. The point of the holiday is not to celebrate barbecue as a food, though, but barbecue as a gathering, particularly as a social event that brings people together. South Africa has a long history of divisions between groups of people, and Braai Day is an event intended to unite them. In an interview with American National Public Radio, the originator of the holiday compared the mixing of cultures in South African history with boerewors, a South African sausage often grilled at braais. "You've got sausage-making skills from Europe that came with the European settlers to Africa," he said. "Then you've got spices and the knowledge of how to use them from the East, stuff like coriander, nutmeg, cloves and then in Africa it was very typical to cook all your food on a fire. So boerewors is, it's probably the best analogy, foodwise, of the rainbow nation."[10] Braai Day is celebrated on September 24.

South Africans grill a variety of foods at a braai, including sosaties, a kind of pork and lamb kebab with a fairly elaborate marinade. C. Louis Keiplodt, an important South African food writer from the 1930s and 1940s, identified sosaties as being a prime Afrikaner dish.

Typical sosaties recipes begin with lamb, pork, or beef (lamb is most typical), cubed to the correct size for skewers. The meat goes into a previously boiled marinade that usually includes vinegar, turmeric, curry powder, coriander, white or brown sugar, a few other spices, and apricot jam—a hallmark of sosaties is the fact that apricots will go on the skewers along with the meat. The meat marinates in the refrigerator for a few hours, then goes on skewers interspersed with dried apricots, onions, and bacon. In many recipes, while the skewers cook on the grill the marinade goes back into a saucepan to be boiled a second time, to then be used as a sauce for the sosaties. Often, cream or butter is added to the marinade at either the first time it is boiled or the second time (or both), resulting in a much richer sauce for the final product.

Tarzan Roast

Tarzan Roast shows up in Justin Bonello's *Cooked in Africa*, where he writes that he got the idea for the roast from South African writer Braam Kruger.[11] The concept is simple, and is probably quite an old method of cooking meat. The addition of a wheelbarrow to the cooking process makes it somewhat easier than it might be otherwise.

Briefly stated, the Tarzan Roast has the cook hang a leg of lamb from a tree, dangling on a rope, held near a fire. The process, as Bonello describes it, is this: The cook starts with a seven-and-a-half-pound leg of lamb, with the shank intact. The shank is a part of the leg that forms a natural loop to tie a rope to. Bonello recommends placing sprigs of rosemary, chilies, and garlic in slits all around the leg, then soaking the leg of lamb in a marinade that includes oyster sauce, onions, and orange and lemon juices. While the leg soaks, a fire is built in a metal wheelbarrow, which will allow the cook to move the fire as the wind changes during the four to six hours it will take to cook the meat. Because of the long cooking time, the meat will be both cooked and smoked, so Bonello suggests burning a fruitwood to give additional flavor to the meat. When the fire is ready, the leg of lamb is hung from a branch of a tree (making sure the branch is high enough not to catch fire), and Bonello recommends using a sheepshank knot, since it is both appropriately named and because the rope can be adjusted up and down easily with that particular knot. The used marinade goes into a baking tray that sits on a stool below the hanging leg, while the fire is to one side of the leg. A forked stick should be used to prop the leg so that it hangs near the fire, downwind, and so that the leg can be rotated slowly during the cooking time. The meat should be close enough to the fire that the cook can hold his hand between the meat and fire for only a few seconds. Rotate the meat a quarter-turn every fifteen minutes or so, and baste it enough that the meat stays moist. The roast should be done in four to six hours, depending on the wind and the size of the fire.

India

As almost anyone who has visited an Indian restaurant will know, India has a tradition of open-fire cooking in the tandoor, although it is less well known that there are actually two kinds of stoves used in India. A tandoor is big, heavy, and hot—temperatures average around a thousand degrees—and so tandoors usually only appear in restaurants. If an Indian home has an open-fire stove, it is a smaller sigri, which is simply a grill.

The essence of the tandoor is its shape and the material it is made from. A tandoor usually resembles a barrel or large tub, and can be made from cement or clay—anything that will hold heat. Although it takes some time to get a tandoor hot, once it is hot it will stay hot for a considerable time, which means that the cook needs to use less fuel overall than with another type of stove. The design of the tandoor is simple and ancient, and tandoors are prevalent throughout central Asia, appearing in Russia and former Soviet Republics, as well as India.

The tandoor has an interesting history in India. Although the roots of it are old, its widespread popularity is a recent phenomenon, dating back to the mid-20th century. Before 1947 the area that today is India and Pakistan was controlled by the British, and when the British pulled out in 1947 the two states were created, India as a Hindu state and Pakistan as a Muslim state. Enormous numbers of people moved to be in the correct state, including Kashmiris who moved out of the area between the two countries (control of Kashmir has been a major source of contention between India and Pakistan). The Kashmiris had a long tradition of tandoor use that other Indians did not, and many of the Kashmiris who moved to New Delhi, India's capital, opened restaurants that quickly became popular. Hence, tandoori, the food that comes from a tandoor, became popular at roughly the same time barbecue became a widespread phenomenon in America.[12]

Tandoor recipes are often quite flavorful, particularly because the meat can be marinated in several different sauces before it is cooked. The 2007 cookbook *Indian Barbecue*, printed in New Delhi, contains a recipe for Chicken Tikka Marinated in Cottage Cheese that could be made in a tandoor or on a grill.[13] The recipe calls for two very different marinades. The cook first lets cut-up chicken breasts marinate in a mixture of lemon juice, garlic paste, and salt for a few hours. The lemon juice flavors the meat and also works as a tenderizer, since the juice is acidic. The chicken is then moved to a second marinade made of cottage cheese, cream, corn flour, and some seasonings, where the chicken marinates for at least another three hours. At the end of the process the chicken is grilled on skewers and served with tomatoes, onions, and cucumber slices.

A method of cooking that is unique to the tandoor is that for baking bread. Rather than cooking on a rack or on the floor of the oven, dough is stuck to the sides of the tandoor, a technique that helps to maximize the baking surface in the tandoor. Nan is a traditional flatbread baked in a tandoor, but there are other breads that can also be baked on the sides of the tandoor, including Russia samsa bread. The central Asian version of nan has a decorative hole punched in the center of the bread, which results in bread that is crispy around the hole and soft and chewy around the outside of the ring. The hole also makes it so the baker can retrieve the bread with a long, hooked pole rather than using his or her hands.

Korea

Like other Asian countries, the Koreas have a tradition of grilling, one that includes a clever variation on barbecued short ribs. Ribs are a tough meat, so grilling ribs takes some time; the low heat slowly tenderizes the meat. Asian cooking techniques are usually geared toward quick cooking, though, and the Koreans have discovered a way to cook ribs quickly. The secret is in butterflying the ribs, which means that a single piece of meat about the size of two decks of playing cards is cut in such a way that it becomes a long, thin strip of meat.

There are many different recipes for Korean barbecued short ribs, most of which involve first cutting the meat and then marinating it. To cut the meat, first place one rib on the work surface. Cut the meat from the rib and discard the rib. The next step is to butterfly the rib: Starting at a long end (so that the rib will be as wide as it can be), cut a thin slice of meat that measures (depending on the ribs you have) about 1 1/2 inches wide, 2 to 3 inches long, and about 1/8 inch thick, but DO NOT cut all the way through to the far edge. When you are very close to the far edge, flip the meat over and begin slicing back across the piece of meat, again with a slice about 1/8 inch thick; the goal is to end up with a single long piece of thin meat (if you cut through do not worry; the meat will still taste fine). The process is complicated to describe but fairly simple in practice; searching for a video of the process on the Internet will help you in understanding how to do it. It looks impressive when you slice the rib into one long piece of meat, but many smaller slices will also work on the grill.

Typically, Korean short ribs are then left for a few hours in a marinade that often includes garlic, sugar (either white or brown), soy sauce, vinegar, sesame oil, and mirin (rice wine). The meat is grilled for a few minutes on each side.

Japan

Most barbecuers in America would see grilled tofu as being some sort of abomination, but the ingredient has a long history in Asia, stretching back over 2,000 years, and barbecuing tofu in Japan is nothing out of the ordinary. In the cookbook *Café Japan*, Emi Kazuko provides a recipe for tofu grilled on a skewer with potatoes and eggplant, and a miso-based sauce.[14] The recipe begins with the cook draining, then pressing between a cutting board and a plate, a ten-ounce cake of tofu. The tofu is then cut into eight pieces, ready to be skewered. A potato is also cut into eight pieces and boiled until almost tender, while an eggplant is also cut up but not cooked. Pieces of tofu, potato, and eggplant are alternated on four skewers.

The miso sauce is made by warming a few ounces of miso, some sake, and some sugar in a saucepan, adding a small amount of water, and cooking until the sauce becomes thick. A bit of lime juice goes in a the very end, and the sauce is cooled to room temperature.

The skewers are then cooked over coals until lightly browned and heated through, about two to three minutes. Off the grill, the miso sauce is spread over one side of the skewers, toasted sesame seeds are sprinkled over the sauce, and the skewers are served on a bed of green leaves.

Yakitori is the Japanese take on grilled chicken on a stick, but the twist here is that a sauce is applied four or five times at the very end of cooking, allowing the sauce to caramelize. Yakitori is the most popular street food in Japan, both because it is easy for vendors to make and because it tastes delicious.

Making yakitori is simple. The sauce is usually made of mirin (rice wine) and soy sauce, with other ingredients, such as sugar, sometimes also added. The sauce is boiled in a saucepan, usually for a few minutes to mix the flavors but sometimes for a longer period to reduce the liquid and make it thicker. Chicken, often thigh meat, is threaded onto skewers, which are then grilled. When the chicken begins to brown the sauce is then applied in three or four coats, each coat being allowed to dry over the coals before the next coat is applied. The chicken is ready when it is golden brown.

East Timor

East Timor, situated on an island just north of Australia, was colonized by the Portuguese, and so the country has a grilling culture as well as a ready supply of fresh fish. The book *Cuisines of Portuguese Encounters*, which examines foods from places colonized by the Portuguese, includes a recipe for grilled fish that is very typical of grilled fish recipes around the world.[15] The recipe begins by calling for two groupers, although this recipe would probably work for almost any fish, the fresher the better. After cleaning, the fish are rubbed inside and out with a mixture that includes garlic, Tabasco sauce, saffron, and lemon juice. They are then wrapped in either banana leaves or aluminum foil, which means that these fish are technically steamed rather than grilled, and placed over a fire for about twenty-five minutes. The traditional accompaniment for the fish is white rice.

The Caribbean

Some grilled foods are popular in the islands of the Caribbean, and grilling is facilitated by the fact that one of the most popular types of stoves in the area is the coal pot. A coal pot is shaped somewhat like a capital Y, with a wide bowl sitting on a squat cylindrical base. The coals sit on a rack at the bottom of the bowl, and one side of the base is open, so that air flows up from the base, through the hot coals. Cooks either place cooking pots directly on the coals or on a gridiron that sits at the top of the stove. Coal pots are popular for foods that require a long cooking time, as the price of the charcoal is relatively inexpensive, and because the charcoal, made from local materials, imparts its flavor to the food.

Some of the barbecuing techniques in the Caribbean are descended from those used by the Taino Indians who were there when Columbus arrived. Jerk barbecue, described below in the section on Jamaica, partially comes from the Tainos, and a tradition of making roast pig survives in Puerto Rico. There, the pig is basted with a sauce of citrus juice, annatto, and oil, and served with roasted plantains, rice, and a mixed salad.[16]

Jamaica

Jerk barbecue is the most popular type of barbecue in Jamaica. The essence of jerk is the spices applied to meat before cooking, particularly allspice (also called the Jamaican pimento) and chilies, which give jerked meat some heat—jerk is usually eaten with something sweet or bland to help cut the heat. Jerk probably originated with the combination of several different cultures in Jamaica. The Taino Indians preserved meat by hanging it on racks over a low fire, drying the meat and smoking it at the same time. The Africans who were brought to the island brought with them a love of spices, and they seem to have influenced the particular combination that is characteristic of jerk spice. Traditionally, jerking has been associated with the Maroons who live in highland Jamaica, descendants of escaped slaves who lived in barely accessible villages far from whites. Jerking became their main method of meat preservation, usually used on the wild boars that inhabit the region. Although jerked meat is popular today throughout Jamaica, the particular blend of spices used by the Maroons, and the specific type of wood used to cook the meat, are known only to the Maroons.

There is a fair amount of disagreement of just where the word "jerk" came from. According to food researcher Lynn Marie Houston, it may have originated with the movement used to turn the meat over and over as it cooks over a fire. It may also have been an English corruption of the Spanish word *charqui*, which referred to the native method of preserving meats. In an even more complicated explanation, Houston writes that it may have been "an English version of a Spanish bastardization of an Indian word that supposedly referred to preparation of pork in the style of the Quechua Indians of South America."[17] While this particular theory is tangled, it is a good example of what happened when many different cultures came together in the early years of New World exploration.

Jamaicans originally used jerking to preserve the wild boar that roamed the island, and then switched to domesticated pigs. Today all types of jerked meat can be purchased in Jamaica, from pork to chicken to sausage to lobster. Pork and chicken are the two most popular types of meat served at jerk huts, the round shacks that serve their own jerked meat.

Jerk seasonings are usually applied to the meat before it is cooked via a rub. The rub is a combination of a number of spices and herbs. Typical jerk seasoning includes allspice, cinnamon, and thyme as specific ingredients, and usually something to provide some heat, such as cayenne pepper or chipotle chili powder. Other spices complementary to allspice and cinnamon, like nutmeg, sometimes appear in jerk seasoning, as do other ingredients typical in barbecue rubs like garlic powder and black pepper. Finally, some jerk rubs include white or brown sugar, which increase the sweetness and also give the grilled meat a darker appearance.

The jerk seasoning does not necessarily need to be applied as a rub. In *Jerk: Barbecue from Jamaica*, Helen Willinsky relates a recipe for jerk marinade, to be applied to the meat both before and during cooking.[18] The marinade includes spices like allspice, thyme, cinnamon, and nutmeg, as well as a hot pepper and onions and scallions. Soy sauce, vinegar, and cooking oil are used as the liquids in the marinade. Making the marinade is simple; the ingredients are blended briefly in a food processor, resulting in a thick mixture with a consistency somewhere between a liquid and a paste.

Willinsky also includes a recipe for chicken that uses the marinade.[19] For that recipe, two chickens, cut into serving pieces, are marinated for at least four hours, then grilled. Authentic Jamaican jerk is cooked over allspice wood, but, since that may be hard to come by, Willinsky recommends using apple or hickory wood, or charcoal.

The chicken should be turned every ten minutes or so while cooking, and basted frequently with the unused portion of the marinade. The chicken should be cooked until the juices run clear when pricked with a fork and internal temperature is 165 degrees.

Argentina

Three things combined to make beef eating, and barbecue, a big part of the food culture of Argentina. The country was colonized by the Spanish, who had an existing tradition of grilling. Early in the colonization process, escaped horses made their way to the pampas—the prairies—where their wild descendants bred like crazy and provided the mounts for the Argentine cowboys. The pampas also proved to be an ideal place to raise cattle, which quickly became a central part of the Argentine economy, and beef was both inexpensive and widely available.

Francis Mallmann is an Argentine-born, French-trained chef with restaurants in Argentina and a cookbook, *Seven Fires: Grilling the Argentine Way*, which is a good introduction to Argentine wood-fired cooking. The seven fires of the cookbook title are the seven possible ways to cook with fire, as defined by Mallmann. *Parrilla* is cooking with a grill, *chapa* is cooking on a piece of cast iron (such as a skillet) over a fire, *infiernillo* is cooking between two fires (say, with one above the food and another below it), *horno de barro* is cooking with a stove like an Indian tandoor, *rescoldo* is cooking by covering the food with hot coals and ashes, *asador* is cooking large pieces of meat on a rotisserie by a fire, and *caldero* is cooking in a Dutch oven. Clearly, Mallmann has spent some time thinking about outdoor cooking.

Two things come through in looking at Mallmann's cookbook. First, he is someone who has spent time learning how the gauchos—South American cowboys—cooked generations ago. His cookbook includes a recipe for cooking an entire 1,400 pound cow, described below. Second, Argentine cooking is very socially oriented. Mallmann recommends cooking four pounds of meat per person, an eyebrow-raising number that he explains by describing the context of barbecues in Argentina. These are not just meals but social occasions, and the assumption is that guests will not simply stay for an hour or so but will stay for many hours, eating and talking until long after the sun has gone down. Thus, the four pounds of meat per person is not for a single midday or evening meal but for a few meals, eaten leisurely over the course of the day.

An example of cooking for a gathering can be seen in his instructions for a Sunday Asado, or barbecue. This is a big grill featuring sausages, short ribs, and beef tri-tip, with a number of side dishes, including roasted vegetables. The shopping list for the meal calls for nearly twenty pounds of meat, and the vegetables would probably add another ten to fifteen pounds of food, *for only twelve guests*. By American standards, this is extreme.

The shopping list for the asado begins with a whole standing rib roast, weighing nearly ten pounds. A few pounds of tri-tip, short ribs, and fresh sausages (which can be Italian sweet, hot, chorizo, or any combination) are also on the list, as are a few pounds of sweetbreads. For vegetables, the cook should procure around five pounds of baking potatoes and five pounds of sweet potatoes, another few pounds of onions, and six large bell peppers—red, green, or yellow are all okay. Six baguettes and a pound and a half of provolone round out the shopping list.

Mallmann provides a timeline for when tasks need to be done for this asado. Much of the planning, and the shopping, happens the day before, while the actual meal preparation does not start until about five hours before the meal, when the meat is brought out of the refrigerator, rinsed, and allowed to come to room temperature. While this is usually not usually advisable because of the risk of microbes growing on the food at room temperature, South Americans tend to like their meat *very* well done, a cultural holdover from the days before refrigeration when "well done" was the best way to avoid food sickness. Mallmann was trained in France—he operated a restaurant in a tourist-oriented area of Argentina and spent time in France during the off-season—and his cooking technique seems to be a response to the fussiness of classical French cooking. Most of the meats listed above are cooked with only salt and pepper as their seasonings. The vegetables are cooked in the ashes of the fire, and the provolone is used in a cheese dish to be served as an appetizer with the bread.

Entire Cow

When there are many, many mouths to feed, one option is to cook an entire cow. It is quite a job (Mallmann called it a "cross between a banquet and a construction project"), but it will produce vast amounts of meat, provided it cooks correctly.[20] The traditional American way to cook a large piece of meat like this would be put the fire in a pit and have the meat at ground level, but Argentine cooking customarily uses a fire at ground level and puts the meat above and to one side of the fire. Mallmann provides a recipe for cooking an entire cow; he cooks it the Argentine way, with the meat in a truss, propped up with a block and tackle (and since the meat weighs about 1,400 pounds, that will need to be a very heavy-duty block and tackle). One of the amazing things about his recipe is its simplicity: It takes about nineteen hours and requires heavy lifting, but beyond those two aspects it is quite a simple recipe.

Mallmann's instructions begin by having the cook procure a medium cow weighing about 1,400 pounds that has been butterflied and the skin removed. About nineteen hours before the planned meal, the cook builds a fire out of twenty large logs, allowing it to burn for about an hour. During that time the cook brings two gallons of water to a boil, adds two cups of salt, and lets the water cool while dissolving the salt in the water. This salt water will be used to baste the meat while it cooks.

After the fire has burned for about an hour, the cow, mounted in a truss, is sprinkled with salt water and then moved into position at a 45-degree angle, with the bone side facing the fire. A piece of corrugated metal should be placed over the meat to allow it to better cook, and the coals should be raked to distribute heat evenly across the entire piece of meat. Every two hours more salt water should be sprinkled on the meat, and logs should be added as needed to keep the meat cooking.

Two hours before the meal, the metal should be removed and the cow brushed with more salt water; then the cow should be turned over and again brushed with salt water. The bone side will now be facing away from the fire, and the meat toward the fire should crisp as it cooks. When the time arrives for the meal, the cook should carve the meat that is ready—some of it may still need to continue cooking. Mallmann recommends chimichurri to accompany the meat.

Chimichurri

Chimichurri is somewhat similar to pesto, and functions as Argentina's version of barbecue sauce, appearing on grilled steaks, chicken, or other meats. The main ingredient in chimichurri is fresh parsley, which makes it resemble pesto, and fresh oregano also frequently appears as well. Chimichurri generally includes a few garlic cloves, and the garlic, parsley, and oregano are all chopped fine. A combination of olive oil and vinegar (usually red wine vinegar) makes up the liquid in the chimichurri. Salt and red pepper flakes are also usually added, while other ingredients, like onion or lemon juice, sometimes appear in recipes. Chimichurri can be used as both a marinade for meats and a sauce to accompany grilled meats.

Uruguay

Like Argentina, Uruguay is a country with a large cattle industry, and so *carne asada* appears often on that country's dinner tables. In the cookbook *Nirmala's Edible Diary*, Nirmala Narine includes a recipe for *carne asada* from Uruguay in which the meat is marinated and then grilled on skewers instead of being grilled in a large piece of meat.[21] Her recipe calls for a pound of beef tenderloin, cut into one-inch cubes, to be marinated in a mixture that includes apple juice, white wine, garlic, lime juice, and olive oil. The kebabs are grilled as usual, but then Narine also relates a recipe for Caruso dipping sauce, named after Enrique Caruso and popular in Uruguay. The sauce features sautéed shallots and garlic, wine, mushrooms, cream, cayenne pepper, and chunky peanut butter. The Caruso sauce should be served alongside the kebabs.

Mexico

Barbacoa, the Spanish root of "barbecue," is still popular throughout Mexico, but its precise definition changes throughout the country. In general, it refers to meat that has been cooked underground, but the exact method of preparation is different in different places. In Mexico City it is lamb, wrapped in maguey leaves and cooked underground, while in some parts of northern Mexico it is a cow's head cooked for hours and then scraped of meat. Other barbecued dishes are regionally popular. *Cochinita pibil*, which translates roughly as "buried baby pig," is a dish popular in the Yucatán Peninsula, and is either a suckling pig or pork shoulder cooked underground. *Cabrito* is a kid goat, often roasted over a charcoal fire, popular in the area around Monterrey, in northern Mexico.

In the book *Smokestack Lightning*, Lolis Eric Elie describes watching the process of making the northern type of barbacoa at a pit in Brownsville, Texas, a city on the border with Mexico. At around nine in the morning, cow heads are rinsed and wrapped in aluminum foil, then stacked in a brick-lined pit that has already been heated with burning wood (the wood is dragged out of the pit before the heads go in). The heads are covered with wet burlap sacks, a heavy metal plate covers the pit, and finally dirt is shoveled over the plate to hold in the heat. At midnight the pit is uncovered and the meat is peeled from the skulls and placed into metal roasters that keep the meat warm until it is sold later that day.[22]

A recipe for the central-Mexico style of barbacoa, using lamb, comes from the *Mexican Cook Book for American Homes*, a mid-20th-century Mexican cookbook that includes a description of the entire process.[23] There are two interesting things about the recipe. First, maguey leaves line the barbecue pit. Maguey leaves look something like enormous aloe leaves—they are fleshy and can be four or five feet long, and their juice imparts a certain taste to the lamb. The second interesting thing about the recipe is that, rather than let the cooking juices simply run to the bottom of the pit, a casserole dish with rice and chickpeas is placed below the meat to collect the drippings, making a natural side dish to the barbecue in the process.

The instructions for making barbacoa begin with the typical instructions for underground cooking: Dig a pit of the appropriate size (in this case, about four feet deep and two feet square), line the pit with stones, fill the pit with firewood, set the wood on fire, and let the wood burn down to coals.

While the wood is burning, the cook soaks a half-cup of rice and a half-cup of chickpeas in water to soften them, then drains the water. The rice and chickpeas go into an earthenware casserole dish with sliced potatoes, carrots, chilies, and epazote leaves, which are an herb native to southern Mexico.

When the wood has burned down to coals, the next step is to line the pit with maguey leaves, but the leaves need to be processed first. Each leaf should be cleaned, then roasted over the fire until it is limp. This will make the leaves begin releasing their juice, which will flavor the meat. The hole should be lined with the long leaves, making sure they overlap and extend onto the ground above (the top of the leaves will need to be held down with rocks). When finished, the hole will look something like a flower.

A grate is then lowered into the pit. The earthenware casserole goes onto the grate, and a lamb, in five sections, is placed over the casserole, which will catch the drippings from the cooking meat.

The tops of the maguey leaves are then folded down over the meat, covering it completely. The leaves are covered with a metal or wooden lid, more maguey leaves are placed upon the lid, and then a palm mat covers those leaves. Finally, a layer of mud goes over the palm mat, sealing everything in so that while the meat cooks it is also steamed.

A fire should then be burned on top of the mud and kept going for five to six hours. At the end of the process everything is unsealed and both the meat and the rice-chickpea dish in the earthenware pot are served.

Carne asada is popular throughout Latin America, and what differentiates *carne asada* in different regions is what is cooked along with the meat. In the cookbook *Savoring Mexico*, Sharon Caldwallader gives a recipe for *carne asada* from the central lowlands of Mexico that includes some fruits and vegetables that are grilled alongside the meat.[24] In her recipe, halved potatoes, peeled and halved onions, and halved and cored apples are first grilled until almost tender. At that point two pounds of beef tenderloin, sliced a quarter-inch thick, are added to the grill, along with a few large zucchini, halved and quartered. Everything should finish at about the same time, and everything should be served on a large platter, along with a pot of refried beans.

Tacos al pastor is a grilled meat dish popular throughout Mexico, and it has an international connection. *Al pastor* means "of the shepherd," and refers to the nickname for Lebanese immigrants who moved to Mexico in the early 20th century. Those immigrants brought foods with them, including *shawarma*, a lamb dish where the meat is grilled vertically, so the meat sits beside the fire instead of over it and the juices do not drip into the fire. With *shawarma*, thin slices of lamb are served on pita bread. The general concept was brought into Mexican culture, but the lamb was shifted to pork and the pita changed to a tortilla. Chilies were added to a marinade for the meat, and slices of pineapple were added to the finished soft-shelled taco.

Hawaii

Yes, Hawaii is part of the United States, but its cultural influences set it apart from other states. Its cuisine is strongly influenced by a number of far-flung countries, including China, Japan, Portugal, and England, as well as older native traditions. The specific tradition that connects with barbecue is, of course, the luau, which traditionally features Kalua Pig, a pig barbecued underground.

The method of roasting the pig is not significantly different from how other cultures roast animals in underground pits. As *The Pacifica House Hawaii Cook Book* described it in 1965, "the cavity of a carefully cleaned fat porker is filled with large hot porous rocks as the carcass rests upon a bed of banana leaves supported on a basket-like piece of wire mesh. More banana leaves and stalks are placed over the pig, then basket and all is lowered into the imu—the pit which is also well filled with hot rocks." As with other meals of this sort, the meat is roasted along with vegetables. "Laulaus, bananas and sweet potatoes are placed around the pig and all is covered with ti leaves, wet gunny sacks and soil. Hours of steaming result in a meal deluxe with an unforgettable flavor." While the pig may be the center of the feast, other dishes make an appearance as well. "Poi—the Hawaiian staff of life, lomi salmon, chicken luau, limu or seaweed, squid, opihis, and pipikaula (Hawaiian jerky) help round out the menu. For dessert one can usually select from several—coconut cake, haupia, or assorted island fruits."[25]

RESTAURANTS

Fogo de Chão

Fogo de Chão, pronounced "fo-go dee shoun," is a chain of Brazilian steakhouses that began in Porto Alegre, Brazil, in 1979, and spread to the United States. The restaurants' founders, Jair and Arri Coser, are two brothers who grew up in Brazil's cattle country; their restaurant focuses on serving plenty of meat prepared the way Brazil's gauchos, or cowboys, historically prepared their own meat: on rotisseries in front of an open fire (Fogo de Chão translates as "bonfire"). Unlike most upscale American steakhouses, where diners pay for each individual item they order, Fogo de Chão charges a single price for a meal. While restaurants do have buffets where diners can get salad and side items, Fogo de Chão is known for the chefs who wander the dining room carrying various cuts of meat on skewers, slicing off pieces as desired (diners are given a card with a red side and a green side with the instructions to turn up the green side when they want meat and the red side when they have enough). The restaurant grills a variety of meats, from sirloin and filet mignon to chicken, pork sausage, pork ribs, and lamb.

Other International Restaurants

Many of the dishes discussed above can be found at international restaurants, even if those restaurants are not specifically international barbecue restaurants, and some of the dishes may begin appearing at American-style restaurants, particularly those specializing in steak or other beef-heavy meals. As of the writing of this book, beef prices are high and will probably remain high for the foreseeable future, as more and more American beef is exported worldwide, particularly to China. The high prices are causing some restaurant chefs to be creative in the cuts of beef they use. For example, a cut from the shoulder referred to as the petite tender is relatively small (only one serving), flavorful, and, most importantly for restaurants, inexpensive. The only question for restaurant chefs is what to do with it. Anthony Dee, the corporate executive chef at Eddie Merlot's, a small steakhouse chain, was quoted in *Nation's Restaurant News* as considering using it in a Korean barbecue dish. "Bulgogi in a restaurant like ours wouldn't really fly," he said, and added that "maybe I could do some version of it."[26] Basing dishes on international barbecue recipes gives chefs a different way to approach cuts of meat that do not easily fit into American-style dishes.

American Barbecue Goes International

In the same way that international barbecue restaurants have begun appearing in America, American-style barbecue restaurants have started appearing in other countries. Bodean's BBQ, in London, bills itself as "London's Original BBQ Smoke House." Their website mentions that their barbecue is Kansas City style. The website for Blues Bar-B-Q in Paris states that it is "the first American Barbecue restaurant in Paris."[27] Both of those restaurants push their American-ness: Bodean's shows sporting events from American ESPN, while the interior of Blues Bar-B-Q includes a Texas state flag and paraphernalia from the University of Texas. Along with the restaurants that exclusively serve barbecued food, there are also a number of restaurants internationally that specialize in American-style food that include a barbecue item or two on the menu. Jazz City, an American-style restaurant in Sydney, Australia, includes a Backyard BBQ Beef Burger which, as at many restaurants in the United States, only has the "BBQ" in its name because it has barbecue sauce on it.

5

BARBECUE IN THE ARTS AND POPULAR MEDIA

B arbecue appears in a wide range of types of popular culture, from books to movies to music to Internet websites. Its appearance in popular culture is a reflection of barbecue's place in American culture, but barbecue sometimes picks up additional cultural baggage when it is used by creators of popular culture. In the 1800s barbecue appeared in writing about the South, since it was largely a Southern phenomenon, while by the early 20th century it also picked up an association with the West. Barbecues are social affairs, so writers sometimes use barbecues to show groups of people interacting.

LITERATURE

Because the written forms of popular culture encompass so many types of writing, barbecue has appeared here in many different ways. Some specific types of writing, like cookbooks, feature barbecue recipes, while other types of writing, like poems or travelogues, have examined other aspects of barbecue.

Barbecue and Cannibalism

In the 2008 book *Savage Barbecue*, Andrew Warnes contends that barbecue had little, if any, connection to Native Americans, and was instead a tradition invented by Europeans. As Warnes writes, the primitive cooking style of barbecue

A 1593 representation of cannibals in the New World. Courtesy of the Library of Congress, LC-USZ62-45105.

contrasted with the Europeans' more civilized cooking styles in the same way that the natives perceived barbaric civilizations contrasted with the Europeans' more advanced civilizations. Warnes's argument is overstated, but he is correct that, in the past, barbecue has been associated with that most primitive of customs, cannibalism.

A few examples show the association. The first is from the first appearance of "barbecue" in the English language, Edmund Hickeringill's *Jamaica Viewed*. Hickeringill was an Englishman assigned as a captain to Jamaica, and he composed a very early description of the colony. Among other things, he wrote that, when high-ranking natives died, their slaves were supposed to be killed and burned on a pyre with their owner, but sometimes the slaves were "Barbacu'd and eat[en]."[1] The accusation of cannibalism does not seem to be merely an example of a European assigning a primitive custom to a group he believed to be primitive since, as he writes, instead of being eaten the slaves were sometimes sold to the English. Using the word barbecue was probably an appropriate way to describe what happened to the unfortunate slave, and it is interesting (although grotesque) that a method for cooking animal meat was also applied to cooking human meat. Barbecue also appeared in association with cannibalism in a satirical British poem published in 1867, but with a twist at the end of the poem that contrasted the primitives with the British. In "The King of the Cannibal Isles," the king tells about the many people he has eaten, including "whole troups / Of Lord May'rs in soups," although he is becoming "a-weary / of mission-eery / and traveller barbecue." Instead of eating people, he decides to move to England to eat "London-killed veal . . . a dish that is fit for savages!"[2] Presumably, this was during a time of concern about the quality of English meats.

The Geographic Connection in Writing about Barbecue

During much of the 20th century, when barbecue was mentioned in writing, it was often associated with a particular geographic area, and depending on the area it was associated with, the writer picked up on an existing narrative about that area. The three areas writers usually associated with barbecue were the South in general, the West focusing on Texas, and the West focusing on California. When making a connection between barbecue and the South, writers often alluded to a pre–Civil War past when upper-class whites depended on enslaved blacks for labor (but this was always presented in a positive way); when writing about barbecue and Texas, cowboys cooking barbecue were usually discussed; and when writing about barbecue and California, authors usually alluded to modernity and newness. This geographic association might or might not be independent of the specific location a writer wrote about. For example, a newspaper article about barbecuing in Dallas, Texas, would probably mention cowboys barbecuing on the open prairie, even if the article was specifically about a brand new barbecue restaurant in downtown Dallas that had nothing to do with cowboys. An article about a backyard barbecue in Chicago might mention that it was a part of the barbecuing trend that came out of California, even if there was no real connection between the barbecue in Chicago and the state of California. Making the connection to the geographic location gave the writers a particular preexisting narrative they could tap into and use in their article.

The connection between barbecuing and the South goes back well into the early 1800s, but the particular narrative that sprung up around barbecuing did not evolve until the years after the Civil War. This is what has been called the "Moonlight and Magnolias" view of the South, the idea that the South was a place of tradition and peace, where white supremacy was cheerfully accepted by the blacks who served the whites. This narrative was popular in the years before the civil rights era, but afterward became difficult to perpetuate because it did not align to the reality of what was happening in the South. When it came to barbecue, this narrative had some truth to it: Blacks were the typical cooks on plantations both during and after slavery, and barbecue was commonly associated with blacks in the South.

This narrative can be seen in a few different magazine and newspaper articles from the 1940s and 1950s. In January 1942, *Vogue* published an article titled "Texas Plantation Party"—while another narrative around Texas will be looked at below, this particular article uses the Moonlight and Magnolias view of the South rather than mentioning cowboys, and the use of the word "Plantation" puts this article firmly in the deep South rather than in the West. The article is three pages long, two of which feature full-page photos; the third page contains four smaller photos and some text. The text informs the reader that the barbecue in question took place at a working cotton plantation near Galveston, Texas. The "guests motored, in true Texas fashion, a careless, hundred-odd miles, arriving just before two o'clock."[3] Once there, they dined "at a long table, under the cedars near the house," on chicken, pig, and baby goat, all of which had been cooking since the night before. Behind the guests "stood old 'Uncle' Green, the cook—long, lean, and dark, wrapped in a huge white apron." After the barbecue the guests were treated to Negro spirituals, sung by a group of blacks, and then they toured the plantation, "past the little cabins, the fields of corn and cotton, the herds of Hereford cattle." The photos complement the text, and further bring out the vision of the South seen in the text. One full-page photo shows the diners sitting at a table under the trees, attended to by black servants. Another shows seven black performers singing spirituals after the meal, as the white guests look on. One page has a collection of four photos. At the top of the page, black gardeners tend the lawn of the plantation house. Another photo shows "Uncle" Green (who is black) standing over the barbecue pit, while a third picture features black cooks cutting and serving meat to a few white guests. A last photo shows blacks standing in front of, as the caption indicates, "one of the dozens of 'field hands' cabins at Deer Hills," which is the name of the plantation. Taken as a whole, the article sticks with the Moonlight and Magnolias vision of the South, particularly in its portrayal of the roles of blacks and whites. Whites live lives of leisure—the barbecue guests spend an hour driving to the barbecue in the middle of the day, and have plenty of time for the barbecue, the singing, the tour of the plantation, and the drive home. The whites presumably have this leisure because the black servants are hard at work cooking and serving the meal. However, the article's focus on black labor serves to put blacks, essentially, at the center of the article. Black workers appear in all six of the photos that accompany the article, while whites only appear in half of those photos. Only three people are named in the article text: the plantation owner and his wife ("Mr. and Mrs. D. W. Kempner") and the black barbecue cook, "Uncle" Green. In this article, because of the text and the photos, whites recede into the background while blacks are firmly in the foreground.

A second example, from 1951 (nine years after the previous example), is a more typical example of the Moonlight and Magnolias portrayal of the South. With a close reading, this article also says quite a bit about race relations in the mid-20th century, and about how blacks and whites interacted when it came to food preparation. "Sea Island Picnic" was written by Clementine Paddleford, one of the most popular food writers in the 1950s and 1960s. At the time the article was published she had a daily food column in the *New York Herald Tribune* and a weekly food column syndicated in newspapers across the country; "Sea Island Picnic" appeared in her national weekly column. For the article, Paddleford traveled to a corporate-owned island just off the coast of Georgia, where she dined on barbecue prepared at the only hotel on the island. Paddleford set the stage in her typically florid writing style, and she so closely followed the Moonlight and Magnolias view of the South that she, in fact, writes about the moonlight. "The moon held a semi-tropical beauty to make the heart ache for things gone by," she writes, as she describes walking away from the campfire. "Here on the islands during Colonial days flourished a luxurious and colorful life. The islanders formed an aristocracy of wealth and power and dwelt each to himself, confessing allegiance only to King Cotton of whom they held their domains in fief. Gone! All is gone."[4] A cool island wind hurries her back to the fire. "The Four Souls Quartet was warming to moonlight, to fireshine, to beer—'Put on my shoes, walk all over God's Hebben.' Long fingers of flowing moss dripped from the oaks, swaying to every little push of the breeze."[5] Like the previous article, Paddleford writes about the lives of luxury whites experienced while, again, a black singing group (pictured in a photo that accompanied the article) provides entertainment.

The "Sea Island Picnic" was actually a barbecue, and when it comes to describing the pitmaster, Paddleford's descriptions are strangely vague. Ben McIntosh was the pitmaster, and he was most likely black, but Paddleford never explicitly says so. The sole physical description Paddleford gives of McIntosh is that he "was a dark shadow tending the chicken over a pit of red-eyed coals."[6] If she does not clearly state his race, she does provide a clue to it in the way he talks: she quotes him talking in dialect rather than standard English, much like she quoted the all-black quartet as singing about "God's Hebben." Her exchange with McIntosh is a good illustration of both race relations at the time and the control blacks had over food preparation (and how they could lose that control). Paddleford's goal as a food writer was to obtain a recipe to print in her column, and McIntosh's boss asks him to give her the sauce recipe in language that is somewhere between a request and a command: "Tell her how you do that sauce, won't you, Ben?" McIntosh responds with a "Yassir," and then says that he does not have a standard recipe. "I takes some vinegar, I takes some ketchup," he says, instructions that are useless for Paddleford, whose recipes were repeatedly tested by home economists before being printed.[7] Luckily for her, McIntosh's boss gives her a good recipe: "I've seen that sauce made hundreds of times," he says. "Do it this way." And then she lists the recipe.

A second location often mentioned by writers who wrote about barbecue is what might be called the Cowboy West, often centered on Texas. In this narrative, barbecue comes from the cowboy culture of the late 1800s, when high cattle prices in the East and vast numbers of cattle in the West (particularly in Texas) combined to put cowboys in high demand. That this narrative focuses on Texas rather than other states is understandable, for two reasons. First, many of the largest cattle ranches were located in Texas, and the longest cattle drives began in Texas after the Civil War as cowboys moved enormous herds of cattle north to railways in Colorado, Kansas, and Missouri. Of course, Texas was in no way the only cattle state in the late 1800s—with cattle prices remaining high through the 1880s, ranches sprang up throughout the plains states during that time. However, something else happened to make cowboys and Texas synonymous in many Americans' minds. In the years after the Civil War, slavery was a topic few Southerners wanted to talk about. In states like Georgia and Mississippi, local history was inexorably tied to slavery. In Texas, though, there was another narrative they could use to talk about the past, one that focused not on the slavery that made Texas break off from the Union but instead on the cowboys who were so important to the state's economy. By focusing on cowboys, the historical narrative could also encompass events like the Alamo, as well as gunslingers and desperadoes, if one loosened the definition of "cowboy" from a word that indicated an occupation to a word that referred to anyone who rode a horse anywhere in the Western states. Barbecue's connection to the cowboys must have seemed logical in that these were men who lived their life among beef—surely barbecues must have been happening all the time.

There is a connection between cowboys and barbecuing, but it is the same connection most people in the South had to barbecuing—they sometimes ate barbecue. Food writer Lolis Eric Elie discussed the connection with B. Byron Price, executive director of the Cowboy Hall of Fame and Western Heritage

Center in Oklahoma City, who has researched the subject. According to Price, cowboys ate barbecue when they stayed in one place for an extended period of time, like a week or so at headquarters. When they were out moving cattle there was not enough time to cook barbecue (which might take twelve hours), and when they were moving they also did not have access to the right kind of meat to barbecue—when they needed meat they usually killed a calf, which did not give them that much meat. "I haven't seen a single mention of a barbecue sauce, much less any recipe of any kind," Price said. "Barbecuing became obviously more prevalent later on, I'd say from about the last quarter of the nineteenth century to World War II."[8] He traced the popular link between cowboys and Texas to the Texas centennial of 1936, when the state received quite a bit of national publicity. Price went on to say that, by 1936, some of the oldest barbecue places in Texas, like Kreuz Market, were operating, but they were selling mostly sausage, not beef. Of course, barbecue would have come to much of Texas the same way it came to most of the American South: through the influx of slave owners and their slaves, moving west across the continent. The rewriting of the story of Texas described above not only made Texas history, focusing on cowboys, a proper subject after the Civil War, but in the process also wrote blacks out of the state's history entirely, leaving a question mark in terms of where barbecue came from.[9]

The cowboy connection has often been mentioned in articles about barbecuing. A syndicated article appearing in the Corpus Christi, Texas, newspaper in 1971 focused on barbecuing in Texas and repeated a few dubious stories about its history. "I have heard that barbecue came about when cowboys gathered about campfires and cooked their low grade beef," the author wrote, "that which was not acceptable for the Northern markets. To enhance the flavor of the poor meat, they made a sauce with whatever ingredients they had on hand."[10] Grading is, of course, done at a slaughterhouse and not on the prairie, and during the late 1800s meatpackers would have accepted almost any animal that made its way to the slaughterhouse. One of the assertions that shocked readers of Upton Sinclair's *The Jungle*, published in 1905, was that meatpackers merrily slaughtered animals that were obviously diseased while government inspectors were either distracted or had gone home for the day.

The author of that article also managed to take an old story about the origin of the word "barbecue" and give it a Texas connection. The story, which the Oxford English Dictionary has called "ridiculous," is that the word comes from a French description of barbecuing a whole animal: *barbe a queue*, beard to tail. The Texas connection written about in that article is that, supposedly, a group of Frenchmen wandered into Texas from Louisiana, killed a calf, and barbecued it.

A few years before that article appeared, Walter Jetton, who became famous as Lyndon B. Johnson's barbecue chef while Johnson was in the White House, published a cookbook in which he wrote that he believed "that barbecue started in Texas in the old cowboy days." His explanation was that cowboys on the range took jerky, or dried, lean beef, with them to eat because it could be stored without refrigeration for weeks "without too much of a toxic effect. It might kill you or me, but these cowpokes were mostly young and tough." Since jerky only required lean meat, once the cowboys killed a cow they had quite a bit of meat left over, so they roasted it over a fire, and this became the modern barbecue (interestingly, in Jetton's telling the cowboys developed the barbecue themselves, but they learned how to make jerky from the Indians).[11]

A significant aspect of the Texas cowboy origination story is that it disregards a population group that looms large in the history of Texas and that also has a strong barbecue culture: Mexicans and Mexican Americans. Barbacoa, which in this case is meat from a cow's head that has been cooked underground, is still very popular among Hispanics in south Texas. Even though Mexican culture has had an impact on Texas, during the 19th and 20th centuries white Texans have tried to minimize the impact of Mexican culture, and so barbecue in Texas is popularly believed to have come from white Europeans (either cowboys or grocers) rather than blacks or Hispanics.

A third location often associated with barbecue during the 20th century was California. By the 21st century this association had almost completely faded away, but during its heyday, around the 1960s, California was often mentioned in conjunction with barbecue. When journalists wrote about barbecue and mentioned California, they tapped into a narrative with two important parts. First, the narrative focused on modernity and contemporary trends, in the same way that the Southern narrative tapped into an image of bygone years. Second, the California narrative played fast and loose with the definition of barbecue. The postwar years were, after all, when barbecue went mainstream, when the popular definition of barbecue shifted to being a synonym for outdoor grilling.

An example of connecting California and barbecue comes from *The General Foods Kitchens Cookbook*, published in 1959. As was mentioned in chapter 2, the book provides a menu for a "California barbecue," which is certainly not a traditional Southern-style barbecue. The complete menu is avocado-grapefruit salad, charcoal-broiled steak, baked potatoes with sour cream and chives, buttered broccoli, pineapple fruit bowls, and coffee. Of these dishes, only the steaks were to be cooked on the grill. The introduction to the menu is a good example of the California narrative popular in the postwar years. "From Seattle south to San Diego, there's scarcely a house on the Pacific Coast without its outdoor dining place—patio, lanai, terrace, or barbecue corner. And the Far Westerners, who live outdoors for perhaps more of the year than anybody else in the country, take meals outdoors as a matter of course." The authors of the book went on to write that Westerners had "developed outdoor cookery to a fine art, and will try just about anything on their grills. But when they invite their friends over for an outdoor meal, you can be pretty sure it's going to be steak—and a whopper of a steak—cooked over charcoal to a harsh darkness on the outside, and a warm pink within."[12]

Barbecue in Fiction Writing

Barbecue appears in fiction, often associated with the geographical ideas discussed above. For example, the classic Western *The Virginian*, published in 1902, features a barbecue early in the book where the title character meets the local schoolmarm, his love interest in the book. The author obviously made the connection between cowboys and barbecue, but the barbecue itself (that is, the cooking and the eating) is not described at all; most of the chapter devoted to the barbecue centers on conversations held while the guests danced. There is, however, a strange parallel to the *Vogue* article described above, where guests at a Texas barbecue travel long distances to attend, as the Virginian travels 118 miles, by horseback, to attend the barbecue (when he arrives his horse is given food and he is given whiskey). The only description of the barbecue occurs after it is over: "The fiddles were silent, the steer was eaten, the barrel emptied, or largely so, and the tapers extinguished."[13] *Gone with the Wind*, set around the time of the Civil War, also includes a scene set at a barbecue. The 1936 book takes place in the South and very much uses the Moonlight and Magnolias view of the South. Like *The Virginian*, *Gone with the Wind* uses the social aspect of the barbecue to advance the plot, as the barbecue is where Scarlett O'Hara first meets Rhett Butler. Slaves are portrayed as being very much a part of the lives of the protagonists of the book, and the barbecue scene includes descriptions of slaves cooking and serving, and also having their own barbecue behind the barn, away from their white owners.

Travelogues

During the 19th century, European visitors crisscrossed America, and many of them wrote about their experiences. While barbecues are not mentioned in some of the more famous travel accounts, such as those by Alexis de Tocqueville or Charles Dickens, they were occasionally mentioned by writers who wanted to give their readers insights into America. One example was published in 1838 in *The Monthly Magazine*, a magazine from London. "Sketches of Kentucky" was written "By an Englishman from the Backwoods," and described the landscape ("beautiful woodland pasture, extending as far as the eye can reach") and people of Kentucky ("a race of people frank and open in their manners").[14] The author also described a political barbecue in Frankfort, beginning with the tradition's supposed origin—essentially, that Kentuckians were predisposed to both visiting each other and arguing about politics, and since their houses were too small for very many to gather at once, their entire affair was moved outside, to "some pleasant grove in the vicinity of a cool spring."[15]

Today, there are travel books that focus specifically on barbecue. Vince Staten and Greg Johnson's *Real Barbecue* describes the best barbecue restaurants the authors visited while traveling across the country, with several paragraphs devoted to each restaurant. Lolis Eric Elie's *Smokestack Lightning: Adventures in the Heart of Barbecue Country* recounts his travels with a photographer, looking for both good barbecue and also the personal stories behind barbecuers and barbecue restaurants. *Texas Monthly* publishes annual lists of the best barbecue restaurants in Texas, and other food- and travel-related magazines also occasionally publish articles on restaurants and barbecue-related events (such as festivals) around the country.

Cooking Literature

Barbecue's appearances in cooking literature parallel its appearances in American culture in general. Until the years around World War II, barbecue was popular in the South and something of a peculiarity outside of that area, but after World War II, barbecue moved to the mainstream, both in American society and cooking literature.

The earliest cooking literature in America was cookbooks, and the earliest of these were copies of English cookbooks, printed in either America or England. Barbecue occasionally appeared in British cookbooks, but the concept came from the colony of Jamaica, rather than the mainland American colonies. For example, *The Experienced English House-keeper*, by Elizabeth Raffald, from 1769, included a recipe titled "To barbicue a Pig," where the cook roasted a stuffed young pig for four hours. Those types of dishes made their way into American cookbooks in the next century, although it is difficult to tell if the American cookbook writers modified the British recipes or created their own. When barbecue recipes did begin to appear in cookbooks, they were usually those written by Southern authors. Both *The Virginia Housewife*, from 1838, and *The Kentucky Housewife*, from 1839, contain recipes for barbecued dishes, although *The Virginia Housewife*'s barbecued shoat recipe, discussed in chapter 2, is a baked dish, as opposed to the more traditional barbecue described in *The Kentucky Housewife*. Barbecue recipes were rare, though, in cookbooks that were meant for a mainstream audience and that did not have a connection to the South. *Miss Beecher's Domestic Receipt Book*, from 1846, and Elizabeth Lea's *Domestic Cookery*, from 1851, were two of the more popular cookbooks of the mid-1800s, and neither contains any reference to barbecue.

By the end of the century, cooking literature was more or less defined by the home economics movement. Home economics tried to professionalize housewives' work by studying the best techniques for women to use in their work, and to train women in that work in schools and colleges. Cooking was a central focus for home economists, and they wrote cookbooks, academic journals, textbooks, and curriculum for schools. Barbecue was not a good fit for this literature for two reasons. First, barbecue was strongly identified with the South, and the early leaders of the home economics movement were New Englanders who believed their own foods were most representative of American foods. While the overall focus of the movement was on professionalizing housewives, there was also a strong tendency to see the movement in terms of educating and Americanizing immigrant women so that they could provide proper meals to both their own families and the families of their prospective employers, when they would be employed as cooks. The baked beans, cornbread, and clam chowder of New England were of course proper foods for a new American to cook; barbecue was more than a little suspect.

A second problem with barbecue was that it was the antithesis of home economics cooking. *Perfection Salad* is the title of a history of the early home economics movement, and the book is named after a dish popular in the early 1900s which was, essentially, a lettuce salad suspended in a mold of gelatin. Here, nature, represented by the lettuce leaves, was held in place by the skill of the cook, in the form of the gelatin. The cook had won out against nature, which was a main goal of home economics. Barbecue was the opposite of all of this. Barbecuing happened outside, in nature, on rough plank tables in shady glens. Standardization was a major preoccupation for home economists (they are the ones who determined just how large measurement cups and spoons should be, for example), and the process of barbecuing was impossible to standardize. Cooking time and cooking temperature were just too variable to result in a particular recipe. The other problem with barbecue, of course, was that it was so masculine: men were always the cooks at barbecues, and they were often the majority of the eaters. This was not the sort of thing home economists were interested in, and so they largely ignored its existence.

In Southern cookbooks, however, a strange sort of hybrid barbecue recipe appeared in the 19th and 20th centuries, and still shows up in recently published cookbooks. The method of cooking those dishes is neither grilling nor slow cooking for hours, but more frequently, roasting in the oven. The recipes are curious because they come from a culture with extensive experience with traditional barbecuing. A very early example is "To Barbecue Shoat," a recipe that appeared in 1838 in *The Virginia Housewife*. A shoat is a young pig, and the recipe directs the cook to take a front quarter of the pig (minus the leg), stuff it with "rich forcemeat," and put it in a pan with water, garlic, salt, pepper, red wine, and mushroom ketchup, a condiment formerly at least as popular as tomato ketchup. The dish is baked until the meat is sufficiently cooked, and then the drippings in the pan are thickened with butter and flour. This results in roasted pork with gravy, something very different from what most people would call barbecued pig. Ninety years later a recipe for Barbecued Chicken appeared in a church cookbook from Cameron, Texas. The recipe has the cook roast a chicken in the oven in a pan of water for a few hours, then add more ingredients to the water to make a barbecue sauce that is spooned over the chicken.[16] A more recent example comes from Paula Deen's *The Lady & Sons Savannah Country Cookbook*, published in 1997. That book contains a recipe for Barbecue-Style Pork Chops that, by adding the word "Style," at least indicates that it is not a replacement for barbecue but rather an approximation of it. The recipe has the cook brown pork chops in a pan, then bake them topped with a mixture of tomatoes, ketchup, brown sugar, Worcestershire sauce, mustard, and salt.[17]

An indication of just why cookbook authors who must have been familiar with traditional barbecue included these kinds of recipes in their books is given in a cookbook from 1913, Martha McCulloch-Williams's *Dishes and Beverages of the Old South*. That book contains pages of descriptions of pre–Civil War barbecues the author had attended in her youth, but it also includes a recipe for barbecued lamb that is roasted in the oven. At the end of the recipe, though, she writes that the recipe "is as near an approach to a real barbecue, which is cooked over live coals in the bottom of a trench, as a civilized kitchen can supply."[18] McCulloch-Williams here sets up a contrast between the masculine barbecue, cooked outside over a trench and tended by men, and the feminine, "civilized" kitchen, where women worked to prepare food. As "real" barbecue was cooked outside by men, the imitation cooked in a kitchen was as close as a woman could get to producing barbecue.

In the 20th century, barbecue became a mainstream phenomenon; in the early 20th century, the definition of "to barbecue" shifted from describing a particular way of cooking meat for a long time at a low temperature to being a synonym for outdoor grilling. The process of this shift had a few components. First, a number of different trends converged, described below, to make outdoor grilling a popular activity. Even though this new activity was different from traditional barbecues in some significant ways (a smaller number of people involved, a very different way of cooking the meat, etc.), the activity was close enough to many people's conceptions of barbecue to warrant calling this activity a "barbecue" (and this new activity had its roots in the West, with no cultural tradition of the older-style barbecues).

A second component of the shift in meaning was the popularization of the new definition of "barbecue" in women's magazines and other cooking-related literature. The barbecue fad might have died a quick death had it not been for the fact that this new kind of barbecue was phenomenally useful for two groups: food companies and producers of women's magazines.

Barbecue's usefulness for food companies is obvious. As barbecue became mainstream, a new type of meal was suddenly available to build marketing campaigns around. Much like the Thanksgiving meal, a set number of dishes quickly became associated with a barbecue meal, and food companies marketed their versions of those dishes as the proper ones to serve at a meal. Food companies sell both finished dishes and ingredients for dishes, so a major component of marketing since the early 20th century has been to offer recipes that feature a company's products as ingredients. Those recipes essentially extended the food companies' reach even further into consumers' lives. Women of the time could have purchased ready-made potato salad at their local supermarket, but many instead made their own, using recipes from advertisements in women's magazines.

Barbecue was also useful for producers of those magazines. A central problem of any publication produced on a fixed schedule is the question of what to write about next, and the popularity of barbecue gave writers a topic that could be written about for four or five months out of each year, with specific ideas recycled every few years. Barbecue's popularity rose not just because it was an enjoyable activity but also because it was heavily promoted in the magazines a majority of women read during the 20th century. Barbecue appealed to both food companies and women's magazines, and in the mid-20th century the food sections of women's magazines were, largely, extensions of the food companies, with food editors accepting story ideas and recipes from home economists at the food companies.

It should be noted, though, that in order for barbecue to be an acceptable topic for the women's magazines, the definition of barbecue *had* to change from what it had been. Traditional barbecue, the slow cooking at a low temperature, simply did not work as a topic for the women's magazines (which, along with the food sections of newspapers, produced the vast majority of cooking literature in the 20th century) for a number of reasons. First, while the concept of traditional barbecue is simple, the directions for it are fairly complex and involved, to the point where they rarely show up even in barbecue cookbooks. Cooking meat for ten or twelve hours is a process that requires a considerable amount of judgment regarding when the meat is fully cooked and when it should be turned or how much wood should be added for smoke. In talking to people who barbecue the traditional way, I found that all of them learned how to do it from a family member or a friend. It seems that the complexity of barbecuing is such that it must be experienced to be learned, rather than absorbed from written instructions. Even today, when traditional barbecuing is more mainstream than it ever has been, instructions for making traditional barbecue rarely appear in cooking magazines or cookbooks.

Another reason that traditional barbecue did not appeal to the women's magazines of the 20th century was its lack of potential variations. Looking through those magazines reveals that almost everything seems to have ended up on a grill, from hamburgers to steak to bologna to Spam. This variety meant that a nearly endless series of articles could be produced on the topic of barbecue, each article focusing on a different type of meat that could be grilled. Traditional barbecue focuses on only a few types and cuts of meat, for good reason, since this type of cooking often works best for tough cuts of meat.

Even before the women's magazines picked up on the barbecue trend, barbecue recipes began appearing in cookbooks aimed at men. This was an extremely small niche. Men's cookbooks usually dealt with outdoor cooking, particularly while camping or hunting. This was the only type of cooking that was generally seen as being proper for men to do, and many of these cookbooks were written by men. Frank Bates's *Camping and Camp Cooking*, from 1914, gave the following instructions for barbecued meat: "Ribs of mutton, thin pieces of beef, rabbits, squirrels or almost any other flesh can be prepared in this manner. Lay your meat on the broiler over hot coals, so as to singe the outside immediately. After a few minutes, move away from the intense heat a little and cook till done through, basting frequently with the following dressing"; the recipe given for dressing was fairly simple.[19] Vinegar, canned tomatoes, red peppers, black pepper, salt, and a little butter were the ingredients for the dressing, simmered together until well mixed.

A few things are notable about these two sets of instructions, one for barbecuing the meat and the other for making the sauce. Even at this early period, in 1914, "barbecue" is already being used as a synonym for outdoor grilling, rather than the more traditional definition of roasting over a low fire for hours. In the context of a book on camp cooking this can hardly be surprising; spending eight or twelve hours watching a chunk of meat cook would scarcely be an enjoyable job for anyone but the most dedicated barbecuer. In fact, the author offers something of an apology for the time involved in cooking this dish, adding at the end of the sauce recipe that "The preparation of this dish is a lot of work, but it pays."[20] Regarding the sauce recipe, the fact that the author refers to it as "dressing" rather than sauce means that the term "barbecue sauce" had not yet become common. The recipe itself is fairly standard, with peppers, vinegar, and tomatoes, but there are no sweeteners—no white or brown sugar, and no molasses. This is not entirely surprising because this was right around the time that ketchup became appreciably sweeter as manufacturers moved away from using benzoate, a preservative that was developing a reputation for being unhealthy, to using relatively large amounts of sugar to do the same job. Later, in many parts of the county, barbecue sauce would follow ketchup's lead in sweetness.

The idea of the outdoors became popular in the 1920s. There were probably two things that fueled this fascination with the outdoors. The outdoors—that is, forests and streams and campsites—became easier to get to with the popularity of the automobile, which allowed those Americans with cars to drive to whichever part of the countryside they wanted to, whenever they wanted to, without having to check train schedules and railroad maps. At the same time, the outdoors, in many people's minds, was becoming a more and more distant thing. The 1920 census was the first to find more Americans living in the city than small towns or the countryside, so thirty or forty years previously most Americans were appreciably closer to the outdoors than they were in 1920. Thus, as more and more magazine articles were written about motoring through the countryside, and as camping sites for motorists appeared across the country, there was an equivalent desire to bring the outdoors back home, or to look for it just outside the back door. This led to the development of the backyard barbecue.

Historian Ripley Golovin Hathaway has traced the development of the backyard barbecue to the convergence of a number of trends, including increased car ownership, the vogue for building and using porches, and the popularity of the backyard barbecue's immediate ancestor, the picnic, which also occurred in a strictly outdoor setting. Hathaway points out that the first article on backyard barbecue to appear in a national magazine was published in 1924. Simply titled "The Backyard Barbecue," the article ran in *Woman's Home Companion*, one of the most popular women's magazine of that time. The article's subtitle, "Just the right picnic for a big hungry crowd," linked this new type of social occasion to the outdoor meal most readers would have been familiar with.[21] The suggested menu is interesting because, in spite of this being the earliest article on the topic, the suggested dishes closely match what could be found at any later barbecue, including those of the early 21st century. Chicken, steaks, chops, and roasts are all suggested as possibilities for grilling. Potato chips; salad; a dish containing sliced tomatoes, cucumber, and onion; and fresh fruit and melon are all on the list, as is cottage cheese with sliced green peppers, which is not typical for today's barbecues. Milk, iced tea, and coffee are the suggested beverages. The 1924 article was the first of a new wave of cooking literature that focused on barbecues, a wave that continues to this day.

Looking through the cooking literature of the mid-20th century shows a progression in the audience's perceived knowledge of barbecuing, and World War II seems to have been a turning point in the maturing of the barbecuing public. Barbecue-related cooking articles from after World War II are not much different from the articles of today, with allowances made for different food preferences. Articles from before World War II, though, feel somewhat unformed, as if the authors were not quite sure of how much their audience knew about barbecuing. An example of this can be seen in *Sunset's Barbecue Book*, from 1939, two years before America joined World War II. The mainstream barbecuing trend came out of the West, and *Sunset*, the Western-oriented magazine, capitalized on the association as much as possible. Their barbecue book is divided into two parts, and each part shows its difference from more recent barbecue books. The first part of the book is made up of plans for building barbecue grills, with architect's drawings for each grill. One problem with writing about barbecue at this point was the fact that so few people actually had an outdoor grill, so early barbecue literature had to work to rectify that problem. All the grills in *Sunset's* book were permanent, and the plans ranged from a quick and easy grill consisting of two short, parallel cinderblock walls with a grate over the top, to a three-foot-square pit "to service approximately 350 to 600 persons."[22] Barbecue books today assume that the reader either owns a grill or can easily obtain one, and so the only information in 21st-century barbecue books regarding grills is often a brief description of the types of grills, leaving it to the reader to obtain whichever type of grill he or she desires. In the 1930s, though, there do not seem to have been many grills available to buy, so for most people the only option was to build their own (permanent barbecue structures were popular at that time, though, so building may have been preferable to buying whatever types of portable grills were available).

The second part of the book features recipes, much like today's barbecue cookbooks, but the types of recipes offered were different. Most of the recipes were for dishes that went along with the barbecue, not for items to be put on the grill. The book features a wider selection of side items than most barbecue books today, and items that may be surprising to encounter at a barbecue. Corn chowder is included, as is macaroni and cheese. Baked potatoes are there, understandably, because at that time, steak was a popular item for outdoor grilling. No all-purpose barbecue sauce recipes are included, only recipes for sauces that go along with specific dishes.

World War II ended in 1945, and after this barbecue (which in this case was synonymous with outdoor grilling) went mainstream. Thousands of barbecue-related articles appeared over the next several decades in magazines and newspapers, and many cookbooks focusing on barbecue were published. Looking at much of the barbecue literature of the mid-20th century reveals that authors were often in a quandary because of some conflicting ideas surrounding barbecue. Cooking was a woman's job, and so the proper audience for food literature was perceived to be women, as seen by the fact that much of the writing appeared in women's magazines. Barbecuing, however, was widely seen to be a man's job, with its connections to the outdoors and to hunks of raw meat, and so it stands to reason that literature about barbecuing, all those cooking articles and cookbooks, would properly be read by men. The problem was that a conflicting view, fairly widespread in cooking literature, held that men were natural-born cooks, and that it was women who needed to read the literature because they did not know how to cook. This caused problems for writers of barbecue literature because, by definition, they were writing to a group of people who did not need to read what the authors were writing.

There were reasons many people believed that men could naturally cook and women had to be taught how to do it well. On the female side, the home economics movement, which tried to professionalize housewives, had perhaps done too good a job convincing the public that home economics, which especially focused on cooking, was a necessary subject for all women to take in school. This was something of a zero sum game: In order to make home economics look like a necessary subject for schools (which would, in turn, bolster the home economists' credibility and employment prospects), home economists claimed that women were naturally inept in the kitchen. On the male side of the equation, two things made men look like good cooks. First, professional cooks were usually men. Second, while men rarely ventured into the kitchen, the kinds of cooking associated with them was cooking that was, at its heart, not very complicated and not technically challenging. Along with grilling, the only other cooking activity commonly associated with men was making pancakes on the weekend. Pancake mixes were widely available by the late 1800s, and these mixes simplified the cooking process. As for barbecue, grilling was a man's kind of cooking. It mostly involved putting pieces of meat on a grill and then watching them to make sure they did not burn too badly and that they were turned when they needed to be. This is not that difficult, especially when compared to something like making a cake. Making a cake has many points of possible failure, ranging from incorrectly measuring the ingredients (the ratios have to be precise) to having different layers of the cake cooked at different rates (pans should always be rotated midway through baking) to having part of the cake peel off while applying the frosting. Because grilling is easier, and because the cook can experiment quite a bit while producing a perfectly good piece of meat, men were perceived to be better natural cooks than women.

This attitude produced some notable dissonance in postwar barbecue literature. For example, the authors of the *Better Homes and Gardens Barbecue Book*, from 1959, realized they had a something of a difficult time on their hands. The book was named after one of the most popular women's magazines of its day, but having "barbecue" in the title meant that it should have been targeted to men. The introduction to the book indicated that it was targeted to both sexes, and the authors had a pretty good idea of just who did what at a backyard barbecue. "For Dad the chef: Here's all the how-to for thick, charcoal-broiled steaks, plump barbecued chickens, and juicy rotisserie roasts. . . . To keep Mom happy: Ideas for specially wonderful salads, vegetables, beverages, and easy top-it-all-off desserts. Shuck off that busy-day hurry-worry, and get the fire started. Coming up: A fresh-air feast!"[23] In short, Dad did the grilling while Mom did pretty much everything else. When the authors turned to speak only to men, though, their language became a bit confusing. At the beginning of a section on meats the authors resorted to buttering up the chef: "This is Dad's domain. Sit back, Mom; admire Chef. He has the fascinating how-to on big steaks, [and] other juicy meats that take to charcoal. There's rotisserie roasting, cooking on skewers, grilling whole meals in foil; plus how-to-talk-knowingly with the meat-man."[24] This language reflects the idea that men were natural cooks who should be admired, and who had "the fascinating how-to on big steaks, [and] other juicy meats that take to charcoal," but, of course, if they knew all about this, why would they have to read the book? This was a central problem in food writing aimed at men in the mid-20th century.

Other male-oriented food writing cranked up the he-man talk. The prewar *Outdoor Cooking*, from 1940, began with a chapter titled "Come and Get It! or Caveman Feeds Girl Friend." The caveman connection shows up often in writing about outdoor cooking, but the text of the chapter moved into strangely Freudian territory. "There's something free and easy about entertaining the girl friend at camp or anywhere in the open," the authors wrote, "with the old pipe and campfire hitting sixty, the hand roving into the nut sack or gypsy stew in the old black kettle, or slapping down a 2-inch sirloin on your spitting hot grid to show her a real sizzling steak in 15 minutes flat without making her nose curl up at the smell of smoke from too much fat dropping into the coals."[25]

The tension in barbecue books between men's real-life lack of experience in cooking and the perception that men are natural cooks still results in some odd cookbooks. *BBQ 25*, a 2010 book by Adam Perry Lang, is different from other barbecue books, starting with the pages it is printed on. Instead of regular paper pages it has pages made from stiff cardboard, the kind of pages usually seen in books for toddlers who enjoy sucking on books and drooling. True to its title the book contains twenty-five barbecue recipes, and the cover trumpets the fact that these are "Now made foolproof." The first few pages of the book are a "Glossary of Techniques" describing each type of technique used, and each technique is given a name like "season 'like rain'" or "kiss with smoke," which is then referred to in the recipes.[26] Each recipe is on a two-page spread, with color photos of the finished product and of some of the steps involved in making the dish, and each recipe has numbered instructions. While this is informative, there are also aspects of the book that insult the reader. Each page has elements that look as though someone wrote in the book, and one of the elements is the word "Start" with an arrow pointing to the already numbered step one in the recipe. After the last step it looks as though someone wrote "Done" and under-lined the word. These appear on each recipe in the book.

Once the barbecue fad caught on after World War II, articles and books about barbecue became a staple of the publishing industry, and continue to be to this day. The books that focus on barbecuing can be divided into several groups, the largest of which is traditional cookbooks (that is, books that feature page after page of recipes with little other material). The vast majority of these books use barbecue as a synonym for outdoor grilling, and usually completely ignore the older "low and slow" style of traditional barbecue. Barbecue cook-books tend to be filled with recipes for entrées, and if side dishes make an ap-pearance, it is usually in a small chapter at the back of the book. Other than the subject matter, there is little to differentiate these books from the many other cookbooks published each year.

Another type of barbecue book is one that is more reflective. These books often have aspects of memoirs to them, and sometimes take a more sociologi-cal approach to barbecue. The sociological approach can be seen in Lolis Eric Elie's *Smokestack Lightning: Adventures in the Heart of Barbecue Country*, in which he and a photographer crossed the country looking for good barbecue restaurants. The book is more than just a restaurant guide; Elie writes quite a bit about the connection between barbecue and different parts of American culture. For example, he travels to Mexia, Texas, for the Juneteenth celebration. Juneteenth is an African American holiday, a commemoration of the day Texas slaves found out they were free, and Mexia has a large, public barbecue during the celebration. Elie writes about the barbecue and the festivities surrounding it, but he also writes about how the celebrations used to be bigger, with more people involved, and he talks with locals about how things have changed in the local community over the years.

There are also hybrids of genres. For example, the subtitle of *Peace, Love and Barbecue*, by Mike Mills and Amy Mills, is "Recipes, Secrets, Tall Tales and Outright Lies from the Legends of Barbecue." This is a good description of the book, which is a mixture of recipes and memories from Mike Mills, who is well known among competition barbecuers for having won many of the biggest competitions, and who is in charge of a number of barbecue restaurants in Illinois and Las Vegas.

Magazines

As of this writing (2014), there are no magazines devoted solely to barbecue, but barbecue does appear often in some magazines. As described above, magazines featuring cooking advice and recipes often include barbecue recipes. Regional magazines like *Texas Monthly* regularly have articles on barbecue restaurants and festivals in Texas. Some barbecue societies have publications; for example, the Kansas City Barbecue Society publishes the *Bull Sheet* for its members, with lists of upcoming barbecue contests and advertising related to barbecuing.

MUSIC

Barbecue has traditionally been associated with African Americans, and the music that has come from black culture, such as jazz and blues, has many examples of the use of barbecue as a subject. Barbecue tends to be used in music in one of two ways. Many songs focused on barbecue are, simply, about barbecue. Frankie "Half Pint" Jaxon's "Gimme a Pig's Foot and a Bottle of Beer," from 1940, is about the singer's desire for something to eat and drink, although the way the lyrics are phrased makes it apparent that the singer is also itching for a fight. However, many songs that seem to be about barbecue use the food as a metaphor for something else. In Bessie Jackson's "Barbecue Bess," from 1935, the singer advertises her barbecue for sale: "I'm selling it cheap because I got good stuff, and if you try it one time you can't get enough . . . if you want my meat you can come to my house at twelve." One of the more well-known barbecue songs is Louis Armstrong's "Struttin' with Some Barbecue." The song originally had no lyrics, which would seem to mean the song should be taken at face value but for the fact that, in the black community of the time, barbecue referred to an attractive woman.

Old Hat Records has released an album titled "Barbecue Any Old Time: Blues from the Pit, 1927–1942," which features barbecue-themed songs. Among the artists included is Barbecue Bob, and the booklet included with the CD has a publicity photo of Barbecue Bob standing next to a barbecue pit, dressed in white cook's clothes, strumming a guitar.

MOVIES

Barbecue appears most often in movies as a type of gathering rather than as a type of food. It is generally used as a way to bring people together. For example, *Baptists at Our Barbecue*, a 2004 film, is probably best described as a Mormon romantic comedy. Tartan Jones, a thirty-year-old unmarried Mormon man, moves to the town of Longfellow, in an effort to shake up his life (the state Longfellow is located in is never defined, although it seems to be the American West). The population of the town is exactly split between Mormons and Baptists and, in an effort to bring the town together and to impress the woman he eventually ends up with, Jones arranges a barbecue for the entire town. The barbecue does not have its intended effect; the movie juggles a number of subplots, and the barbecue of the title is actually something of a minor occurrence in the film.

Barbecue has deep ties to African American culture, and barbecues show up relatively often in African American films. For example, *Johnson Family Vacation*, also from 2004, follows Nate Johnson and his family as they travel from Los Angeles to Missouri for an annual barbecue with the extended Johnson family. The barbecue includes a competition with nine Johnson families for the "Family of the Year" award, and Nate is in particular competition with his brother, for both the award and his mother's attention. The way "Johnson Family Vacation" uses the barbecue is interesting in that the competition brings Nate Johnson's immediate family (that is, his wife and children) closer together while the focus on the competition keeps them apart from their extended family. Prior to the beginning of the film, Nate and his wife moved into separate houses and split the children as well, but when they all arrive at the barbecue Nate's wife announces that not only are they still together but they are renewing their vows (Nate's mother expresses surprise that they are still together at all). While Nate's children play with their cousins there is no real bonding shown, but there are scenes of the cousins cheating at the games. In short, the movie plays against the expectations of barbecues bringing large groups together and instead focuses on the way barbecues can maintain existing conflicts.

TELEVISION

Because of its popularity in American culture, barbecue also appears on television, most frequently in reality television, but in other types of television programs as well.

Reality Television

Reality TV occupies a space somewhere between documentaries and scripted TV. Some shows are largely just "what happened," with crews filming the events and then putting together the program later, when editing the video. Other shows are much closer to scripted programs, although reality TV shows do not have writers or professional actors in order to keep the costs down (the low cost is the reason reality TV is so popular with TV channels). On those types of shows directors are more heavy-handed in suggesting scenes or in giving the on-air talent things to say.

Like most television shows, reality shows thrive on conflict. Higher-quality shows bring it about organically, by focusing on people in situations with a high amount of conflict (for example, people whose job is to repossess cars) or by building the show around a competition. Lower-quality programs build the conflict awkwardly by obviously pushing people into situations where there is conflict.

An example of the lower-quality show is *Mystery Diner*, which has an episode built around barbecue. The premise of *Mystery Diner* is that a restaurant owner has a problem of some sort (an employee is stealing money or a competitor seems to have stolen a secret recipe) and a group from the program helps the owner by using hidden cameras and undercover store employees who work for the program. The barbecue episode focused on Cooper's Barbecue, a Fort Worth, Texas, restaurant. The owner heard from customers and friends that a food truck in nearby Arlington had a barbecue sauce identical to his own, which was a family secret. At the beginning of the episode sauces from both establishments were analyzed by a lab, which declared them to be identical. The host of the program and his helpers then went on to help the store owner identify who was stealing the recipe.

There appears to be quite a bit of controversy on the Internet regarding the "reality" part of *Mystery Diner*. When performing a Google search for "Mystery Diner," the first link returned is to a page titled "Mystery Diner. 100% faked, i'll tell you why"; the second link is to the show's official website at the Food Network.[27] There are a variety of complaints about the show, ranging from the fact that store employees on some episodes can be seen appearing on other reality TV shows to inconsistencies between how restaurants on the show operate and how restaurants operate in real life.

In watching the *Mystery Diner* episode relating to the barbecue sauce recipe, it is difficult to tell how much is real and how much, if anything, is faked. The *Mystery Diner* team first focuses on the head chef, Bobby, who is responsible for making the sauce, and they find out that he makes it in front of the entire kitchen staff, holding back seemingly no secrets about the sauce. Both Bobby and the owner's nephew, who manages the restaurant, are approached by diners (working undercover for the show) who want to buy the recipe to bottle it. Bobby sends them to the nephew, and the nephew agrees to sell the recipe for $5,000 and 3 percent of the sales of the bottled sauce. When the owner finds out, he fires the nephew and sends him away.

The show hits some sour notes. The conflict in this episode largely comes from interactions between the restaurant owner and the show's host, Charles Stiles, while they watch hidden camera video of what is happening in the restaurant. Stiles constantly needles the owner, provoking responses from him as the owner fumes about the conduct of his employees. Another problem is the show's emphasis on the importance of the barbecue sauce recipe. Near the beginning of the program Stiles meets the restaurant owner and asks him about the secret to the restaurant's success. "Barbecue sauce," the owner says, and when Stiles repeats that phrase, the owner responds with, "No doubt about it." This seems surprising, given that the emphasis for almost any barbecue restaurant is the taste of the meat, not the barbecue sauce. At the end of the program the restaurant owner says that, because of what has happened, he has decided to start bottling and selling his barbecue sauce with his name on it. This means that his competitors, including food trucks, can openly use his barbecue sauce, which was the cause of the problem to begin with. (Ironically, when the nephew tried to sell the sauce he stipulated that Cooper's name could not be on the bottle and that the sauce could not be sold in the geographic region—two stipulations that would have avoided the problem of competitors using the sauce.) Ultimately, the danger of a competitor stealing Cooper's sauce recipe is probably not much of a danger at all. Cooper's uses a Texas-style cafeteria format for the restaurant, so the customer stands near the barbecue pits and tells the staff what meats they want, and the meats are served on butcher paper. Customers have the option to have their meat dipped in the barbecue sauce when it comes off the pit, or they can use the bottled barbecue sauce sitting on the table. There is quite a difference in taste between the dipped or bottled sauce because the pan of dipped sauce has large amounts of drippings from every other piece of meat that was dipped into it. That sort of taste is impossible to replicate in a bottled sauce, and so the authentic Cooper's "taste" is probably safe.

While Cooper's does exist as a barbecue restaurant, and the sauce may have been a family secret, there is nothing on this particular episode that makes the use of a barbecue restaurant stand out. The stolen barbecue sauce recipe could have been any stolen recipe from any restaurant, and in this way the show's focus on barbecue is essentially reduced to window dressing.

A second example of a reality show that had an episode focused on barbecue, and one that better brings out the importance of barbecue, is *Food Wars*, which airs on the Travel Channel. The premise of *Food Wars* is that, in most instances where there is a food that is identified with a particular place (such as cheesesteaks in Philadelphia or deep-dish pizza in Chicago), there are multiple restaurants that claim to have the best example of that food. The first third of an episode focuses on one restaurant that is prized for making a given food, the second third focuses on another restaurant that also has its supporters, and then the last third of the show is a blind taste test competition between the two restaurants. Because of the show's format, conflict is inherent in the program, and so the producers do not need to work very hard to bring out that conflict.

The *Food Wars* episode that focused on barbecue looked at the two famous barbecue restaurants in Lockhart, Texas: Kreuz Market and Smitty's. As was outlined in chapter 3, Kreuz Market was originally a grocery store and butcher shop opened by German immigrants near the turn of the 20th century, where unsold meat was sold as barbecue. Eventually, Kreuz Market became famous for its barbecue, and was sold to the Schmidt family. In 1999 Rick Schmidt, owner of Kreuz Market, felt that his sister Nina, who owned the building the business was housed in, was charging too much for rent, so Rick moved the business a few blocks away.[28] Nina opened her own barbecue restaurant, Smitty's, in the old Kreuz Market building, and so Lockhart, with a population of about 13,000 people, now has a number of famous barbecue restaurants (Black's Barbecue, also in Lockhart, is also nationally known). This episode of *Food Wars* focused on the competition between Kreuz Market and Smitty's.

The episode was both informative and entertaining. Camille Ford is the host of the program, and she is good at engaging people to talk with her, whether she is talking with a cook at Smitty's or sitting down to eat barbecue with a self-professed Kreuz Market "superfan." Rather than make the two restaurants seem like carbon copies of each other, the show points out differences between the two. Kreuz Market, according to the show, uses electric smokers for at least some of its meat, and a very standardized recipe for its sausage. Smitty's uses Kreuz Market's original barbecue pits, and the sausage is made up of roughly 85 percent beef and 15 percent pork (the same as Kreuz Market), except that the 85/15 ratio is simply a guideline. As a cook says, the actual ratio changes from day to day, and if he is not cutting any pork that day, there may not be any pork in that day's sausage.

The final part of the show is the blind taste test, on this episode judged by one fan of Kreuz Market, one fan of Smitty's, a local food critic, a rodeo star, and a local radio personality. The judges tasted both brisket and sausage from each restaurant and could only vote for one restaurant. The show lingers over each judge as he gives his vote, and, after the fourth judge has voted, it is a tie between the two restaurants. Ultimately, the final judge votes for Kreuz Market.

One problem with the program is its insistence that there can be only one winner and one example of the "best" barbecue. The difficulty with this attitude is highlighted during the taste test when one judge complains that, after blind tasting selections from both restaurants, one of the restaurants has excellent brisket while the other has excellent sausage. A further problem comes from the show's desire to make the stakes appear to be much higher than they actually are. Coming out of a commercial break late in the show the host says that this "barbecue food war between Kreuz Market and Smitty's is tearing apart the town," while showing images of a mob of people moving toward a building, and then the host says that the point of the taste test is "to finally decide who serves the best brisket and sausage in the Lone Star state," ignoring the fact that this is simply a taste test between two barbecue restaurants in a single town in Texas.

Unlike the *Mystery Diner* show, barbecue was an important aspect of the *Food Wars* episode. The program's producers show how the food is made, both in terms of the grinding of the meat for sausage and the actual cookers where the barbecue is made. That barbecue is the focus of an episode of *Food Wars* points to the passion many people have about barbecue; it also points to the idea that, for many people, there is only one restaurant that produces the best barbecue in town (and perhaps the best barbecue in the state).

A third example of a reality show that focuses on barbecue is *BBQ Pitmasters*, a series oriented around competition barbecuing. Instead of following teams that are competing in an existing competition, the program uses existing teams who compete specifically on the show. The format of each episode is simple: Three teams of two contestants are given particular meats to barbecue, and three judges then appraise the cooked meat. The winner advances to the next round of competition, with the winner of all rounds being awarded a certain dollar amount ($50,000 in the season examined below) and free entry into a specific barbecue competition (the Kingsford Invitational barbecue competition, in this season).

Unlike the other reality shows discussed above, *BBQ Pitmasters* is an hour long, and the producers have done a good job of designing a standard format for episodes that fills the time but also moves along at a brisk pace. By using a barbecue competition as the setting for the show, the producers usually do not need to resort to gimmicks to try to increase the pressure on the teams, and thereby to artificially increase the conflict as well. Competition barbecuing brings its own pressures and conflicts.

A closer look at one episode shows how *BBQ Pitmasters* handles its subject. This particular episode was filmed at the Hog Wild Festival in Mobile, Alabama, although it was likely filmed either just before or just after the festival, since the contestants set up in the middle of a wide open area with no one around them. Three pairs of competitors, each with a different competition name, from three different states, were involved, and each cooked barbecue in a different way. Only one person in each pair of competitors was introduced and named on camera, giving the impression that each team had, essentially, one chef and one assistant, although that may not have been the reality of the situation. The format for the show basically demanded this, though, because during the judging each team only sends one person to watch the judging and comment on it.

On this particular episode the competitors were Sara Horowitz, of Nacho Mama, from El Paso, Texas; Chuck Baker, of Barrel House BBQ, from Lynchburg, Tennessee; and Mark "Pig Daddy" Little, of Team Bibs, from Winston-Salem, North Carolina. The three judges are heavily involved in barbecue in one way or another. Myron Mixon is referred to on the show as "the winningest man in barbecue" because he has won many competitions, including grand champion at the Memphis in May competition on three different occasions. George "Tuffy" Stone was also involved in competition barbecuing, and is the owner of a restaurant named "Q Barbecue." Finally, "Big Bob" Gibson, the third judge, also owns a barbecue restaurant, and is a local judge brought in just for this particular episode.

This episode is from the program's fourth season, and over time the producers have made changes to the structure of the show. By the fourth season the producers seem to have found an overall structure that allows the show to flow naturally and also highlight the conflicts that arise during a cooking competition.

The program begins with the three sets of competitors lined up before the judges, who are seated on a raised platform. The competitors are briefly introduced, the judges are briefly introduced, and then the judges announce the meats that will be cooked for that episode's competition. On this particular episode, the meats were whole pork shoulder and chicken. As soon as they retrieve their meats from a cooler on the ground, the competitors move to their barbecue grills and begin cooking.

In the next part of the show, where the contestants cook their food and the judges talk to each other, *BBQ Pitmasters* differs from other reality shows in the element of education in the program. When the contestants go to their grills with their raw meat, the contestants first describe their grills, and onscreen graphics give more information about the grill and the method each competitor uses to cook the meat. On this episode, each contestant used a different kind of grill. Horowitz used a gravity-fed pit, and while she poured glowing coals onto wood packed into the pit, an onscreen graphic informed viewers that a gravity-fed pit is a "Pit heated by a chute of charcoal that burns from the bottom up, fed by gravity." Contestant Little brought a large indirect cooker and, again, onscreen graphics informed the viewer that this used a "Firebox set away from meat to cook indirectly." Baker brought a pile of cinderblocks that he assembled into a box measuring about a four-foot cube with a metal door, and the judges commented that almost any structure can be used to make good barbecue. During this part of the program, the cooks also talked about the wood they used, including hickory and fruitwoods.

This educational element shows up often during the program. Whole pork shoulder is a very large cut of meat that is probably not familiar even to many barbecuers, so while the judges discussed where it comes from, a graphic of a pig, showing the various cuts that come from a pig, appeared on screen. As the cooks began preparing the meat, each one described just how he or she planned to cook the meat and what tricks they planned to use to make a better tasting or better looking final product (one used an injection of whiskey and cola while another decided to use a fancy cut on the chicken drumsticks). The judges also talked among themselves about the challenges in preparing the foods, and just what the competitors needed to consider.

The competitors had twelve hours to cook the meat, so obviously quite a bit was cut from the program. With an hour-long show, the pace of the program might be described as leisurely, but in some ways it does a good job of mimicking the leisure involved with cooking barbecue (minus the alcohol consumption). Much of the enjoyment from the program comes in watching the teams good-naturedly rib each other, and also from seeing the teams realize that something has gone wrong and try to correct it (in this episode one competitor realized that the problem with a cinderblock barbecue is that it is very hard to modulate the temperature).

The last third of the program is the taste test, and much of this part of the program is taken directly from competition barbecuing. Each team puts pieces of finished meat onto a bed of greens, in a Styrofoam box, one box for each type of meat, and presents the boxes near the judges' table. Since the shows revolve around festivals, the person receiving the boxes is often a festival queen or someone else associated with the festival. Each team also randomly selects a number, one through three, that will be the number the judges use to identify the teams during the taste test.

The food is judged based on its taste, tenderness, and appearance in the box. The judges do not technically know which team fielded which box but there are likely ways they could ferret out information. For example, on this episode Sara Horowitz, who had attended culinary arts school, had cut her drumsticks so that they resembled lollypops, with all of the meat at one end of the drumstick. The judges knew she was formally trained as a chef while the other two competitors were not, and could possibly guess that that was her entry.

As the judges go through each box and make comments about it, the competitors sit in a tent, watching the judging on a video screen. This provides an interesting dimension to the judging; the competitors are vocally proud of the positive comments from the judges and usually acknowledge their negative comments, often saying that yes, they knew that the meat was too dry but they hoped the judges would not notice. At the end of the program, the judges announce their ratings, beginning with the third-place winner. The first-place winner advances to the next round and the chance to win $50,000 and a spot at the Kingsford Invitational barbecue competition.

While the show is squarely focused on barbecue, there are some possible criticisms of the program. For one, it does not show much of the realities of competition barbecuing. Competition barbecuing is expensive for the teams involved, in terms of both money and time, not only because they need to get themselves to the competition but also because they need to get their grills there as well, by driving them to the site. The expense involved may account for why one of the competitors on this particular episode (the team that built their grill out of cinderblocks) had never been involved in any competition before. This is a missed opportunity for the show: It would be interesting to know more about competition culture, how these people specifically make ends meet, and why they compete. Likewise, by skipping roughly eleven hours of the twelve the teams have to make their food, the program does not show the main component of barbecuing, which is the waiting. Again, it would be interesting to find out what the teams do during this time, and just what needs to be done at the grill during the hours the meat is cooking.

Cooking Programs

Cooking shows may be seen as the video equivalents to cookbooks, but shows are usually more oriented toward entertainment while cookbooks are more oriented toward providing information. While cooks may watch a show to find out about a new dish, they will probably use some sort of printed recipe when they themselves make the dish, either downloaded from the program's website or copied down from the television screen. In this way, cooking programs are usually less useful than cookbooks for actual cooking. However, when it comes to barbecue, the informational aspect of the show can be extremely useful for new cooks because so much of the barbecue cooking process is based on experience. For example, *Paula's Home Cooking*, with Paula Deen, has an episode where Deen makes what she calls Drunk Chicken, a dish usually referred to as beer can chicken, since an entire bird is propped up on a can of beer as it cooks, which keeps the inside of the chicken moist. The episode is similar to other cooking shows in that the audience watches Deen put together the various dishes for a meal while she talks about what she is doing. In this particular episode, though, she begins by visiting a hardware store and talking to a clerk about a drum grill, which resembles a barrel lying on its side with a door cut into it to access the inside. This is the type of grill she uses to cook the chicken, and her discussion with the clerk is informative for viewers. Later, when she puts the chicken on the grill, she shows the difficulty of placing the narrow beer can on the grate and warns of the danger of accidentally tipping over the chicken. When the chicken is nearly done cooking, Deen shows the viewer a tip for checking the chicken: If the legs and wings can be moved easily, the chicken is nearly done. Although these things can be communicated through print, video works more effectively. A more extreme example of video working better than print for communicating complicated information can be seen in the technique of butterflying pork ribs for Korean barbecue. Ribs are a tough meat that usually needs to be cooked for a long time, but butterflying makes the rib meat very thin and quick to cook. The technique, which involves continually cutting a section of rib and then turning the rib over, never quite cutting entirely through the meat, until the cook is left with a long, thin ribbon of meat, is complicated to explain in print but easy to understand on video.

Documentaries

There are a few documentaries that look at barbecue. For example, *Barbecue: A Texas Love Story* (2004) examines some of the cultural aspects of barbecue in the Lone Star state, although it focuses on restaurant food rather than individuals making barbecue. The filmmakers follow the University of Texas student barbecue club on some of their travels to taste barbecue around the state, but much of the film focuses on other groups and individuals, such as a restaurant owner who lost his restaurant in a fire, only to see other people from the community contribute money and labor to help him rebuild. The movie also has interviews with some of the reporters and editors at *Texas Monthly*, which has a yearly survey of the top fifty barbecue restaurants in the state. For one year's survey ten reporters traveled 21,000 miles and ate at 360 restaurants. *Barbecue: A Texas Love Story* is an interesting movie that does cover some of the important aspects of barbecue in Texas. However, it also falls back on the cowboy origin story in explaining its beginnings in that state, rather than discussing blacks who came west during slavery, or the German immigrants who moved in during the 1800s (which is somewhat odd since numerous scenes are filmed at Smitty's, in Lockhart, which is the archetypical German immigrant grocery store).

INTERNET

There is quite a bit of information about barbecue on the Internet, and the sites that have the information can roughly be divided into three types of websites. One source of information comes from the food and barbecue industry. Barbecue industry leaders like Weber (maker of grills) and Kingsford (charcoal) have websites with recipes and how-to videos for consumers. Food corporations like Kraft also have some barbecue recipes and information. A second source of information is non-industry websites that focus on barbecue. AmazingRibs .com is a good example of this sort of site, which covers all aspects of barbecue, from cooking to competition to reviews of products. Of course, a problem with privately run websites is that they either disappear or, more often, stop receiving updates and linger on, unchanged, for years. And a third type of site is that which is not specifically oriented toward barbecue but that has barbecue information. YouTube.com, for example, has many videos relating to barbecue that can be useful for someone without experience in cooking a certain type of food, or in using a certain kind of grill.

OTHER TYPES OF POPULAR CULTURE

Architecture

Architecture is also a part of popular culture. In this case, the architecture is that of barbecue restaurants, and as with all restaurants, the architecture of barbecue restaurants has two goals. The first is functional: to house the business, to keep out the elements, and to shelter the people and equipment inside. The second goal of barbecue restaurant architecture is to attract the customer's attention and to bring him or her into the restaurant. Of course, many barbecue restaurants that have been around for decades are housed in buildings that are not inviting at all, but, with the perverse logic that often goes with being a barbecue aficionado, this lack of invitation is itself an invitation.

Barbecue restaurant architecture has gone through a number of phases over the years. As has been discussed earlier in the book, the first places that sold barbecue were merely shacks set up along the road with no inside seating. These shacks were originally made simply to shelter the contents within, but with the development of the automobile, signs were added to attract customers' attention. Someone walking by, or passing on a wagon or horseback, could easily ask the attendant what was for sale, but someone driving a car at twenty or thirty miles per hour would have to slow down or stop to find out what was for sale, unless there was signage. The photo on page 164, taken near Fort Benning, Georgia, in 1940, shows the kind of large signs that sprouted up on roadside restaurants. As often appears today at independent restaurants, the signs advertise both the restaurant and branded products sold at the store. Because the brand owner often paid for the signs, the brand name is frequently larger than the store name; for example, on the right side of the photo "Dr. Pepper" is displayed much larger than "Big Chief Barbecue!" above it. The size of the signage is somewhat ridiculous when compared to the rest of the structure, as the signs are actually taller than the visible storefront beneath them. However, after the advent of the automobile, signs became an important and necessary part of restaurant advertising.

A particular thing to note about that photo is the area immediately in front of the building. The gravel area could be a parking lot or it could very possibly be a road that passes very near to the building. The photo on page 165, of a Pig Stand restaurant in Dallas, Texas, from the 1920s, shows cars parked along

Barbecue stand near Fort Benning, Georgia, from 1940. Note the profusion of signs where brand names are larger than the restaurant name. Courtesy of the Library of Congress, LC-USF34-056482-D.

the curb right next to the restaurant. The Pig Stand did not have inside seating, so customers either took their food elsewhere, ate while standing near the Pig Stand, or ate in their cars. Like many businesses of the time, there was no parking lot near the building; parking lots were a development that came slightly later in the transition from a horse-drawn/walking culture to a car culture. Again, the Pig Stand had ample signage to attract customers and let them know what was sold at the restaurant.

Another development in barbecue restaurant architecture came with changes in health regulations in the early 20th century. Restaurants were required to have solid floors instead of floors made of packed dirt or sawdust. Pit barbecues became illegal in most places, except for restaurants that were grandfathered in with the new regulations. As Robb Walsh has pointed out, the sanitary laws affected the racial characteristics of barbecue. In Texas most black-owned barbecue shops, which used pit barbecuing, had to shut down, while those owned by recent European immigrants (such as Kreuz Market or Louie Mueller's), which used brick pits in established buildings, continued to operate just as they had before the laws came into place.[29]

Pig Stand restaurant in Dallas, Texas, in the 1920s. From the collections of the Texas/ Dallas History and Archives Division, Dallas Public Library.

The barbecue places that survived grew slowly, often ending up with a ramshackle appearance as their owners expanded as needed, usually in a fairly random manner. Authors Vince Staten and Greg Johnson have called the resulting style the "Sowhaus" style of architecture: "a new wing on the . . . side, a take-out window out back, a picnic area, indoor restrooms. . . . The place has grown in all directions, like a sow fattened up."[30]

In the past few decades, as barbecue has shifted from a primarily regional food with limited popularity to food that is nationally known with a considerable popularity, two different styles of architecture have come to dominate barbecue restaurants.

The first style is a continuation and variation of the Sowhaus style mentioned above. In this style of architecture the building, both its interior and exterior, are mostly afterthoughts to the primary function of the restaurant: making barbecue. Not so much selling it, though; an emphasis on selling means an emphasis on marketing, which in turn means taking the time and money to improve the building by doing things like making it look more inviting or having better signage. This type of architecture is the type prized by many barbecue aficionados, and it is certainly possible to find examples of this style of architecture. One example is Smitty's, in Lockhart, Texas, about an hour from San Antonio, a restaurant that is often considered to be the epitome of central Texas barbecue (it was originally a grocery store that also sold barbecue).

I visited Smitty's the summer of 2013 and was struck by several aspects of the restaurant. According to its postal address, the restaurant is located along a fairly quiet downtown street one block from US 183, a busy highway that runs through town. In reality, though, the parking lot for the business fronts the highway, and customers usually enter through the rear of the building. It appears that there was originally an alleyway behind Smitty's, and then another row of buildings that fronted US 183, but those buildings seem to have been torn down long ago, and all that is left is a large dirt lot where customers park. Customers entering from the parking lot first come in to a very hot, small room where the barbecue pits are located, and where customers order, pay for, and pick up their meat. Most barbecue places in Texas indirectly grill their meat, and Smitty's is no exception, so, on the floor near the door, at one end of the pits, were a few burning logs whose heat was sucked into the brick pits. This made the room quite hot—on the day the author visited, the temperature outside was about 98 degrees Fahrenheit and the room was noticeably hotter than that. After picking up their meat the customers then move into the dining room, which was, thankfully, air conditioned. The dining room was a long, large room with lines of tables and folding chairs and a counter at one end. At the counter the customer orders, picks up, and pays for side items and drinks.

There are many aspects of the Smitty's experience that are unique. The only utensils given out are plastic spoons and knives; there are no forks. There are also no plates for the meat, which is given out on butcher paper. Customers pay for their meat in one room and the rest of their food in another, and there is no barbecue sauce, only hot sauce.

The uniqueness extends to the architecture as well, and is why Smitty's is a good example of that first type of restaurant, one that puts more care into making barbecue than into its architecture. In a town with two other nationally known barbecue restaurants (Kreuz Market and Black's Barbecue), Smitty's does almost nothing to advertise itself in the town other than having a few stand-up signs in the parking lot, near the highway running by the lot. (Black's has several large signs throughout the town and Kreuz Market's large building, standing by itself on the north side of town beside US 183, has several large signs on it.) Smitty's signage on the downtown street side (as opposed to the highway side) is minimal. The author's GPS directed him to park on the downtown street side, and there are a few signs for Smitty's hanging overhead on that side of the building, but no indication as to how to enter the building. The doors on that side of the building are painted black and the windows have dark tinting (which is not unusual in south Texas). The author entered one of the doors and found himself in what looked like an old grocery store, with shelves lining the walls, but otherwise completely empty. Another door to the room led to a hallway (painted black) that ran the length of the building (front to back), and that also led into the restaurant's dining room. The layout of the building indicated that it clearly began as a grocery store facing the street, but over time the barbecue pits in the back of the building became the focus of the business, so that the restaurant reoriented itself to face what had been the back of the building. The dining room has doors that face out to the street, but these are barricaded so that it is impossible to use those doors. There are no signs on the outside of the building that indicate which side should be entered by customers. Inside, there is not much in the way of signs that explain to a new customer just how the ordering and paying process works. It is hard to imagine this process (obtaining food and paying for it at two different places) existing in a brand-new business, except at a restaurant that is supposed to replicate this experience. In fact, the situation is almost entirely the same at Kreuz Market, which opened its doors only a few years before, with the exception that Kreuz Market does have signage indicating where customers should go first and second to order their food. In short, ordering and eating food at Smitty's is a complicated affair, and this complication is reflected in Smitty's architecture, with its warren of different rooms inside the building and overall lack of signage for customers.

This, then, is an example of the first type of barbecue architecture, one that was developed over a long period and that is focused on simply housing the business, rather than attracting customers or making an inviting atmosphere. The second type of modern barbecue restaurant architecture is oriented in the opposite way. It seeks to attract customers and make an inviting atmosphere. The more extreme versions of this type of architecture are obviously made by professionals, people whose work and training is not just in architecture but more specifically in the restaurant and food service industry. Of course, having defined these two types of architecture, it is important to point out that these are two sides of a continuum, and any particular restaurant may exist at any point along this continuum.

A set of restaurants on the other side of the continuum is the Famous Dave's chain. Those restaurants are professionally designed and decorated with the intention of attracting as many customers as possible. As a chain, they use a template for the layout and look of their restaurants that does not vary much based on location. The following observations come from the Manhattan, Kansas, restaurant, but other locations around the country look very similar.

At the Manhattan restaurant, the building is surrounded by a parking lot and clearly has a front door for customers. Inside that door is a small entryway with a host station; the host escorts patrons to their table. The restaurant is laid out with a large central seating area, with several smaller seating areas on either side of that. The tables at the booths that line the walls, and in the middle of the rooms, are set with checkerboard tablecloths and stands for paper towel rolls that function as napkins—the paper-towel-as-napkin motif is typical at barbecue restaurants.

The interior design uses two different themes that often appear in newer barbecue restaurants. The first theme works to make the impression that the restaurant has been in existence for a long time, and that the interior design has been thrown together in a haphazard style—essentially, an attempt to recreate the previously mentioned "Sowhaus" style of architecture. The walls are wood paneled, and the paneling is covered with signs and hung with bric-a-brac, like old pots and pans and calendars. Many of the signs have a pork theme, such as "Welcome to Hog Heaven USA" and "Swine Dining Area—No bone throwin' in aisle." Another large sign reads "Don't tell us how good it is just come back," and beside that, "Don't forget our Famous Dessert." Among all the wood paneling there is a large stone fireplace, somewhat incongruously placed between the main seating area and a side room, with a mantel featuring a picture of Robert Burns, and a stuffed elk's head mounted on the stone about halfway to the ceiling.

A second theme used in the interior decorating is that of the outdoors, in terms of eating barbecue while sitting in a backyard. The ceiling in the main dining area is open to the rafters, which are lined with strings of white lights of the sort sometimes strung overhead at evening backyard parties. Along one side of the room is a long open window that leads to the kitchen; above the window is what looks like the side of a roof. A colorful sign reading "Dave's Home Cookin'" is perched on one side of the roof, and the window and the roof give the impression that all of this is one side of a building, and customers are actually sitting outdoors, under the stars. Rudy's, a chain based in Texas, takes the outdoor theme much further by using a much larger main dining area filled with full-sized picnic tables and fake buildings along the walls that have real shingles.

The interior of the Famous Dave's restaurant does look professional and inviting, but the irony is that, in its attempts to recreate what one might think of as a real barbecue restaurant, the interior actually looks much more like an Applebee's or other chain restaurant, and much less like a barbecue restaurant that has been in operation for decades, and just happened into its interior decorating.

Barbecue Competitions

One major change to the world of barbecue since the 1980s has been the increasing popularity of barbecue competitions. The largest competition as of this writing is the American Royal, in Kansas City, which attracts hundreds of competitors each year, and was also one of the first competitions (the American Royal itself began as a cattle show in 1899, and the barbecue competition was added as an event in 1980).

Competition barbecue is, essentially, a sport, with several governing organizations with different sets of rules, a year-long calendar of competitions, and championship cook-offs at the end of the season. The Kansas City Barbecue Society, or KCBS, is by far the largest of the governing organizations, sanctioning over 400 contests in 2013 (that is, the contests use rules and judges from the KCBS, and contest winners earn points in the ongoing season). Other organizations are the Memphis Barbecue Network and the Lonestar Barbecue Society.

A competition I was involved in provides an example of what many competitions are like. The contest took place in Parsons, Kansas, a small town (10,000 residents) a few hours south of Kansas City, in mid-October 2013. The competition was part of the town's Balloons, Bikes, Blues & Barbecue Festival, an event with an explicit tourism component, sponsored by the local Chamber of Commerce. The competition essentially began on Friday afternoon as teams arrived and began setting up along two streets that bordered a large park. Most teams brought an RV to sleep in and several grills, ranging from inexpensive units available at any Wal-Mart to custom-built grills mounted on their own trailers. Only twenty-three teams arrived at the event, and because KCBS rules require twenty-five teams to be a sanctioned event, two of the teams split into two more teams to make up the difference.

On Friday evening a cooks' meeting was held that combined a recitation of the rules by two KCBS representatives assigned to the competition and a dinner provided by the event organizers. Teams were also issued the numbered Styrofoam boxes they would use to turn in their food. At some point during the evening all teams' meat was inspected by the representatives to make sure the meat was cold and that no preparation had been done, other than cutting fat from the meat. By eleven o'clock that night most teams had fired up their grills and begun cooking their largest pieces of meat. A KCBS competition focuses on four types of meat: pork ribs, pork shoulder, beef brisket, and chicken. During the night teams checked their fires and meat temperatures every hour or so—any longtime competitor has stories of problems that occurred during the night, from blown fuses on grill fans to pellet stoves, which slowly feed pellets of fuel to the fire, mistakenly feeding six hours' worth of fuel all at once.

The competition requires about one judge per team, and the judges arrived Saturday morning in time for a meeting at 10:30, when they were reminded of the contest rules. Judging began at noon, when teams had a ten-minute window to turn in their box of chicken, followed, at half-hour intervals, by the ribs, pork, and brisket. At the end was a final judging of what is technically an "anything else" category but which, at this competition, was desserts (not all teams enter this category because it does not count for KCBS points, but since it did bring both money and bragging rights, most teams entered). Each entry was judged for appearance in the box, taste, and tenderness. The winners of each category, and the grand champion, were announced about an hour after judging was completed.

In observing the competition, I noted a number of tensions that exist in competition barbecue. One set of tensions is between the public and private aspects of the event. The competition was inherently public. Anyone could enter as a competitor, provided they paid the entry fee. Grills were set up in the street, along a major park; people walking by were free to talk to the competitors, and most competitors were quite willing to talk to people. The competition was part of a major festival in the town, the type of event that towns and cities across the country rely on to bring in tourist dollars. At the same time, large parts of the competition were not oriented toward the public. At most competitions it is illegal for the competitors to sell the barbecue they make, and this results in a certain amount of confusion for members of the public who attend the competitions expecting to be able to purchase barbecue. The judging of the competition was closed to both the public and the competitors, and in the morning meeting, judges were reminded that they were not supposed to fraternize with competitors before judging. After the event, teams can see all scores the judges awarded them and other competitors, but those are merely numeric scores ranging between two ("Inedible") and nine ("Excellent"), and I sat with a team during the awards announcement that was clearly mystified that they placed first in one category and eleventh in another, in which they believed they would do well. In an event that was widely publicized in the local newspaper long before the event, large parts of it were closed to the public.

This leads to another set of tensions in competition barbecue, that which exists between the competitors and the judges. Competitions would not exist, of course, without the competitors, and competing is expensive in both time and money. The competitors do not judge the barbecue; that is left to judges who have gone through a half-day training session and who usually have judged many other competitions previously. The overlap between the two groups is quite small. From what I saw at the Parsons barbecue, judges tended to be at least a decade older than competitors and included many more women than participated in the competition. The judges do not know whose barbecue they are judging at any particular time, and the names of the teams are never later revealed to the judges. Rather than being paid in cash, judges are paid in barbecue. To judge the taste and tenderness of the barbecue, the judges place a sample in front of them, and anything they do not eat can be taken home (most judges bring plastic bags and a small cooler for just this reason). Like the competitors, the judges often travel long distances, and the food makes up for the time and effort involved in judging—as will be explored next, each box of meat submitted to judges costs hundreds of dollars to produce, and most of the resulting barbecue *tastes* like hundreds of dollars were spent to produce it. The barbecue I sampled at a barbecue contest was far better than anything produced at a restaurant.

Another set of tensions revolves around the expense of competition barbecue. It is a relatively expensive hobby for many contestants. Costs for each event include the entry fee for the contest, which is usually several hundred dollars; optional fees, such as the cost of a larger space at the event; and the cost of the meat. Teams generally bring two or three briskets, pork butts, and racks of ribs, as well as a few packs of chicken thighs, and the meat itself can add another few hundred dollars to the weekend cost. Most teams shopped for meat at their local grocery store, and Sam's Club has a reputation for having good barbecue meat (Sam's Club has further garnered support from competition barbecuers by donating meat to Operation BBQ Relief). Beyond a certain quality level (available at most grocery stores) competitors generally agreed that spending more money on higher-priced meat did nothing to help a team's chances of winning, and the epitome of the competitor with more money than sense is the team that purchases Wagyu beef for its brisket (no one brought Wagyu beef to the competition I attended, although several competitors used this as the example of teams that had gone too far). Wagyu is a Japanese cattle breed known for its marbled fat, and it is very expensive—although it is a different cut of meat, in late 2013 vendors on Amazon.com were selling raw five-pound Wagyu tenderloins for about $330.

Teams also incur costs through the RVs they bring and the grills they use. Contestants can sink an almost unlimited amount of money into their grills, but most will quickly concede that the money is really spent on ease of use rather than quality of product, as exemplified by the fact that all types of grills allowed by the KCBS were used at the contest (no gas and no electric are allowed), and all types of grills have a chance of winning. All of this money adds up. In a meeting the morning of the competition, the KCBS representatives reminded the judges that each box of food submitted by competitors represented several hundred dollars' investment. For this reason, most teams only compete at a few contests each year.

Successful competitors (who usually compete at dozens of contests each year) make money in several ways. The most obvious is through winning competitions, which pay in both cash and free entry in the following year's event. Competitors can get sponsorships, and these are often friends with businesses with some money to essentially donate to them. Higher-level competitors with more wins can sell products like rubs and sauce that are often bought by their competitors (at the event this author attended one competitor admitted to doing just that). Finally, a few teams that are very well known among the barbecue competition community offer classes in how to win competitions.

This points to the final tension in competition barbecue: the tension between competition and cooperation (or friendliness). While there is money to be won at contests, the contestants tend to be a fairly social lot, and even teams that compete at only one or two events per year will usually know competitors from other events. The most secrecy seems to revolve around recipes used for sauces and rubs, and while teams may vent their frustrations at the awards ceremony, the ire is usually directed toward judges and the opacity of the judging process rather than at other teams.

One way the friendliness of the competitors comes out is through an organization named Operation BBQ Relief. The group was started in 2011 in Joplin, Missouri, after a tornado ripped through much of the town, killing 140 and injuring over 1,000. As a way to help out, competition teams from eight states moved into the area to serve barbecue to displaced residents and relief workers. Two aspects of competition barbecue proved to be especially useful in this situation. Barbecue has always been a method of cooking to feed large numbers of people, and some competitors have custom-built grills that can barbecue very large amounts of food at once. Also, the set-up competitors use is designed to be self-sufficient, since not every contest will have available electricity, water, or nearby toilets or showers, and competitors are used to supplying their own meat and fuel for the fire. In a disaster situation like Joplin, the self-sufficiency kept the teams from putting more pressure on an already-fragile infrastructure where food, water, and shelter were at a premium. Since Joplin, Operation BBQ Relief volunteers have worked at many different disaster sites, including wildfires in

Colorado, a fertilizer plant explosion in Texas, and hurricane-affected areas. In the aftermath of Hurricane Sandy in 2012, volunteers cooking at nine different locations across two states cooked over 100,200 meals in twelve days.

Barbecue Tourism

Tourism is an extremely mature industry in America, and it is possible to find tours on almost any subject imaginable. As more people identify themselves as "foodies," tours and travel information have been created to cater to that market.

There are numerous local festivals across the country that feature barbecue in one way or another. Both the American Royal, in Kansas City, and the Memphis in May festival are large annual events that have barbecue competitions associated with them that, by themselves, attract hundreds of competitors, and many more onlookers, every year. Most barbecue competitions are associated with local festivals or events. By hosting these events, local boosters hope to generate more tourism dollars and bring more visitors to their cities.

In terms of tours, as of the summer of 2013 both Kansas City and Memphis had companies that organize tasting tours of barbecue restaurants. I went on

Cooking on a cinderblock grill at a festival. Photograph courtesy of the State Archives of Florida, Florida Memory, http://floridamemory.com/items/show/120507.

the Memphis tour, run by a company called Tastin' Round Town, during which the group visited six restaurants in about four hours. The six restaurants showcased a variety of barbecue, from traditional Memphis-style ribs to Texas brisket. While the restaurants were all within a few minutes' driving distance from each other, they were in significantly different neighborhoods, and this allowed the guide to talk not just about Memphis barbecue but also about the history of Memphis. Memphis became important in the late 1800s as a regional hub for industry and a destination for travelers, and Beale Street, as the center of black life in the city, also became a center of black life in the region. In the 1960s and 1970s, though, as the upper and middle class moved to the suburbs, Memphis experienced a profound population loss that it has not yet recovered from, and during this time large sections of Beale Street were razed in urban renewal projects. The tour guide recounted this history and spoke about how the city was working to recover from the problems it had experienced, giving specific examples of recovery such as the revitalization of Beale Street and the Memphis in May festival, which includes a large barbecue festival. The guide connected the resurgence of the economy and tourism in downtown Memphis to the relatively recent national popularity of Memphis barbecue, in this way tying barbecue into a larger story of Memphis in the late 20th and early 21st centuries.

Other areas have tried to capitalize on the popularity of barbecue. A number of chambers of commerce in central Texas seem to have banded together to create the Texas BBQ Trail, which is actually two roads, US 183 and Texas 95. These two roads pass through Luling, Lockhart, Elgin, and Taylor, all of which have well-known barbecue restaurants. Pamphlets for the trail are available at tourist locations throughout Texas and the group has a website, http://www.texasbbqtrails.com.

NOTES

INTRODUCTION

1. Lolis Eric Elie, *Smokestack Lightning: Adventures in the Heart of Barbecue Country* (New York: Farrar, Straus and Giroux, 1996), 22.

2. http://www.merriam-webster.com/dictionary/barbecue, accessed 23 July 2013.

CHAPTER 1

1. Robert F. Moss, *Barbecue: The History of an American Institution* (Tuscaloosa: University of Alabama Press, 2010), 9.

2. "Andrés Bernáldez, History of the Catholic Sovereigns, Don Ferdinand and Doña Isabella. Chapters 123–131," *The Four Voyages of Columbus: A History in Eight Documents, Including Five by Christopher Columbus*, ed. Cecil Jane (New York: Dover, 1988), 120–24.

3. Gonzalo Fernandez de Oviedo y Valdes, *Historia General y Natural de las India*, vol. 3 (Madrid: Imprenta de la Real Academia de la Historia, 1853), 50. The author is extremely grateful to Dr. Lola Norris, in the Spanish department at Texas A&M International University, for her translation from the original Spanish.

4. Oviedo y Valdes, *Historia*, vol. 3, 50.

5. Gonzalo Fernandez de Oviedo y Valdes, *Historia General y Natural de las India*, vol. 1 (Madrid: Imprenta de la Real Academia de la Historia, 1853), 265–66.

6. Oviedo y Valdes, *Historia*, vol. 1, 266.

7. Edmund Hickeringill, "Jamaica Viewed," in *Caribbeana*, ed. Thomas W. Krise (Chicago: University of Chicago Press, 1999), 46.

8. Jessica B. Harris, "Caribbean Connection," in *Cornbread Nation 2: The United States of Barbecue*, ed. Lolis Eric Elie (Chapel Hill: University of North Carolina Press, 2004), 17.

9. Quoted in Moss, *Barbecue*, 11.

10. John Duncan, *Travels Through Part of the United States and Canada in 1818 and 1819*, vol. 1 (New York: W. B. Gilley, 1823), 297–99.

11. "From the Boston Post," *Littell's Living Age*, October 18, 1851, 118.

12. Library of Congress, Online Slave Narratives, Wesley Jones Interview, 390153, 2.

13. "Kentucky Barbecue on the Fourth of July," *The Family Magazine; or, Monthly Abstract of General Knowledge*, May 1, 1838, 5.

14. "The Barbecue," *Indiana Palladium*, July 24, 1847, 1.

15. "The Richland Festival," *Niles' National Register*, September 29, 1838, 5.

16. John Steele Henderson, "'A Poor Dinner It Was': 1860 and the Politics of Barbecue," *Southern Cultures* 1, no. 3 (Spring 1995): 411–12.

17. "Barbecues and Political Changes," *Hagerstown Mail*, August 14, 1829, 2.

18. "The Best Liquor," *New York Observer and Chronicle*, July 15, 1852, 30.

19. "Big Barbecue to Blue and Gray," *Atlanta Constitution*, May 11, 1900, 1.

20. "Emancipation Day," *Galveston Daily News*, June 20, 1894, 4.

21. "How to Roast an Ox," *Boston Daily Globe*, September 1, 1895, 9.

22. *Better Homes and Gardens Barbecue Book* (New York: Meredith Press, 1965), 145.

23. *Better Homes and Gardens Barbecue Book*, 24, 20, 63.

24. Horace Kephart, *Camp Cookery* (New York: Outing Publishing Company, 1910), n.p.

25. Kephart, *Camp Cookery*, 50.

26. George A. Sanderson and Virginia Rich, *Sunset's Barbecue Book* (San Francisco: Lane Publishing, 1939), 5.

27. Cynthia Lindsay, "The Procal: His Habits and Habitat," *Harper's*, May 1960, 35–36.

28. Clementine Paddleford, Memo to Staff, August 29, 1956, Box 82, file 1, Clementine Paddleford Collection, University Archives and Manuscripts, Richard L. D. and Marjorie J. Morse Department of Special Collections, Kansas State University, Manhattan, Kansas (hereafter referred to as "Paddleford Collection").

29. The Editors of *Fortune*, *The Changing American Market* (Garden City, NY: Hanover House, 1953), 198, 200, 202–3.

30. Ted Hatch, "For the Male Cook in All His Glory!" *The American Home*, June 1940, 30–33.

31. Clifford Edward Clark Jr., *The American Family Home, 1800–1960* (Chapel Hill: University of North Carolina Press, 1986), 201.

32. Edward T. Paxton, *What People Want When They Buy a House* (Washington, D.C.: U.S. Government Printing Office, 1955), 51–52.

33. Clark, *American Family Home*, 228.

34. James Beard, *Cook It Outdoors* (New York: M. Barrows and Co., 1941).

35. Ernest Dichter, "The Sex and Character of Food," *Motivations* 1, no. 2 (April 1956): 4.

36. Robert D. Buzzell and Robert E. M. Nourse, *Product Innovation in Food Processing, 1954–1964* (Boston: Harvard University Press, 1967), 79.

37. Editors of *Fortune, Changing American Market*, 25.

38. Ripley Golovin Hathaway, "In Xanadu Did Barbecue," in *Cornbread Nation 2: The United States of Barbecue*, ed. Lolis Eric Elie (Chapel Hill: University of North Carolina Press, 2004), 94.

39. Sanderson and Rich, *Sunset's Barbecue Book*, 35.

40. "$50.13 for an Outdoor Grill." *McCall's*, July 1955, 102–4.

41. Helen Evans Brown and James A. Beard, *The Complete Book of Outdoor Cookery* (Garden City, NY: Doubleday, 1955), 13.

42. Brown and Beard, *Outdoor Cookery*, 22.

43. *Betty Crocker's Outdoor Cook Book* (New York: Wiley, 2009), 12.

44. "You can assemble this Barbecue-Incinerator in less than half an hour!" Pamphlet for the Incin-O-Grill, undated, Box 221, folder 14, Paddleford Collection.

45. Timothy D. Baker and William G. Hafner, "Cadmium Poisoning from a Refrigerator Shelf Used as an Improvised Barbecue Grill," *Public Health Reports* 76, no. 6 (June 1961): 543–44.

46. Gretchen L. Lamberton, "Men Become Experts at Barbecuing," *Winona Daily News*, July 29, 1962, 2.

47. Bette Doolittle, "Barbecue Boom," press release from the Grocery Manufacturers of America, June 21, 1957, Box 221, file 14, Paddleford Collection.

48. Julian Kilman, "Suggested Barbecue Menu for Army of Outdoor Eaters," July 7, 1958, Box 221, file 14, Paddleford Collection.

49. *How to Become a Cookout Champion* (Foothill Ranch, CA: Kaiser Aluminum & Chemical Corp., 1959).

50. "Georgia Barbecue Booms Roosevelt," *New York Times*, October 14, 1931, 3.

51. "100,000 Oklahomans Feast at Barbecue," *New York Times*, January 10, 1923, 3.

52. Ian Urbina, "Kentucky Politics, Served With a Helping of Ribs at an Annual Barbecue," *New York Times*, August 6, 2007, A14.

53. Tom Wicker, "Spareribs and World Affairs at LBJ," *New York Times*, December 28, 1963, 1, 10.

54. "Johnson Serves Australians Texas-Style Bean Barbecue," *New York Times*, October 23, 1966, 3; Benjamin Welles, "Johnson Spends a Busy Colorful Day in Salvador," *New York Times*, July 8, 1968, 17.

55. www.kcbs.us/about_history.php, accessed February 1, 2013.

CHAPTER 2

1. Ripley Golovin Hathaway, "In Xanadu Did Barbecue," in *Cornbread Nation 2: The United States of Barbecue*, ed. Lolis Eric Elie (Chapel Hill: University of North Carolina Press, 2004), 94.

2. *Betty Crocker's Outdoor Cook Book* (New York: Wiley, 2009), 11.

3. http://static.hpba.org/fileadmin/Statistics/TotalCW_Shipments—87-2005.htm, accessed December 30, 2013.

4. The Editors of Good Housekeeping, *Grill It!: Good Housekeeping Favorite Recipes* (New York: Hearst Books, 2005), 8.

5. Good Housekeeping, *Grill It!*, 9.

6. Good Housekeeping, *Grill It!*, 9.

7. *Betty Crocker's Outdoor Cook Book*, 15.

8. *Betty Crocker's Outdoor Cook Book*, 25.

9. *Betty Crocker's Outdoor Cook Book*, 27.

10. Amazon.com was accessed March 3, 2013; the method of searching was to drill into the Patio, Lawn & Garden department, then Grills & Outdoor Cooking, and then Barbecue Utensils.

11. Frances Trollope, *Domestic Manners of the Americans* (London: Whittaker, Treacher, & Co., 1832), 51.

12. Lettice Bryan, *The Kentucky Housewife* (1839; reprint, Columbia: University of South Carolina Press, 1991), 95–96.

13. Bryan, *Kentucky Housewife*, 168.

14. Vince Staten and Greg Johnson, *Real Barbecue* (New York: Harper and Row, 2007), 255.

15. Lolis Eric Elie, *Smokestack Lightning: Adventures in the Heart of Barbecue Country* (New York: Farrar, Straus and Giroux, 1996), 84.

16. George H. Gallup, *The Gallup Poll: Public Opinion 1935–1971*, vol. 1 (New York: Random House, 1972), 637.

17. Eric Schlosser, *Fast Food Nation: The Dark Side of the All-American Meal* (Boston: Houghton Mifflin, 2001), 197.

18. Helen Evans Brown and James A. Beard, *The Complete Book of Outdoor Cookery* (Garden City, NY: Doubleday, 1955), 133.

19. *Better Homes and Gardens Barbecue Book* (New York: Meredith Press, 1965), 51–57.

20. Rick Rodgers, *Kingsford Complete Grilling Cookbook* (Hoboken, NJ: Wiley, 2007), 152–78.

21. *Quasar Microwave Cooking* (Matsushita Electric Industrial Co. Ltd., 1981), 76.

22. Martha McCulloch-Williams, *Dishes and Beverages of the Old South* (New York: McBride Nast, 1913), 159.

23. *Buckeye Cookery and Practical Housekeeping* (Marysville, OH: Buckeye Publishing, 1877), 176.

24. Horace Kephart, *Camp Cookery* (New York: Outing Publishing, 1910), 84.

25. Brown and Beard, *Complete Book of Outdoor Cookery*, 98.

26. *Better Homes and Gardens Barbecue Book*, 41.

27. Arthur Coleman and Bobbie Coleman, *The Texas Cookbook* (New York: A. A. Wyn, 1949), 37.

28. Celine Steen and Joni Marie Newman, *500 Vegan Recipes* (Beverly, MA: Fair Winds Press, 2009), 215.

29. Tested Recipe Institute, *The Art of Barbecue and Outdoor Cooking* (New York: Bantam, 1971), 157.

30. Tested Recipe Institute, *Art of Barbecue*, 157.

31. McCulloch-Williams, *Dishes and Beverages*, 274–75.

32. McCulloch-Williams, *Dishes and Beverages*, 274–75.

33. Library of Congress, Online Slave Narratives, Wesley Jones Interview, 390153, 2.

34. Steven Raichlen, "Have Barbecue, Will Travel: Tracking Sauces Down South," *New York Times*, June 30, 1999, F5.

35. Walter Jetton, *Walter Jetton's LBJ Barbecue Cook Book* (New York: Pocket Books, 1965), 13.

36. Jetton, *LBJ Barbecue Cook Book*, 14.

37. Robb Walsh, *The Texas Cowboy Cookbook* (New York: Broadway Books, 2007), 179.

38. Staten and Johnson, *Real Barbecue*, 214.

39. Shifra Stein and Rich Davis, *All About Bar-B-Q Kansas City–Style* (Kansas City: Barbacoa Press, 1985), 128.

40. McCulloch-Williams, *Dishes and Beverages*, 275.

41. William Bircher, *A Drummer-Boy's Diary: Comprising Four Years of Service with the Second Regiment Minnesota Veteran Volunteers, 1861 to 1865* (St. Paul, MN: St. Paul Book and Stationery, 1889), 127–29.

42. Bircher, *Drummer-Boy's Diary*, 129.

43. Molly O'Neill, *One Big Table: A Portrait of American Cooking* (New York: Simon & Schuster, 2010), 402.

44. Bryan, *Kentucky Housewife*, 192.

45. Bryan, *Kentucky Housewife*, 193.

46. Mrs. A. E. Kirtland, *New Southern Cook Book* (Montgomery, AL: 1906), 53.

47. McCulloch-Williams, *Dishes and Beverages*, 206.

48. Colonel Halstead C. Fowler, comp., *Recipes Out of Bilibid* (New York: George W. Stewart, 1946), 55.

49. Marion Harland, *Common Sense in the Household* (New York: Scribner, Armstrong, 1873), 173.

50. "The Kentucky Barbecue," *New York Times*, November 7, 1897, 3.

51. John Egerton, *Southern Food: At Home, on the Road, in History* (New York: Knopf, 1987), 277.

52. *Joys of Jell-O* (White Plains, NY: General Foods Corporation, n.d. but probably 1963), 58.

53. Myron Mixon with Kelly Alexander, *Smokin' with Myron Mixon* (New York: Ballantine, 2011), 139.

54. Bryan, *Kentucky Housewife*, 387.

55. George A. Sanderson and Virginia Rich, *Sunset's Barbecue Book* (San Francisco: Lane Publishing, 1939), 65.

56. McCulloch-Williams, *Dishes and Beverages*, 282.

57. Sanderson and Rich, *Sunset's Barbecue Book*, 70.

58. Sanderson and Rich, *Sunset's Barbecue Book*, 70.

59. Sanderson and Rich, *Sunset's Barbecue Book*, 70–71.

60. Sanderson and Rich, *Sunset's Barbecue Book*, 71.

61. The Women of General Foods Kitchens, *The General Foods Kitchens Cookbook* (New York: Random House, 1959), 137.

62. Jetton, *LBJ Barbecue Cook Book*, 8–9.

63. "Regional Food," *Vogue*, August 1947, 114.

64. "Regional Food," *Vogue*, 114.

65. "Regional Food," *Vogue*, 114.

66. "Potluck Party, Barbecue Style," *Better Homes & Gardens*, May 1961, 72–73.

67. "Barbecues and Garden Suppers," *Better Homes & Gardens*, June 1943, 37.

68. Sanderson and Rich, *Sunset's Barbecue Book*, 55.

69. Women of General Foods, *General Foods Kitchens Cookbook*, 136.

CHAPTER 3

1. Vince Staten and Greg Johnson, *Real Barbecue* (New York: Harper and Row, 2007), 236–37.

2. John A. Jakle and Keith Sculle, *Fast Food: Roadside Restaurants in the Automobile Age* (Baltimore: Johns Hopkins University Press, 1999), 171.

3. Menu reprinted in Robert F. Moss, *Barbecue: The History of an American Institution* (Tuscaloosa: University of Alabama Press, 2010), 220.

4. Quoted in John Shelton Reed, Dale Volberg Reed, and William McKinney, *Holy Smoke: The Big Book of North Carolina Barbecue* (Chapel Hill: University of North Carolina Press, 2008), 237.

5. Staten and Johnson, *Real Barbecue*, 31.

6. John Shelton Reed, "Barbecue Sociology: The Meat of the Matter," in *Cornbread Nation 2*, ed. Lolis Eric Elie (Chapel Hill: University of North Carolina Press, 2004), 80–81.

7. Quoted in Moss, *Barbecue*, 173.

8. Jakle and Sculle, *Fast Food*, 172.

9. Jakle and Sculle, *Fast Food*, 173.

10. http://www.pitch.com/kansascity/kc-disasterpiece/Content?oid=2178534, accessed July 1, 2013.

11. http://www.pitch.com/kansascity/kc-disasterpiece/Content?oid=2178534, accessed July 1, 2013.

12. http://nrn.com/archive/regional-barbecue-players-debut-less-costly-fast-casual-variants, accessed June 9, 2013.

13. Reprinted in Jakle and Sculle, *Fast Food*, 17.

14. Menu for the Old Southern Tea Room. Box 178, file 39, Paddleford Collection.

15. Calvin Trillin, "A Reporter at Large: American Royal," *New Yorker*, September 26, 1983, 110.

16. John T. Edge, "Patronage and the Pits: A Portrait, in Black and White, of Jones Bar-B-Q Diner in Marianna, Arkansas," in *The Slaw and the Slow Cooked: Culture and Barbecue in the Mid-South*, ed. James R. Veteto (Nashville: Vanderbilt University Press, 2011), 44.

17. Moss, *Barbecue*, 213–14.

18. Moss, *Barbecue*, 214–15.

19. Jack Hitt, "A Confederacy of Sauces," *New York Times*, August 26, 2001, SM28.

20. Stephen Smith, "The Rhetoric of Barbecue," in *Cornbread Nation 2: The United States of Barbecue*, ed. Lolis Eric Elie (Chapel Hill: University of North Carolina Press, 2004), 65.

21. Smith, "Rhetoric," 65.

22. Reed, "Barbecue Sociology," 81.

23. Lolis Eric Elie, *Smokestack Lightning: Adventures in the Heart of Barbecue Country* (New York: Farrar, Straus and Giroux, 1996), 3.

24. Steven Raichlen, "Stalking 4-Star Barbecue in the Lone Star State," *New York Times*, July 24, 2002, F4.

25. Jakle and Sculle, *Fast Food*, 32.

26. Lolis Eric Elie, "When Pigs Fly West," in *Cornbread Nation 2: The United States of Barbecue*, ed. Lolis Eric Elie (Chapel Hill: University of North Carolina Press, 2004), 121.

27. "New Nashville Restaurant Serves Barbecue and Blessings." *Tennessee Tribune*, March 21, 2013, 2A.

28. Reed et al., *Holy Smoke*, 68–69.

29. Doug Worgul, *The Grand Barbecue: A Celebration of Kansas City Barbecue* (Kansas City: Kansas City Star Books, 2001), 16–18.

30. Moss, *Barbecue*, 195–96.

31. Trillin, "Reporter at Large," 97.

32. Trillin, "Reporter at Large," 98.

33. Elie, *Smokestack Lightning*, 17.

34. Christine Miller Ford, "Food Network Winners' Barbecue Joint Is a Showstopper," *State Journal* (WV), April 15, 2011, 26.

35. http://nrn.com/archive/qa-roland-dickey-jr-dickey-s-barbecue-restaurants, accessed May 5, 2013.

36. Reed et al., *Holy Smoke*, 240.

37. http://nrn.com/seafood-trends/menu-tracker-new-items-kfc-little-caesars, accessed May 5, 2013.

38. Menu from the 5 Points, Alabama, location, http://www.jimnnicks.com/images/menu9/Menu9_Dine-In.pdf, accessed July 18, 2013.

39. Alexa Schirtzinger, "Where There's Smoke," *Santa Fe Reporter*, January 2, 2013, 30.

40. http://nrn.com/latest-headlines/burger-king-launches-barbecue-inspired-summer-menu, accessed May 4, 2013.

41. http://nrn.com/latest-headlines/hard-rock-caf-menu-looks-barbecue, accessed May 5, 2013.

42. As of the writing of this book, the most recent top 10 list available is from 2011, from the Nation's Restaurant News website, http://nrn.com/us-top-100/top-100-chains-us-sales, accessed June 9, 2013. The complete list is McDonald's, Subway, Starbucks, Burger King, Wendy's, Taco Bell, Dunkin' Donuts, Pizza Hut, KFC, and Applebee's Neighborhood Bar & Grill.

43. Reported in Mark Brandau, "Old Carolina Barbecue Company," *Nation's Restaurant News*, June 10, 2013, 14.

44. http://nrn.com/archive/growth-chains-dickey-s-barbecue-pit, accessed May 5, 2013.

45. *Nation's Restaurant News*, June 24, 2013, 27, 32, 38.

46. http://nrn.com/latest-headlines/famous-daves-aims-develop-better-barbecue-niche?page=1, accessed May 4, 2013.

47. Reed et al., *Holy Smoke*, 248.

48. http://www.southernfoodways.org/assets/TennesseeBBQ_Rendezvous_John.pdf, accessed May 5, 2013, 5.

49. See Raichlen, "Stalking 4-Star Barbecue," for more information about the feud.

50. Elie, *Smokestack Lightning*, 57.

51. Elie, *Smokestack Lightning*, 57.

52. Elie, *Smokestack Lightning*, 58.

53. Addie Broyles, "Lockhart Barbecue Family Buries the Hatchet with New Restaurant Near Austin," http://www.austin360.com/news/lifestyles/food-cooking/lockhart-barbecue-family-buries-the-hatchet-with-2/nRpkB/, accessed July 27, 2013.

54. Calvin Trillin, *The Tummy Trilogy* (New York: Farrar, Straus and Giroux, 1994), 20.

CHAPTER 4

1. Francis Mallmann, *Seven Fires: Grilling the Argentine Way* (New York: Artisan, 2009), 14.

2. Lynn Visson, *The Art of Uzbek Cooking* (New York: Hippocrene Books, 1999), 94.

3. Visson, *Art of Uzbek Cooking*, 105–6.

4. Visson, *Art of Uzbek Cooking*, 131.

5. Ursula Heinzelmann, *Food Culture in Germany* (Westport, CT: Greenwood Press, 2008), 141–42.

6. Heinzelmann, *Food Culture in Germany*, 55.

7. Glenn R. Mack and Asele Surina, *Food Culture in Russia and Central Asia* (Westport, CT: Greenwood Press, 2005), 107.

8. Peter Heine, *Food Culture in the Near East, Middle East, and North Africa* (Westport, CT: Greenwood Press, 2004), 128.

9. Cherie Y. Hamilton, *Cuisines of Portuguese Encounters* (New York: Hippocrene Books, 2001), 215.

10. http://www.npr.org/blogs/thesalt/2013/08/27/214592906/braai-day-aims-to-bring-s-africans-together-over-barbecue, accessed November 28, 2013.

11. Justin Bonello, *Cooked in Africa* (New York: Penguin, 2010), 43.

12. Steven Raichlen, *Planet Barbecue* (New York: Workman Publishing, 2010), 102.

13. *Indian Barbecue* (New Delhi: Lustre Press/Roli Books, 2007), 48.

14. Emi Kazuko, *Café Japan* (Chicago: Contemporary Books, 1999), 29.

15. Hamilton, *Cuisines of Portuguese Encounters*, 184.

16. Lynn Marie Houston, *Food Culture in the Caribbean* (Westport, CT: Greenwood Press, 2005), 117.

17. Houston, *Food Culture in the Caribbean*, 92–93.

18. Helen Willinsky, *Jerk: Barbecue from Jamaica* (Freedom, CA: Crossing Press, 1990), 15.

19. Willinsky, *Jerk*, 43.

20. Mallmann, *Seven Fires*, 104.

21. Nirmala Narine, *Nirmala's Edible Diary* (San Francisco: Chronicle Books, 2009), 129.

22. Lolis Eric Elie, *Smokestack Lightning: Adventures in the Heart of Barbecue Country* (New York: Farrar, Straus and Giroux, 1996), 32–36.

23. Josefina Velazquez de Leon, *Mexican Cook Book for American Homes* (Mexico City: Academia Velazquez de Leon, 1971), 260–63.

24. Sharon Cadwallader, *Savoring Mexico* (New York: McGraw-Hill, 1980), 138.

25. Don FitzGerald, *The Pacifica House Hawaii Cook Book* (North Hollywood, CA: Pacifica House, 1965), 7–8.

26. Bret Thorn, "Cut Costs," *Nation's Restaurant News*, November 4, 2013, 18.

27. http://www.bluesbarbq.fr, accessed February 1, 2014.

CHAPTER 5

1. Edmund Hickeringill, "Jamaica Viewed," in *Caribbeana*, ed. Thomas W. Krise (Chicago: University of Chicago Press, 1999), 46.

2. "The King of the Cannibal Isles," *Fun*, June 29, 1867, 170.

3. "Texas Plantation Party," *Vogue*, January 1942, 64.

4. Clementine Paddleford, "Sea Island Picnic," Box 71, file 17, Clementine Paddleford Collection, University Archives and Manuscripts, Richard L. D. and Marjorie J. Morse Department of Special Collections, Kansas State University, Manhattan, Kansas (hereafter referred to as "Paddleford Collection").

5. Paddleford, "Sea Island Picnic."

6. Paddleford, "Sea Island Picnic."

7. However, this testing only took her so far; she once printed a molasses cookie recipe that inadvertently left out the molasses.

8. Lolis Eric Elie, *Smokestack Lightning: Adventures in the Heart of Barbecue Country* (New York: Farrar, Straus and Giroux, 1996), 63.

9. An excellent source for the story of how Texas barbecue came to be associated with German immigrants instead of blacks is Robb Walsh, "Texas Barbecue in Black and White," in *Cornbread Nation 2: The United States of Barbecue*, ed. Lolis Eric Elie (Chapel Hill: University of North Carolina Press, 2004).

10. Mary Faulk Koock, "Star Hostess," *Corpus Christi Caller Times*, August 1, 1971, 103.

11. Walter Jetton, *Walter Jetton's LBJ Barbecue Cook Book* (New York: Pocket Books, 1965), 5.

12. The Women of General Foods Kitchens, *The General Foods Kitchens Cookbook* (New York: Random House, 1959), 137.

13. Owen Wister, *The Virginian* (New York: Macmillan, 1902), 123.

14. An Englishman from the Backwoods, "Sketches of Kentucky," *The Monthly Magazine*, January 1838, 65.

15. Englishman from the Backwoods, "Sketches of Kentucky," 66.

16. *The Christian Church Cook Book* (Cameron, TX: 1927), 8–10.

17. Paula Deen, *The Lady & Sons Savannah Country Cookbook* (New York: Random House, 1998), 51.

18. Martha McCulloch-Williams, *Dishes and Beverages of the Old South* (New York: McBride Nast, 1913), 159.

19. Frank A. Bates, *Camping and Camp Cooking* (Boston: Ball Publishing, 1914), 78.

20. Bates, *Camping*, 79.

21. Quoted in Ripley Golovin Hathaway, "In Xanadu Did Barbecue," in *Cornbread Nation 2: The United States of Barbecue*, ed. Lolis Eric Elie (Chapel Hill: University of North Carolina Press, 2004), 90.

22. George A. Sanderson and Virginia Rich, *Sunset's Barbecue Book* (San Francisco: Lane Publishing, 1939), 35.

23. *Better Homes and Gardens Barbecue Book* (Des Moines: Meredith Publishing, 1959), 5.

24. *Better Homes and Gardens Barbecue Book* (1959), 25

25. Cora Brown et al., *Outdoor Cooking* (New York: Greystone Press, 1940), 1. The full author list is Cora, Rose, and Bob Brown; Cora was Bob's mother and Rose was his wife. Somehow this information makes the quote even stranger.

26. Adam Perry Lang, *BBQ 25* (New York: HarperCollins, 2010), 4.

27. Google search performed July 17, 2013. The website critical of the show is at http://chowhound.chow.com/topics/851426.

28. See Steven Raichlen, "Stalking 4-Star Barbecue in the Lone Star State," *New York Times*, July 24, 2002, for more information on the feud.

29. Walsh, "Texas Barbecue in Black and White," 58.

30. Vince Staten and Greg Johnson, *Real Barbecue* (New York: Harper and Row, 2007), 19.

BIBLIOGRAPHY

"Andrés Bernáldez, History of the Catholic Sovereigns, Don Ferdinand and Doña Isabella. Chapters 123–131." *The Four Voyages of Columbus: A History in Eight Documents, Including Five by Christopher Columbus*. Edited by Cecil Jane. New York: Dover, 1988.

Baker, Timothy D., and William G. Hafner. "Cadmium Poisoning from a Refrigerator Shelf Used as an Improvised Barbecue Grill." *Public Health Reports* 76, no. 6 (June 1961): 543–44.

"The Barbecue." *The Indiana Palladium*, July 24, 1847, 1.

"Barbecues and Garden Suppers." *Better Homes & Gardens*, June 1943, 37.

"Barbecues and Political Changes." *Hagerstown Mail*, August 14, 1829, 2.

Bates, Frank A. *Camping and Camp Cooking*. Boston: Ball Publishing, 1914.

"The Best Liquor," *New York Observer and Chronicle*, July 15, 1852, 30.

Better Homes & Gardens Barbecue Book. Des Moines: Meredith Publishing Company, 1959.

Better Homes & Gardens Barbecue Book. New York: Meredith Press, 1965.

Betty Crocker's Outdoor Cook Book. New York: Wiley, 2009.

"Big Barbecue to Blue and Gray." *Atlanta Constitution*, May 11, 1900, 1.

Bircher, William. *A Drummer-Boy's Diary: Comprising Four Years of Service with the Second Regiment Minnesota Veteran Volunteers, 1861 to 1865*. St. Paul, MN: St. Paul Book and Stationery Co., 1889.

Bonello, Justin. *Cooked in Africa*. New York: Penguin, 2010.

Brandau, Mark. "Old Carolina Barbecue Company." *Nation's Restaurant News*, June 10, 2013, 14.

Brown, Cora, et al. *Outdoor Cooking*. New York: Greystone Press, 1940.

Brown, Helen Evans, and James A. Beard. *The Complete Book of Outdoor Cookery*. Garden City, NY: Doubleday, 1955.

Broyles, Addie. "Lockhart Barbecue Family Buries the Hatchet with New Restaurant Near Austin." http://www.austin360.com/news/lifestyles/food-cooking/lockhart-bar-becue-family-buries-the-hatchet-with-2/nRpkB/. Accessed July 27, 2013.

Bryan, Lettice. *The Kentucky Housewife*. 1839; reprint, Columbia: University of South Carolina Press, 1991.

Buckeye Cookery and Practical Housekeeping. Marysville, OH: Buckeye Publishing Company, 1877.

Buzzell, Robert D., and Robert E. M. Nourse. *Product Innovation in Food Processing, 1954–1964*. Boston: Harvard University Press, 1967.

Cadwallader, Sharon. *Savoring Mexico*. New York: McGraw-Hill, 1980.

The Christian Church Cook Book. Cameron, TX: 1927.

Clark, Clifford Edward, Jr. *The American Family Home, 1800–1960*. Chapel Hill: University of North Carolina Press, 1986.

Coleman, Arthur, and Bobbie Coleman. *The Texas Cookbook*. New York: A. A. Wyn, 1949.

Deen, Paula. *The Lady & Sons Savannah Country Cookbook*. New York: Random House, 1998.

Dichter, Ernest. "The Sex and Character of Food." *Motivations* 1, no. 2 (April 1956): 4.

Doolittle, Bette. "Barbecue Boom." Press release from the Grocery Manufacturers of America, June 21, 1957. Box 221, file 14, Clementine Paddleford Collection, University Archives and Manuscripts, Richard L. D. and Marjorie J. Morse Department of Special Collections, Kansas State University, Manhattan, Kansas (hereafter referred to as "Paddleford Collection").

Duncan, John. *Travels Through Part of the United States and Canada in 1818 and 1819*, vol. 1. New York: W. B. Gilley, 1823.

Edge, John T. "Patronage and the Pits: A Portrait, in Black and White, of Jones Bar-B-Q Diner in Marianna, Arkansas." In *The Slaw and the Slow Cooked: Culture and Barbecue in the Mid-South*, edited by James R. Veteto, 43–50. Nashville: Vanderbilt University Press, 2011.

The Editors of *Fortune*. *The Changing American Market*. Garden City, NY: Hanover House, 1953.

The Editors of *Good Housekeeping*. *Grill It!: Good Housekeeping Favorite Recipes*. New York: Hearst Books, 2005.

Egerton, John. *Southern Food: At Home, on the Road, in History*. New York: Knopf, 1987.

Elie, Lolis Eric. *Smokestack Lightning: Adventures in the Heart of Barbecue Country*. New York: Farrar, Straus and Giroux, 1996.

———. "When Pigs Fly West." In *Cornbread Nation 2: The United States of Barbecue*, edited by Lolis Eric Elie, 121–29. Chapel Hill: University of North Carolina Press, 2004.

"Emancipation Day." *The Galveston Daily News*, June 20, 1894, 4.

An Englishman from the Backwoods. "Sketches of Kentucky." *The Monthly Magazine*, January 1838, 65.

"$50.13 for an Outdoor Grill." *McCall's*, July 1955, 102–4.

FitzGerald, Don. *The Pacifica House Hawaii Cook Book*. North Hollywood, CA: Pacifica House, 1965.

Ford, Christine Miller. "Food Network Winners' Barbecue Joint Is a Showstopper." *State Journal* (WV), April 15, 2011, 26.

Fowler, Colonel Halstead C. *Recipes Out of Bilibid*. New York: George W. Stewart, 1946.

"From the Boston Post." *Littell's Living Age*, October 18, 1851, 118.

Gallup, George H. *The Gallup Poll: Public Opinion 1935–1971*, vol. 1. New York: Random House, 1972.

"Georgia Barbecue Booms Roosevelt." *New York Times*, October 14, 1931, 3.

Hamilton, Cherie Y. *Cuisines of Portuguese Encounters*. New York: Hippocrene Books, 2001.

Harland, Marion. *Common Sense in the Household*. New York: Scribner, Armstrong, 1873.

Harris, Jessica B. "Caribbean Connection." In *Cornbread Nation 2: The United States of Barbecue*, edited by Lolis Eric Elie, 16–18. Chapel Hill: University of North Carolina Press, 2004.

Hatch, Ted. "For the Male Cook in All His Glory!" *The American Home*, June 1940, 30–33.

Hathaway, Ripley Golovin. "In Xanadu Did Barbecue." In *Cornbread Nation 2: The United States of Barbecue*, edited by Lolis Eric Elie, 88–96. Chapel Hill: University of North Carolina Press, 2004.

Heine, Peter. *Food Culture in the Near East, Middle East, and North Africa*. Westport, CT: Greenwood Press, 2004.

Heinzelmann, Ursula. *Food Culture in Germany*. Westport, CT: Greenwood Press, 2008.

Henderson, John Steele. "'A Poor Dinner It Was': 1860 and the Politics of Barbecue," *Southern Cultures* 1, no. 3 (Spring 1995): 411–12.

Hickeringill, Edmund. "Jamaica Viewed." In *Caribbeana*, edited by Thomas W. Krise, 31–50. Chicago: University of Chicago Press, 1999.

Hitt, Jack. "A Confederacy of Sauces." *New York Times*, August 26, 2001, SM28.

Houston, Lynn Marie. *Food Culture in the Caribbean*. Westport, CT: Greenwood Press, 2005.

How to Become a Cookout Champion. Kaiser Aluminum & Chemical Corp., 1959.

"How to Roast an Ox." *Boston Daily Globe*, September 1, 1895, 9.

Indian Barbecue. New Delhi: Lustre Press/Roli Books, 2007.

Jakle, John A., and Keith Sculle. *Fast Food: Roadside Restaurants in the Automobile Age*. Baltimore: Johns Hopkins University Press, 1999.

Jetton, Walter. *Walter Jetton's LBJ Barbecue Cook Book*. New York: Pocket Books, 1965.

"Johnson Serves Australians Texas-Style Bean Barbecue." *New York Times*, October 23, 1966, 3.

Joys of Jell-O. White Plains, NY: General Foods Corporation, n.d. but probably 1963.

Kazuko, Emi. *Café Japan*. Chicago: Contemporary Books, 1999.

"The Kentucky Barbecue." *New York Times*, November 7, 1897, 3.

"Kentucky Barbecue on the Fourth of July." *The Family Magazine; or, Monthly Abstract of General Knowledge*, May 1, 1838.

Kephart, Horace. *Camp Cookery*. New York: Outing Publishing, 1910.

Kilman, Julian. "Suggested Barbecue Menu for Army of Outdoor Eaters." July 7, 1958, File 14, box 221, Paddleford Collection.

"The King of the Cannibal Isles." *Fun*, June 29, 1867, 170.

Kirtland, Mrs. A. E. *New Southern Cook Book*. Montgomery, AL: 1906.

Koock, Mary Faulk. "Star Hostess." *Corpus Christi Caller Times*, August 1, 1971, 103.

Lamberton, Gretchen L. "Men Become Experts at Barbecuing." *Winona Daily News*, July 29, 1962, 2.

Lang, Adam Perry. *BBQ 25*. New York: HarperCollins, 2010.

de Leon, Josefina Velazquez. *Mexican Cook Book for American Homes*. Mexico City: Academia Velazquez de Leon, 1971.

Library of Congress. Online Slave Narratives, Wesley Jones Interview, 390153.

Lindsay, Cynthia. "The Procal: His Habits and Habitat." *Harper's*, May 1960, 35–36.

Long, Christopher. "LEON SPRINGS, TX." *Handbook of Texas Online* (http://www.tshaonline.org/handbook/online/articles/hll37). Accessed July 26, 2013. Published by the Texas State Historical Association.

Mack, Glenn R., and Asele Surina. *Food Culture in Russia and Central Asia*. Westport, CT: Greenwood Press, 2005.

Mallmann, Francis. *Seven Fires: Grilling the Argentine Way*. New York: Artisan, 2009.

McCulloch-Williams, Martha. *Dishes and Beverages of the Old South*. New York: McBride Nast, 1913.

Menu for the Old Southern Tea Room. File 39, box 178, Paddleford Archive.

Mixon, Myron, with Kelly Alexander. *Smokin' with Myron Mixon*. New York: Ballantine Books, 2011.

Moss, Robert F. *Barbecue: The History of an American Institution*. Tuscaloosa: University of Alabama Press, 2010.

Narine, Nirmala. *Nirmala's Edible Diary*. San Francisco: Chronicle Books, 2009.

"New Nashville Restaurant Serves Barbecue and Blessings." *Tennessee Tribune*, March 21, 2013, 2A.

"100,000 Oklahomans Feast at Barbecue," *New York Times*, January 10, 1923, 3.

O'Neill, Molly. *One Big Table: A Portrait of American Cooking*. New York: Simon & Schuster, 2010.

de Oviedo y Valdes, Gonzalo Fernandez. *Historia General y Natural de las India*, vols. 1 and 3. Madrid: Imprenta de la Real Academia de la Historia, 1853.

Paddleford, Clementine. Memo to Staff, August 29, 1956. File 1, box 82, Paddleford Collection.

———. "Sea Island Picnic," Box 71, file 17, Paddleford Collection.

Paxton, Edward T. *What People Want When They Buy a House*. Washington, D.C.: U.S. Government Printing Office, 1955.

"Potluck Party, Barbecue Style." *Better Homes & Gardens*, May 1961, 72–73.

Quasar Microwave Cooking. Matsushita Electric Industrial Co Ltd, 1981.

Raichlen, Steven. "Have Barbecue, Will Travel: Tracking Sauces Down South." *New York Times*, June 30, 1999, F5.

———. *Planet Barbecue*. New York: Workman Publishing, 2010.

———. "Stalking 4-Star Barbecue in the Lone Star State." *New York Times*, July 24, 2002, F4.

Reed, John Shelton, Dale Volberg Reed, and William McKinney. *Holy Smoke: The Big Book of North Carolina Barbecue*. Chapel Hill: University of North Carolina Press, 2008.

———. "Barbecue Sociology: The Meat of the Matter." In *Cornbread Nation 2*, edited by Lolis Eric Elie. Chapel Hill: University of North Carolina Press, 2004.

"Regional Food." *Vogue*, August 1947, 114.

"The Richland Festival." *Niles' National Register*, September 29, 1838, 5.

Rodgers, Rick. *Kingsford Complete Grilling Cookbook*. Hoboken, NJ: Wiley, 2007.

Sanderson, George A., and Virginia Rich. *Sunset's Barbecue Book*. San Francisco: Lane Publishing, 1939.

Schirtzinger, Alexa. "Where There's Smoke." *Santa Fe Reporter*, January 2, 2013, 30.

Schlosser, Eric. *Fast Food Nation: The Dark Side of the All-American Meal*. Boston: Houghton Mifflin, 2001.

Smith, Stephen. "The Rhetoric of Barbecue." In *Cornbread Nation 2: The United States of Barbecue*, edited by Lolis Eric Elie, 61–68. Chapel Hill: University of North Carolina Press, 2004.

Staten, Vince, and Greg Johnson. *Real Barbecue*. New York: Harper and Row, 2007.

Steen, Celine, and Joni Marie Newman. *500 Vegan Recipes*. Beverly, MA: Fair Winds Press, 2009.

Stein, Shifra, and Rich Davis. *All About Bar-B-Q Kansas City-Style*. Kansas City: Barbacoa Press, 1985.

Tested Recipe Institute. *The Art of Barbecue and Outdoor Cooking*. New York: Bantam, 1971.

"Texas Plantation Party." *Vogue*, January 1942, 62–65.

Thorn, Bret. "Cut Costs." *Nation's Restaurant News*, 4 November 2013, 18.

Trillin, Calvin. "A Reporter at Large: American Royal." *New Yorker*, September 26, 1983.

———. *The Tummy Trilogy*. New York: Farrar, Straus and Giroux, 1994.

Trollope, Frances. *Domestic Manners of the Americans*. London: Whittaker, Treacher, 1832.

Urbina, Ian. "Kentucky Politics, Served with a Helping of Ribs at an Annual Barbecue." *New York Times*, August 6, 2007, A14.

Visson, Lynn. *The Art of Uzbek Cooking*. New York: Hippocrene Books, 1999.

Walsh, Robb. "Texas Barbecue in Black and White." In *Cornbread Nation 2: The United States of Barbecue*, edited by Lolis Eric Elie, 48–60. Chapel Hill: University of North Carolina Press, 2004.

———. *The Texas Cowboy Cookbook*. New York: Broadway Books, 2007.

Welles, Benjamin. "Johnson Spends a Busy Colorful Day in Salvador." *New York Times*, July 8, 1968, 17.

Wicker, Tom. "Spareribs and World Affairs at LBJ." *New York Times*, December 28, 1963, 1; 10.

Willinsky, Helen. *Jerk: Barbecue from Jamaica*. Freedom, CA: Crossing Press, 1990.

Wister, Owen. *The Virginian*. New York: Macmillan, 1902.

Worgul, Doug. *The Grand Barbecue: A Celebration of Kansas City Barbecue*. Kansas City: Kansas City Star Books, 2001.

The Women of General Foods Kitchens. *The General Foods Kitchens Cookbook*. New York: Random House, 1959.

"You can assemble this Barbecue-Incinerator in less than half an hour!" Pamphlet for the Incin-O-Grill. Undated. Box 221, folder 14, Paddleford Collection.

INTERNET SOURCES

http://nrn.com/archive/growth-chains-dickey-s-barbecue-pit. Accessed May 5, 2013.

http://nrn.com/archive/qa-roland-dickey-jr-dickey-s-barbecue-restaurants. Accessed May 5, 2013.

http://nrn.com/archive/regional-barbecue-players-debut-less-costly-fast-casual-variants. Accessed June 9, 2013.

http://nrn.com/latest-headlines/burger-king-launches-barbecue-inspired-summer-menu. Accessed May 4, 2013.

http://nrn.com/latest-headlines/famous-daves-aims-develop-better-barbecue-niche?page=1. Accessed May 4, 2013.

http://nrn.com/latest-headlines/hard-rock-caf-menu-looks-barbecue. Accessed May 5, 2013.

http://nrn.com/seafood-trends/menu-tracker-new-items-kfc-little-caesars. Accessed May 5, 2013.

http://nrn.com/us-top-100/top-100-chains-us-sales. Accessed June 9, 2013.

http://static.hpba.org/fileadmin/Statistics/TotalCW_Shipments--87-2005.htm. Accessed December 30, 2013.

http://www.foodsafety.gov/keep/charts/mintemp.html. Accessed October 11, 2013.

http://www.jimnnicks.com/images/menu9/Menu9_Dine-In.pdf. Accessed July 18, 2013.

http://www.merriam-webster.com/dictionary/barbecue. Accessed July 23, 2013.

http://www.npr.org/blogs/thesalt/2013/08/27/214592906/braai-day-aims-to-bring-s-africans-together-over-barbecue. Accessed November 28, 2013.

http://www.pitch.com/kansascity/kc-disasterpiece/Content?oid=2178534. Accessed July 1, 2013.

http://www.primalgrill.org/recipe_details.asp?RecipeID=82&EpisodeID=15. Accessed November 9, 2013.

http://www.rudysbbq.com/page/about. Accessed July 26, 2013.

www.kcbs.us/about_history.php. Accessed February 1, 2013.

INDEX